Missouri's Literary Heritage for Children and Youth

Alice Irene Fitzgerald

Missouri's Literary Heritage for Children and Youth

An Annotated Bibliography of Books about Missouri

Life has loveliness to sell,
  All beautiful and splendid things,
Blue waves whitened on a cliff,
  Soaring fire that sways and sings,
And children's faces looking up
  Holding wonder like a cup.

—"Barter" from *Love Songs* by Sara Teasdale

University of Missouri Press
Columbia & London, 1981

Library of Congress Cataloging in Publication Data

Fitzgerald, Alice Irene, 1911–
Missouri's Literary Heritage for Children and Youth.

Bibliography: p. 238
Includes index.
Summary: An annotated guide to more than 270
books about Missouri, set in the state, or written
by Missouri authors.
1. Missouri—Juvenile literature—Bibliography.
2. Children's literature, American—Missouri—
Bibliography. [1. Missouri—Bibliography]
I. Title.
Z1303.F58   [F466.3]   016.9778   81–3030
AACR2
ISBN 0–8262–0346–9

The illustration on the title page is from *Hannah's House* by Rhoda
Wooldridge, illustrations by Alta Adkins. Used by permission of
Independence Press, Independence, Missouri. The remainder of
the credit lines can be found on p. 256.

*This book is dedicated
to the memory of my parents,
J. W. and Ida Cotten Fitzgerald*

Preface

Missouri's Literary Heritage for Children and Youth: An Annotated Bibliography of Books about Missouri is intended to fill a need that has long been evident in the field of reference material about this important body of literature.

Anyone wishing to acquire books about Missouri, particularly books with Missouri settings by Missouri authors, has had to refer to numerous sources with little guidance about what was available. This annotated bibliography contains information on many widely read books as well as on several books that are now rare and difficult to locate. The comprehensive list includes a total of 301 books about Missouri written by 230 different authors. One hundred seven Missouri authors are identified along with 150 of their books with Missouri settings. (Any author who was born in the state or who has resided there has been considered a Missouri author.) Missouri authors and all book titles are indexed. This annotated bibliography represents a valuable contribution to an appreciation of Missouri's literary heritage and of the increasing need to preserve it.

The primary purpose of the annotated bibliography is to help Missouri's teachers, librarians, parents, children, and youth to locate, select, and evaluate materials for enjoyable and informative reading about their state. But the bibliography also has other far-reaching uses: young readers everywhere can learn more about America in general from these books; and individual and library collections can be more efficiently expanded and maintained through an increased awareness of this important aspect of Missouri's legacy. College teachers of courses in literature for children and youth and of other related fields will also find this volume a valuable resource; many colleges and universities have already initiated seminars and have established courses dealing with Missouri authors and with Missouri in literature for children and youth.

The selections are arranged alphabetically according to author and are numbered in sequence. In addition to the annotations, bibliographical information includes the illustrator, photographic credits, publisher, copyright date, number of pages, suggested age level (in parentheses), and an identification of the genre. While most of the titles are appropriate for ages 5–14, several titles usually considered adult material have been included because of their historical significance or their value as a reference; these books are designated "YA" for Young Adult. Books that are presently out of print are indicated by the symbol "OP."

Since many books for children and youth tend to go out of print quickly, librarians are urged to acquire and conserve Missouri collections. Teachers and parents should encourage readers to make use of interlibrary loan when unable to secure books of their choice in the local library. Missouri has an exceptional network system, and the service is remarkably efficient.

In addition to availability, other criteria were established for the selection of books to be included in the bibliography.

1. The books are identified with Missouri because they describe settings, characters, or events important to the state.

2. The books contain content that can be read by young people themselves or can be read or told to them.

3. Both fiction and nonfiction are included. Since there is a scarcity of up-to-date nonfictional materials, a few books with textbook formats have been selected. Even though some of these textbooks are outdated, they contain excellent information about Missouri's early history and folklore as well as worthwhile bibliographies.

4. While some of the books—such as the biographies of Harry S. Truman and the stories of the Pony Express—have the same or similar titles, each of them is helpful in meeting individual differences as the material is written at various levels of difficulty and is approached from different viewpoints.

5. A few recent publications dealing with local history

are included as exemplary titles. This type of material is abundant in its general scope, and specific titles can usually be located in local libraries and in historical collections, as well as in selected bibliographies of textbooks and other nonfiction books.

6. A few books were included in this bibliography because of their historical value even though they are quaint period pieces and the style of writing is somewhat archaic. As suggested in their annotations, these books could well be read in light of the chronological period for the setting of the story, as well as for the characterizations portrayed and for the events depicted.

7. All the books have been read and annotated by the author-compiler.

I express my sincere appreciation to those who have given assistance in this undertaking. The Daniel Boone Regional Library, Columbia, Missouri, has been continuously helpful in locating books through interlibrary loan. Several books were made available through the Missouri State Library, Jefferson City, and the Missouri State Teachers Association, Columbia. The State Historical Society of Missouri was especially helpful in locating information concerning author identity. Ruth Monsees, Boonslick librarian, identified and made available a number of books; Mary York, elementary curriculum supervisor, St. Louis Public Schools, sent *Heritage of St. Louis*; Emma Jean Clark, director for curriculum and instruction, Kansas City Public Schools, sent *The Story of Kansas City*; and Betty K. Aboussie, art education director, Learning Exchange, Kansas City, Missouri, sent *My Kansas City*. I also express appreciation to Mary Nelson for her efficient typing of the manuscript and to Elizabeth Cauthorn for her careful proofreading.

A. I. F.
Columbia, Missouri
24 February 1981

Contents

Introduction

Missouri has a rich literary heritage characterized by history and legend as well as by present-day realism and future promise. The child's portion of this heritage includes some of the finest works by Missouri authors and by those out-of-state authors whose stories reflect the memorable personalities and the colorful events of this picturesque state.

Missouri authors rank among the great, and many of them hold a special place in Missouri's literary heritage for children and youth. Samuel L. Clemens's characterization as the celebrated Mark Twain is as well known as the characters that he created in his books. Eugene Field, Sara Teasdale, and T. S. Eliot, the poets of St. Louis, have also taken their place in the annals of literature and in the hearts of young readers throughout the world. James S. Tippett, poet and educator born in Memphis, Missouri; Langston Hughes, poet and lecturer born in Joplin; and Carl Withers, gifted folklorist of the Ozark foothills, have each left a legacy to delight the generations to come.

Through her "Little House" books (a ten-volume saga on which the current television series "Little House on the Prairie" is based), Laura Ingalls Wilder has won an enduring reputation. Millions of children have read and loved her stories. Wilder and her family moved to Missouri in 1894. At their Rocky Ridge Farm home at Mansfield, now a museum, she wrote her books—pioneer stories of her own childhood as her family moved from Wisconsin to Kansas, to Minnesota, to Dakota, and finally to Missouri. Her first book was published in 1932 when she was sixty-five; the other seven appeared within the next ten years. In the 1950s new editions were issued with Garth Williams's memorable illustrations. *On the Way Home* is her Missouri story. Illustrated with photographs, this book is the diary of the trip from South Dakota to Mansfield in 1894;

the introduction is by her daughter, Rose Wilder Lane. *West from Home: Letters of Laura Ingalls Wilder*, published in 1974, contains letters to her husband "Manly"—the Almanzo of the book *Farmer Boy*—describing her visit to her daughter in California in 1915.

Missouri has a growing number of contemporary authors who have already become widely recognized and who have won many distinguished awards. Among these are Gertrude Bell, Clyde Robert Bulla, Alberta Wilson Constant, Scott Corbett, Cena Christopher Draper, Aileen Fisher, Shirley Glubok, Robert Heinlein, Edith Thatcher Hurd, Harold Keith, Jean Bell Mosley, Berniece Rabe, Keith Robertson, Rhoda Wooldridge, and Wilma Yeo.

Draper's *Rim of the Ridge* was chosen by the Books across the Sea panel as one of the "American Ambassador Books," a series meant to convey the lives, background, and interests of American young people to readers in Great Britain.

Fisher, a graduate of the University of Missouri–Columbia, received the second annual National Council of Teachers of English Award for Excellence in Poetry for Children. Her stories have also won wide acclaim.

Bulla, one of America's best-known modern writers for young people, was given the Silver Medal of the Commonwealth of California for his distinguished contribution to the field of children's books.

Corbett, a native of Kansas City and a graduate of the University of Missouri School of Journalism, was the 1976 winner of Missouri's distinguished Mark Twain Award.

Bell's awards include the 1965 Missouri Writer's Guild Plaque and first place in the 1966 national contest of the League of American Pen Women.

Rabe received the Society of Children's Book Writers' 1977 Golden Kite Award for her book, *The Girl Who Had No Name*.

Wooldridge, a native Missourian living near Independence, has made history come alive with her stories of pioneer living in the early days of Missouri. While she devotes most of her time to writing and lecturing, she takes time to visit the actual sites that she uses as backgrounds and carefully researches the information for her subjects. As a result, her frontier stories contain authentic details of pioneer living and have been widely recognized not only for their contribution to Missouri's literary heritage but also for their general historical value. In a review of *Hannah's Brave Year* in *Horn Book* magazine (February 1965, pp. 54–55), Virginia Haviland said, "Full domestic detail lends compelling vitality to a book that might have been only one more pioneer story. Hannah is not superman, nor are the other children more than life size. Easily read, with interest beyond the middle group." Mary Soderberg, a reviewer in *Library Journal* (15 October 1964, p. 4220), further stated, "The many details of cooking, planting, harvesting, and small tragedies are simply and clearly described as the brothers and sisters go through the winter together. The story flows smoothly and easily and will be enjoyed by all who like historical fiction."

The list of Missouri's authors who have written books about Missouri could extend well beyond the 150 books included here as could their recognitions and awards. (A list of Missouri authors and their books that are annotated in this bibliography is included in a special index.) This brief introduction to some of them may serve to encourage an increased awareness on the part of teachers, parents, librarians, and others who have the opportunity to bring children and Missouri's literary heritage together.

Other authors have been inspired to write not so much about Missouri but about great Americans who were Missourians and about national and world events and situations that have had significance for the state. Most of these stories are biographies and other nonfiction books that include information about Missouri.

The history of Missouri and the story of Missouri's literature for children and youth go hand in hand. Like its history, the literature, both fact and fiction, begins to take shape in the eighteenth century when Missouri was still an unexplored and unsettled wilderness. During the early days of settlement, flags of three nations symbolized Missouri's changing government, and its centralized location identified the area as the crossroads of a nation. The stories in this volume, for the most part, cover a period from the 1760s to the present time and span the entire geographic area of the state. The settings, some real and some imagined, represent locales as varied and colorful as the cities, towns, and villages that dot the state's landscape.

The character of the people and the culture and traditions that they brought with them are also diverse and individualistic. The authors of the books about Missouri have re-created equally memorable characters in realistic settings, providing the reader a vicarious experience charged with emotion and conviction.

Readers may be surprised to find their hometowns or geographic regions in these stories, although sometimes set in another era. Arrow Rock, Sibley, Columbia, Jefferson City, Warrensburg, Springfield, Ste. Genevieve, and many other familiar places appear. Often readers may recognize themselves or someone they know in such believable characters as those in *Me and Caleb*, or *Treasure of Crazy Quilt Farm*. Then there are encounters with real people including George Caleb Bingham, William C. Clark, and Sacagawea. Interesting as well as amazing stories about local areas, such as Breadtray Mountain located south of Reeds Spring, arise from the folklore of the state.

Exploring a collection of Missouri's literary heritage is an inspiring experience that leaves an indelible impression of the many features of Missouri as well as a greater appreciation of such diverse things as mules, foxhounds, scenic rivers, frontier artists, mischievous boys, baseball, trading posts, Mickey Mouse, peace pipes, pinafores, and the "Saint Louis Blues."

Annotated Bibliography

1. Abisch, Roz, and Boche Kaplan, adapters and illustrators. *Sweet Betsy from Pike.* New York: McCall, 1970. Unpaged. (Ages 3–10) *Fiction*

   Did you ever hear tell of Sweet Betsy from Pike,
   Who crossed the wide prairie with her husband, Ike?
   From Pike County, Missouri, so it is told,
   They made their way westward prospecting for gold.

   This folk ballad tells what happened to Ike, Betsy, their "two yoke of cattle, a large yellar dog, a tall Shanghai rooster, and one spotted hog" as they made their way from Missouri to California. Sweet Betsy's story embodied the difficulties, fears, and hopes of westward-bound immigrants who added new verses as they journeyed across the country to seek their fortunes.

   Sweet Betsy from Pike was adapted from a ballad written by an unknown singer in the 1850s. The artists have created a distinctive picture book through their use of colorful fabric collages of burlap, calico print, felt, rickrack, ribbon, and beads. Their technique lends an air of frontier America to Betsy and Ike's amusing adventures. Music for the ballad is included along with a note about its background. This version is arranged for young children; older readers will enjoy other versions in Earl A. Collins's *Folk Tales of Missouri* and Benjamin A. Botkin's *A Treasury of American Folklore* (Crown, 1944) and *A Treasury of Western Folklore* (Crown, 1951).

2. Adams, Samuel Hopkins. *The Pony Express* (A Landmark Book). Illustrated by Lee J. Ames. New York: Random House, 1950. 185 pages. (Ages 10–15) *Nonfiction*

   Many of the stories about the Pony Express are fictionalized, and this one is no exception. But Adams's story remains faithful to the period and to the major events, and he presents a dramatic account of an enterprise that proved to be a landmark in American history. Although the scenes of the drama unfold across the vast stretch of country between Missouri and California, the Pony Express began at St. Joseph, Missouri, and Missourians held prominent places in the organization. The author clearly recounts the events leading up to 3 April 1860 when the first pony riders set out to get the mail from St. Joseph to San Francisco within ten days. Interesting details are provided about the planning of the route and the schedules, the establishment of the way stations, and the selection and equipment of the riders. For these hard-riding couriers and their horses, each relay through the lonely miles of arduous and perilous country was a merciless test of endurance. Several of these young riders have been characterized in the book along with factual and fictional stories of their bravery and heroism. The names of Bob Haslam, Johnny Frey, Alex Carlisle, Bill Campbell, Warren "Boston" Upson, William F. Cody, and many other pony riders included here reappear in book after book about the exciting adventures of the Pony Express. Other books on this subject that present the material in a variety of styles and at levels of difficulty ranging from second grade through junior and senior high school are also included in this bibliography.

3. Aliki (Aliki Brandenberg). *A Weed Is a Flower: The Life of George Washington Carver*. Illustrated by the author. Englewood Cliffs, N.J.: Prentice-Hall, 1965. Unpaged. (Ages 6–9) *Biography*

Many colorful and appealing illustrations complement the simple, easy-to-read text in this outstanding picture biography for the beginning reader. Each realistic picture expresses the quiet purpose and direction in George Washington Carver's life. The title is drawn from the remark ascribed to Dr. Carver: "A weed is a flower growing in the wrong place." The brief but well-written text is an inspiring story of the black slave born in Missouri in 1860 who went on to become one of America's great scientists. The account highlights his early childhood at the Moses Carver farm where his interest in plants and in learning was respected and encouraged, his struggles for an education, his devotion to people as well as to his work, the distinguished accomplishments that brought him many rewards and worldwide recognition.

4. Allen, Lee. *Dizzy Dean: His Story in Baseball.* New York: Putnam's, 1967. 159 pages. (Ages 12 and up) *Biography*

The memorable career of Jay Hanna "Dizzy" Dean is highlighted by his fame as a pitcher for the St. Louis Cardinals and by his popularity as a sportscaster for the KWK radio station in St. Louis. Dean, the son of an itinerant farmer, was born in Lucas, Arkansas, and spent his childhood traveling throughout the Southwest. Dean's family picked cotton for a living, so he had very little time for schooling; however, for recreation his father played ball with Dean and his two brothers. Dean put on his first baseball uniform at sixteen when he was in the army. In 1930 he was discovered by a Cardinal talent scout and was assigned to the Saints of St. Joseph, Missouri, in the Western League. A year later, he had earned his place in the major leagues with the St. Louis Cardinals. He was one of the original Gas House Gang who helped the Cardinals to win the 1934 World Series. That same year, Dean was voted the most valuable player in the National League. In 1953, at the age of forty-four, he was elected to the Baseball Hall of Fame. After his retirement from baseball, he became a radio sportscaster for both the St. Louis Cardinals and the St. Louis Browns, and while he delighted many fans with his colorful reporting, he horrified others with his grammatical errors. Dean was characterized as boastful, hot-tempered, and sometimes unreliable, but he was also considered a competent player and a good businessman who possessed self-confidence and unusual determination. Certainly he was a hero to his fans and has become an irrepressible legend in the world of baseball. The frontispiece, four tables showing Dean's pitching records, and an index add value to the book.

5. Anderson, A. M. *Grant Marsh: Steamboat Captain* (The American Adventure Series). Illustrated by Jack Merryweather. Chicago: Wheeler, 1959; distributed by Harper, 1969. 220 pages. (Ages 8–12) *Biography*

> *Away, I'm bound away*
> *Across the wide Missouri.*

This highly fictionalized story relates the adventures of Grant Marsh from the time that he became a cabin boy on the Ohio River at the age of twelve to his career as army steamboat captain on the Missouri. After five years of working on Ohio riverboats, he made his first trip to St. Louis, the gateway to the West; two years later, he was back again looking for a job on the Missouri. The entire next section of the book deals with Marsh's life as a deckhand on the steamboats plying the lower Missouri River from St. Louis to St. Joseph. There are vivid descriptions of the landscape along the river, the loading and unloading of cargo, as well as glimpses of the passengers, settlers, gold miners, Indian scouts, trappers, and hunters heading to and from the western plains. Marsh met and married Kathy Reardon in St. Louis, where they made their home until he moved his family to Sioux City, Iowa. By this time, he had become a captain and chief pilot and made most of his trips on the upper Missouri River.

This book would make a fine companion to Veglahn's *Getting to Know the Missouri River*. Anderson's maps of the lower and upper Missouri River would add much to the information in Veglahn's book. While the book's primary appeal is for children aged eight and beyond, its content and readability are especially designed for slower or reluctant readers in the upper grades.

6. Anderson, A. M., and Adolph Regli. *Alec Majors: Trail Boss* (The American Adventure Series). Illustrated by

Jack Merryweather. New York: Harper, 1953, 1963. 204 pages. (Ages 10 and up) *Biography*

Written in an interesting but easy-to-read style, this fictionalized biography of Alexander Majors provides a challenging adventure story for a wide range of readers. Besides being a biography of Majors, the book is also the story of the Old West of army forts, wagon trains, and hardy trailblazers. Few individuals contributed more than Majors did to the development of the West. Although he was highly respected in his day and was a hero to those who followed the western trails, little is known about him. This book is divided into five major sections, each covering a special phase of Majors's life. He grew up on the family farm near Independence, Missouri. Since the Santa Fe Trail was only a few miles away, covered wagons loaded with goods were a common sight, and the stories of trail life so fascinated the boy that he longed to become a trail boss. After several enjoyable years as a farmer, he followed the call of the trail, which led to a highly profitable career in the freight business. His life was not without hardship and danger as he crossed rugged mountains and encountered unfriendly Indians and treacherous weather. He contracted to haul supplies for the U.S. Army and later formed the company of Majors, Russell, and Waddell. His last great venture was the Pony Express, whose brave riders carried the mail from Missouri to California in ten days. The story is appropriate for children in the intermediate grades, but it would be especially suitable for less able readers in the upper grades. While this book is appealing and useful, many readers will find greater satisfaction in Bailey's *Wagons Westward! The Story of Alexander Majors.*

7. Andrist, Ralph K. *Steamboats on the Mississippi* (American Heritage Junior Library). Illustrated with photographs. New York: American Heritage, 1962. 153 pages. (Ages 12–15) OP. *Nonfiction*

This book with its wealth of photographs, many in full

color, has been designed to give young people a deeper
understanding and a more lasting impression of the Mississippi steamboats and the world through which they
moved. While Andrist focuses on the heyday of western
steamboats, he also takes the Mississippi story into the
twentieth century, including today's summertime excur-
sion boats. These and a few sternwheel towboats are reminders that today is the twilight of the steamboat age.
The steamboat era began 150 years ago when Nicholas
Roosevelt took the *New Orleans* downriver through the
chaos of the New Madrid earthquake. The book's first
chapter, "The Year of Strange Happenings," describes in
detail this voyage and the devastation of the earthquake in
the New Madrid area. Other chapters provide interesting
information about river travel before the coming of the
steamboat, a description of the Mississippi–Missouri river
system, and an account of steamboat pioneering on the
Mississippi and its tributaries, including episodes about the
first steamboats on the treacherous Missouri. Sketches of
the "Lords of the River" and "Steamboat Comin'" reflect
the glory and glamour of steamboat days. A glimpse into
life in the river towns and encounters with river cutthroats
and scoundrels offer exciting reading as well as further insight into the past. Stories of steamboat races and wrecks,
along with the tall tales and legends, express the folklore
of the river. Some of these steamboat superstitions are the
subject of a story included from Mark Twain's *Life on the
Mississippi*. The book also contains a list of books for further reading and an index.

8. Archer, Myrtle. *The Young Boys Gone*. Jacket drawing by
   Laura Lydecker. New York: Walker, 1978. 218 pages.
   (Ages 12 and up) *Fiction*

Thirteen-year-old Thad Woodruff had seen his Pa
and his brother Gideon ride off to fight for the South. Just
two weeks later, both were killed in the battle at Carthage
(the first major conflict of the Civil War in Missouri). With
Quantrill on the warpath and jayhawkers, abolitionists,

and bushwhackers from Kansas and Missouri burning, raiding, and trying to force men and boys to fight on one side or the other, Thad faced a dilemma. He could fight for a cause he didn't believe, could allow himself to be dragged off to war by conscriptors, or could obey his father's orders to look after his Ma and sisters. As the threatening raiders approached the Woodruff farm, Thad's decision came quickly and clearly. The family managed to escape with whatever supplies they could carry and sought safety in the wilderness beyond their home. Many times their hardships seemed almost unbearable, but they managed to establish a home in a remote valley. For the duration of the war, they lived off the land deep in this southwestern strand of the Missouri Ozarks. Thad faced the challenge of making moral decisions as well as of ensuring his family's survival. His attitude toward slavery was brought into focus when a runaway slave stole corn from their clearing. He learned that not all Yankees were inhumane when a Union soldier freed him from a trap, and after an encounter with two Confederate soldiers, he even became less certain about aiding the South.

Although the story takes place during the Civil War, the theme and plot are more concerned with a family's struggle to survive in an uninhabited wilderness than with the drama of the war.

As a point of interest, the National Park Service is planning to return the Wilson's Creek National Battlefield area to its 1861 appearance by duplicating as nearly as possible the native ground cover and rural landscape of the 1860s (Missouri State Teachers Association, *School and Community*, January 1980, pp. 40–41). The decisive battle of Wilson's Creek took place a month after the battle of Carthage and involved many of the same soldiers. Both battlefields are a part of this story's setting.

9. Bachmann, Evelyn Trent. *Black-eyed Susan*. Illustrated by Lilian Obligado. New York: Viking, 1968. 159 pages. (Ages 8–12) *Fiction*

For twelve-year-old Susan Meredith, who lived on a
farm in the Ozarks, "There surely wasn't any place on
earth as nice as these hills in Southern Missouri" (p. 9). But
the time was 1936, during the depression, and the Meredith family had to move into town in order to help Grandad with the lumber business. Susan had dreaded the
change, but she soon found that there was no time for
moping as there were plenty of interesting activities to
keep her attention. Sometimes she was uncertain about
her own participation, particularly where her older sisters
and Grandad were concerned. However, as wedding plans
for sister Deborah went forward and the family adjusted
to living with Grandad, Susan was able to expand her own
resources and to discover the world beyond the farm and
the little town of Vista. The story reflects not only the
changing life of a growing girl but also the mood and tone
of the period. The fourteen titled sections lend added appeal.

10. Bailey, Bernadine. *Picture Book of Missouri* (The United
    States Books). Illustrated by Kurt Wiese. Chicago:
    Whitman, 1951, 1966. 32 pages. (Ages 8–11) *Nonfic-
    tion*

The illustrations are the outstanding feature of this
book. Each two-page spread of pictures, alternating color
and black-and-white, illuminate the brief text. A short introduction giving geographical information about Missouri is followed by a summary of the state's history. Some
of the state's resources are mentioned along with a brief
discussion of major cities. The author points out that the
lives of well-known Americans in many fields are woven
into Missouri's story and identifies the contributions of several of these distinguished Missourians.

Maps of Missouri and the Louisiana Territory, a print of
the Great Seal of the State of Missouri and the state flower,
and an index are included. However, the statement,
"Money he [Joseph Pulitzer] left established the University
of Missouri's School of Journalism" (p. 29), is erroneous.

11. Bailey, Ralph Edgar. *Wagons Westward! The Story of Alexander Majors*. Map by James McDonald; jacket and frontispiece by Richard Cuffari. New York: Morrow, 1969. 188 pages. (Ages 11–16) *Biography*

Both a history and a biography, this story covers a crucial period in American history and deals with a subject about which there is scant material. Before the advent of the transcontinental railroad, the developing West depended on wagon trains for goods and supplies. Among the most prominent wagon freighters was Alexander Majors, a Missourian, who took his first train of six wagons to Santa Fe in 1848. Later he was joined by William Waddell, a successful Lexington, Missouri, businessman, and William Hepburn Russell, a Richmond, Missouri, banker and real-estate operator. Together they built an enterprise that had thirty-five hundred wagons on the western trails. The characterizations of these men alone make this book important—the historical background naturally shaped this book, but these men had already shaped that history, just as each of them influenced the operation of their business in his own way. Majors managed the freighting, which included contracts to haul supplies to army posts along the Santa Fe Trail; Waddell remained in Kansas City or in Independence to manage the office; and Russell, using his contacts in Washington, D.C., took responsibility for getting future contracts. Their enterprise extended to include a stagecoach line and the history-making Pony Express. While Majors emerged as a hero of his day, he had his share of sorrow, difficulties, and disappointments. His story remains an exciting adventure into the past when settlements beyond the Missouri and Mississippi rivers relied on his services. As his wagon trains, stagecoach lines, and Pony Express riders crossed the high plains and the Rocky Mountains, they struggled against rough terrain, treacherous weather, and an ever-present threat of Indian attacks. Majors lived to see the turn of the century and, with his wife Susan, found time to travel around the country that he had helped to expand. The book also contains a bibliography and an index.

12. Baird, W. David. *The Osage People* (Centennial Commemorative Issue, 1872–1972). Illustrated with photographs and maps. Phoenix: Indian Tribal Series, 1972. 104 pages. (Ages 10 and up) *Nonfiction*

This modern, up-to-date history of the Osage tribe, written in celebration of their centennial, is also the history of the great Osage Nation, the only Indian reservation in Oklahoma at the present time. An introductory two-page spread describes Sylvester J. Tinker, who was elected principal chief of the Osage tribe in 1970. (He attended Kemper Military School at Boonville, Missouri, for four years.)

The section entitled "Ethnohistory" tells of the proud and ancient heritage of the Osage Indians and would be particularly interesting and appealing to elementary-school students. This section gives an account of the legendary origin of the Osage people as well as a clear description of their appearance, customs, and traditions. Since the dawn of Osage history, their culture has reflected an organized tribal life characterized by traditions and ceremonies. According to Osage mythology, the tribal ancestors once dwelt among the stars and were sent by Wa-kon-da, the life force of the universe, to occupy the earth. After long periods of wandering, the Sky People met and joined with the Land People, thereafter referring to themselves as Children of the Middle Waters and the Little Ones. Most of this book deals with the history of the Osage Indians from the white man's arrival in 1673 to the present. Events are discussed chronologically according to the following themes: "The Osages Meet the White Man, 1673–1803"; "The Americans Arrive, 1803–1839" (these two sections record Osage activities in Missouri); "On the Kansas Reservation, 1839–1871"; "In Indian Territory, 1872–1907"; and "Into the Twentieth Century." The book closes with a look at the future for the Osage, a people with a fascinating history, a substantial culture, and meaningful traditions.

13. Baker, Betty. *The Dunderhead War.* New York: Harper, 1967. 216 pages. (Ages 12 and up) *Fiction*

"I sang about the wide Missouri and dreamed of home. Then I thought of the volunteers who'd never see home again. . . . The War Office should have planned things better. But then, Independence [Missouri] was a sight closer to Santa Fe than Washington was, and the trip hadn't been at all what I'd expected" (p. 190).

The Dunderhead War is one of the few books that give young people a realistic account of the Mexican War that brought California and other parts of the Southwest into the United States. The story, which begins and ends in Independence, Missouri, belongs to Quincy Heffendorf, although the little-known but important part played by the Grand Army of the West and its Missouri volunteers provides an interesting historical backdrop.

The spring of 1846 came earlier than any remembered in Missouri. The spring thaws brought in the mountain men from a heavy beaver-trapping season, and every boat from St. Louis carried emigrants bound for Oregon and California. Young Quincy longed to see the West that was creating so much excitement at his Pa's store and around town. When the first news of the Mexican War reached Independence, two of Quincy's best friends enlisted in the Missouri volunteers. Even though Quincy was too young to enlist, he got his chance to go west anyway when he and his Uncle Fritz became traders and joined a wagon train that followed the route of the Grand Army. While Uncle Fritz's contempt for "an army of dunderheads" caused problems, Quincy and his uncle's fortunes were inseparably linked with those of the volunteers as they traveled together in pursuit of the Mexican army.

14. Baker, Nina Brown. *A Boy for a Man's Job, the Story of the Founding of St. Louis.* Illustrated by Edward F. Cortese. Philadelphia: John C. Winston, 1952. 179 pages. (Ages 9–12) *Fiction*

In August 1763, determined to be a part of an expedition to establish a trading post along the upper Mississippi, two young boys, Auguste and his half-Indian friend

Charlie, set out from New Orleans in a small canoe to overtake Pierre Laclede and his companions. During the months that followed, Charles Ronsard learned his true identity and Auguste Chouteau became a leader of men. Once a suitable site was chosen, Laclede began making plans for the construction of the fur-trading post. But when he was disabled in an accident, he put the fourteen-year-old Auguste in charge of the thirty loyal followers who proceeded with the building of the town named St. Louis. Within a few months, a fort had been built and homes were ready for the workmen's families who would arrive from New Orleans. Among them were Mrs. Laclede and her young children who were to live in the fine house on the hill overlooking the post.

The immature dialogue, especially between Laclede and Auguste, is inconsistent and unconvincing in light of the responsible role given to the fourteen-year-old boy. Interested readers would likely find greater satisfaction in the more mature and more authentic version, *Chouteau and the Founding of Saint Louis* by Rhoda Wooldridge.

15. Baldwin, Clara. *Little Tuck*. Illustrated by Paul Galdone. Garden City, N.Y.: Doubleday, 1959. 96 pages. (Ages 7–10) *Fiction*

Everyone called Jonathan Jacobs "Little Tuck" because he was "sort of a runt for all his ten years" (p. 7) and because he was born in Kentucky, where his family had lived before moving to Missouri. He didn't mind being called Little Tuck or even being teased by his older brothers, but he did mind being left behind when his father and brothers went hunting in the woods. As he set about to prove that he was big enough to help, his adventures caused plenty of excitement. Little Tuck caught a wild turkey, had a frightening experience when he went to salt the cattle, helped to shear sheep, and got treed by a bear while honeybee hunting. He finally gained proper respect and received not only an invitation to go hunting but also a gun of his own. While no particular locale is identified other than the Missouri River valley, the episodes provide young readers with an authentic background of pioneer living.

16. Baldwin, Helen I., Ruth M. Dockery, Nancy L. Garrett, and S. Joseph Gore, project writers. *Heritage of St. Louis*. Picture editor, Helen M. Herminghaus; designer, Richard H. Brunell. St. Louis: St. Louis Public Schools, 1964 (paperback). 201 pages. (Ages 10 and up) *Nonfiction*

"I have found a situation where I am going to form a settlement which might become hereafter one of the finest cities in America." Pierre Laclede left thirteen-year-old Auguste Chouteau in charge of carrying out the plans for that settlement. So began the city of St. Louis. This book was created as a special project, and much of the material has been incorporated into the social-studies curriculum of the St. Louis public schools. The wide range of content covering more than fifty topics is organized into eight sections that include "St. Louis Begins," "Time to Learn," "Steamboat to Space Capsule," "Days of Conflict," "During Leisure Time," "In the Circle of Arts," "In the Working World," and "Tables." As the content indicates, the material is logically organized with an emphasis on those aspects important to an appreciation and understanding of one of the great cities of America. Interesting and informative stories re-create the past, acquaint the reader with the present-day environment, and transmit a heritage that rightfully belongs not only to the youth of the St. Louis community but also to young people everywhere. The city was founded and grew on national and worldwide contributions and influences. Carefully selected photographs, detailed maps, and imaginative drawings clarify the well-written text and reflect the quality of the extensive content. In addition to the section of tables that includes several chronologies and selected references, the book also contains an index.

17. Ball, Zachary (Kelly R. Masters). *Keelboat Journey*. Illus-
     trated by Hans Helweg. New York: Dutton, 1958. 190
     pages. (Ages 12 and up)   *Fiction*

Keelboat Journey is a singular piece of historical fiction
about a keelboat voyage on the uncharted Missouri River
during the early frontier days. The author has re-created
the journey so effectively that the reader soon becomes a
part of the adventure, alert to the dangers along the way,
sensing the treachery of the river, and feeling the appre-
hensions and weariness of the strong, tough crewmen as
they maneuver the long boat with its precious cargo along
its uncertain course upriver. In addition to excellent passages describing the beauty of the wilderness, colorful
character portrayals of the rough, proud keelboatmen
match exciting incidents that challenged the vigorous adventurers, and particularly vivid accounts depict the skill
required to move a heavily loaded keelboat upstream.

Eighteen-year-old Garth Madden, youngest member of
the crew and the hero of the story, signed on the *Tomahawk*
at St. Louis to begin an adventure-filled voyage that was to
play an historic role in opening the way for others to follow. The *Tomahawk* was the first keelboat to reach the headwaters of the Missouri River in 1831, allowing the Missouri
Fur Company to establish a permanent trading post in the
Oregon Territory. While *Keelboat Journey* is seen through
Garth's eyes, the entire cast is firmly bound together
throughout the story. In one of the most striking scenes
reflecting this unity of purpose, the travelers encountered
a mass of driftwood (the act of a traitor) amid the swirling
current of the turbulent, muddy river. As the current became too strong for the boat to be rowed or even poled,
cordelling (dragging on a tow line) was the only way to
move it, but first Garth had to risk his life to rescue the
broken cordelle (tow line). Only Captain Eli and Big Jim
the poleman remained on the craft to keep the prow forward through the swift channel, as, inch by inch, scram-
bling over rocks and underbrush near the riverbank, the
strong, tough keelers dragged the boat many miles at a
stretch.

From *Where Rivers Meet* (Banks and McCall)

The author's *Mike Fink* and James McCague's *Flatboat Days on Frontier Rivers* also provide interesting reading on this subject.

18. Banks, Marjorie, and Edith McCall. *Where Rivers Meet.* Illustrated by John C. Teason. Chicago: Benefic, 1958. 224 pages. (Ages 10 and up) *Nonfiction*

The authentic account of how three great rivers helped to make a great nation is told with the use of some fictional characters. Generous and appropriate illustrations reinforce the easy-to-read text. Besides being a story of the Mississippi, Missouri, and Ohio rivers and the lands to which they led, the book tells about the people—Indians, explorers, traders, trappers, and boatmen who found their way along the rivers, and the farmers and the businessmen who followed them to the river crossroads of America. Chapter headings and subtopics featuring factual information contribute to the historical value of the content as well as to the ease of reading the text. Appendixes include two lists separating the people who really lived from the people who might have lived. The book also contains a generous table of contents, a pronouncing index, maps, and a "where it happened" index.

19. Barrett, S. M. *Shinkah, the Osage Indian.* Illustrated
with photographs. Oklahoma City: Harlow, 1916,
1918. 114 pages. (Ages 10 and up) OP. *Fiction*

This life story of Shinkah, the Osage Indian, not only
provides a lucid account of Indian life in Missouri at the
beginning of the nineteenth century but also gives valuable
insights into the nature and lore of the Osage Indians. The
story begins almost two centuries ago at the winter camp
of a band of Osage Indians in central Missouri. Shinkah's
tribe, known as the Great Osages, was accustomed to
spending the winter along the south banks of one of the
numerous bends in the Osage River between what are now
Cole and Osage counties. Here in the secluded valley en-
closed by the river and the wooded bluff, his people found
safety from their enemies as well as protection from the
winds of winter. Their permanent village farther up the
Osage River was situated near the present town of Rich
Hill, Missouri. The story includes an account of Lieutenant Pike's visit with Chief Pawhuska (White Hair) at the
village of the Great Osages. (History records Zebulon M.
Pike's visit to Pawhuska's village in Vernon County, Missouri, in 1806.) At the time of this story, the Osage Indians
claimed the territory covering Missouri south of the Missouri River, all of Arkansas north of the Arkansas River,
and much of eastern Kansas and Oklahoma. As Shinkah
grew from young childhood to manhood, he roamed the
extent of this land, playing games, hunting, fishing, trading, participating in ceremonies, and engaging in battle
against the enemy along with other warriors of his tribe.
The story closes near the end of the nineteenth century
with the aging Nekoh (Shinko-Shinkah) at the Pawhuska
village of the Osage on their reservation in Oklahoma.
This village bears the name of his long-ago home by the
Osage River in Missouri. As he had prophesied, the traditional life of the Osage was preserved only in the memory
of aged Indians or in the archives of history.

The material in this book is well documented and written with a readability level suitable to the average reader
in the middle grades. It is one of the few stories dealing

with Osage Indian material that is appropriate for this age-group. Unfortunately, the book has long been out of print and is only likely to be found in rare-book collections. Readers would also find *Sports and Games the Indians Gave Us* by Alex Whitney of interest.

20. Barry, James P. *Bloody Kansas, 1854–65: Warfare Delays Peaceful American Settlement* (Focus Books). Illustrated with photographs. New York: Franklin Watts, 1972. 86 pages. (Ages 12 and up) *Nonfiction*

Focusing on Kansas during a ten-year period, the author has attempted to provide a study of the events and influences surrounding the settlement of the state. In keeping with the format of the series, this treatment of the material intends to help the reader to gain an understanding of the entire period of history. The Kansas–Nebraska Act of 1854 opened those two territories for settlement; it also stirred the rivalry between antislavery forces of the northeastern states and the proslavery forces of the South as both groups sent settlers into Kansas. Some of the principals in the story were John Brown and William Quantrill who came from Ohio along with Charles "Doc" Jennison of Wisconsin who joined Jayhawker Jim Lane in the guerrilla warfare that erupted and continued until the end of the Civil War. The title of this book is as misleading as the subject is controversial: While Kansas is the focus of the theme, a great deal of the material concerns Missouri's involvement as a strategic border state. The writing in this book lacks the usual quality of the series; conjectures and sweeping generalizations often overshadow the facts. However, the book is worthwhile for school collections and should send the Missouri-history buff researching the facts. Photographs, maps, a bibliography, and an index add to the book's usefulness.

21. Bell, Gertrude. *First Crop*. Illustrated by Susan Hood. Independence, Mo.: Independence Press, 1973. 164 pages. (Ages 9–12) *Fiction*

Jackson County in western Missouri during the Civil War is the setting for this story dealing with the pressures of General Order No. 11. Young Ambrose Patton was trying hard to remain neutral as he raised his first crop of corn in the late summer of 1863. Pa had joined up with the Confederates, while Uncle Matt had gone with the Union, and Grandpa had left for Nebraska Territory to avoid involvement with either side. Then disaster, desolation, and confusion beset Ambrose when his home, his crop, and even his baby calves were laid waste by Union soldiers. In the following days, Ambrose searched for food and gave help to other sufferers. In a few short days, he learned that fear, confusion, and cruelty existed on both sides of the conflict and that people often suffer as a result of situations over which they have no control. While there are several other books that treat this same subject in a more authentic setting (Loula Grace Erdman's *Another Spring* and Alberta Wilson Constant's *Paintbox on the Frontier*), this easy-to-read selection could be useful on a lower track for the reluctant older reader. *First Crop* was one of the twenty nominations for the 1974–1975 Mark Twain Award.

22. Bell, Gertrude. *Posse of Two*. Eau Claire, Wis.: Hale, 1967. 160 pages. (Ages 10–14) *Fiction*

The pre–Civil War border strife between Kansas and Missouri serves as the backdrop for this midwestern adventure. Shortly after the Mexican War, Ned Belt and his family moved from Kentucky to Clay County, Missouri. Unaware of the growing conflict between Kansas and Missouri, they had been attracted by cheap land and a promising future. But then border outlaws burned their cabin and took their possessions, including Ned's stallion. Ned was determined to recover his horse. In his pursuit, he met another boy whose family had been similarly victimized. Together they managed to outwit the border ruffians and to regain their treasured possessions. This book won the author first place in the 1966 national contest of the National League of American Pen Women.

23. Bell, Gertrude. *Roundabout Road.* Illustrated by Judith Ritchie. Independence, Mo.: Independence Press, 1972. 173 pages. (Ages 9–12) *Fiction*

Roundabout Road is an adventurous tale that travels from St. Louis through Jefferson City to Westport, Missouri, at the beginning of the Civil War. Missouri was already violently involved in a war of its own because the people were divided on the secession issue. Fights and riots were common, and outlaws roamed the countryside. Leaving his wounded older brother in St. Louis, fourteen-year-old Tobe Knight made the dangerous journey alone across the war-torn state. He carried with him a money belt that belonged to his family who lived in Westport, three hundred miles from St. Louis. The long trip would have been considerably easier by steamboat, but troops threatened to close the Missouri River traffic, so Tobe had to ride his bad-tempered, unpredictable horse, Hammerhead. To avoid the soldiers, he took a roundabout road to reach his home. A wild race ends the story as Tobe and Nat and Molly Porter, two friends he acquired along the way, face grave danger within sight of the Porter homestead. While the theme is more suitable for older children, the easy-to-read vocabulary and simple style may only appeal to slow readers and to middle-grade-level children.

24. Bell, Gertrude. *Where Runs the River.* Cover design by Robert M. Brackenburg. Independence, Mo.: Independence Press, 1976. 186 pages. (Ages 10 and up) *Fiction*

Amelia Thurston's courage helps her family and friends to survive hardships and dangers during the Civil War that tore Missourians apart. Amid the confusion of neutrality versus secession and union, neighbors, friends, and even families were caught up in mutual fear and distrust. Johnny Woods, Tobe Flagett, and Joe Shellen were among those Clay County boys who had enlisted in the state guard that was fighting to keep Missouri neutral. But with the inevitable doom of neutrality, choices had to be

From *Roundabout Road* (Bell)

made as civil authority waned in the presence of federal troops. Amelia, drawn into daring circumstances demanding secrecy and dangerous risks, turned often to her special retreat by a stream leading to the Missouri River. While many times she had dreamed of following the river to faraway places and adventure, in the end it was the river that brought happiness to her. Romance suitably integrated with the locale makes this easy-to-read novel interesting enough to recommend to older, slower readers.

25. Benson, Sally. *Meet Me in St. Louis*. New York: Random House, 1941, 1942. 290 pages. (Ages 12 and up) *Fiction*

The story of the Lonnie Smith family of St. Louis in the year 1903–1904 highlights the opening of the Louisiana Purchase Exposition. The story begins and ends with six-year-old Tootie Smith, the youngest member of the family, but three older girls, a college-aged brother, Grandpa, Papa, Mama, and a host of other people also figure in the narrative. Tootie, the mischief maker, is encouraged by her twelve-year-old sister Agnes. Rose and Esther are mostly interested in fancy clothes, parties, and boyfriends but are continually reminded of Tootie's often unwelcome antics. Although Lon is a sophisticated Princeton student, his attention to Tootie is colored by teasing and pranks to which she is usually gullible.

The book is divided into twelve chapters, one for each month of the year. Each chapter is filled with details of activities reflecting the family's status and values as well as with the capers of the imaginative Tootie. Her captivating interest in dolls is sure to amuse and amaze the reader. The description of the 1904 St. Louis World's Fair adds historical significance to the book for readers of all ages. The author, who as a young child lived in St. Louis at the time of the world's fair, dedicated the book to her family.

26. Berry, Erick. *When Wagon Trains Rolled to Santa Fe* (How They Lived Series). Illustrated by Charles Wa-

terhouse. Champaign, Ill.: Garrard, 1966. 95 pages.
(Ages 9–14)   *Fiction*

This fictionalized account of the Santa Fe Trail in 1838
is filled with vivid descriptions of the day-by-day challenges faced by the people in the wagons rolling west.
More than 800 miles of hardship and danger lay ahead of
the sturdy wagoneers on their long journey from Independence, Missouri, to Santa Fe in Mexican territory.
Huge wagons—the Conestogas, the Pittsburghs, and smaller
Dearborns—were heavily loaded with goods brought from
many parts of the country and even from Canada and Europe to be sold or traded to Mexican merchants. These
wagons, pulled by heavy oxen, moved slowly over the
rough terrain, often taking ten days to reach Council
Grove, 150 miles from Independence. Each member of
the wagon train was important for his or her particular
skill. Along with the traders were the bullwhackers, the
herdsmen, and the scouts. Sometimes would-be adventurers and pioneer families joined the train. Together they
lived, worked, and faced the dangers of stampeding buffalo, fierce Indian attacks, unexpected floods, rugged
mountains, and parched deserts. The rich rewards at the
end of the trail were highlighted by the unforgettable
sights and sounds of historic Santa Fe, which was an Indian pueblo as early as A.D. 1200 and had been settled by
the Spanish since 1610.

In this well-written, easy-to-read story, readers share adventures that were a part of the authentic record of the
early days in the American West. The Missouri River
waterfronts and the overland trails across Missouri were a
vital part of this record as were the many Missourians involved in the westward migration. Old prints, engravings,
colorful endpapers and cover, a map, and an index supplement the text.

27. Blassingame, Wyatt. *Bent's Fort, Crossroads of the West*
(How They Lived Series). Illustrated with drawings
and photographs. Champaign, Ill.: Garrard, 1967. 96
pages. (Ages 9–14)   *Nonfiction*

Bent's Fort tells the story of the historic marketplace and refuge on the crossroads of the West and of the two men from Missouri who built it. Charles and William Bent were sons of a well-to-do judge in St. Louis. Eager for adventure, the brothers joined a wagon train traveling the Santa Fe Trail during the summer of 1829. Over this dangerous wilderness trail that led from Independence, Missouri, to Santa Fe, the Bent brothers, along with other merchants, drove wagons loaded with goods to be traded for Mexican silver, fur, mules, horses, and other items to sell back East. Within a few years, Charles became one of the most famous merchants in the Santa Fe trade as he traveled back and forth between Missouri and Santa Fe. But William fell in love with the West and became a mountain man. By 1832 he had a successful business trading with the Indians and decided to build a trading post where he could store his supplies. With his brother's help, an elaborate fort was built on a site located between the modern cities of Las Animas and La Junta, Colorado. For the next sixteen years, the fort, under William's management, was an active center that served as a marketplace and supply station for the enterprising interests of both brothers. It also served as a hotel and refuge for other traders, pioneers, and mountain men. Another Missourian, Kit Carson, who was one of the most famous of these mountain men, often worked at the fort as a hunter. With the last days of Bent's Fort went a way of life that ended a colorful and exciting era in American history.

Attractive old prints, engravings, and paintings of the period enrich the authentic and easy-to-read text. The book also contains a map and an index.

28. Blassingame, Wyatt. *Jim Beckwourth: Black Trapper and Indian Chief* (A Discovery Book). Illustrated by Herman Vestal. Champaign, Ill.: Garrard, 1973. 80 pages. (Ages 7–10) *Biography*

Young readers in the primary grades can share the adventures of a great hunter, trapper, explorer, and innkeeper in this easy-to-read biography of a black man who became a legend in the West. This story of James Pierson Beckwourth (1798–1866) begins with his early childhood on a farm at the edge of the wilderness not far from St. Louis in the year 1807. He attended school in St. Louis and, at the age of fourteen, went to work in a blacksmith shop. While working there, he became fascinated by the mountain men and by the stories that they told about the Far West. After spending a year and a half as a hunter supplying food for government soldiers along the Fever River, he returned to St. Louis and was hired by Gen. William H. Ashley's Rocky Mountain Fur Company. His first trip west was filled with adventure and danger but took him no farther than the head of the Kansas River where he spent the winter. Back in St. Louis the following spring, he joined General Ashley who was leading a party of beaver trappers into the Rocky Mountain area. Beckwourth's ability to survive hardships in the wilderness made him famous among mountain men, and his knowledge of Indian ways earned him the respect of many Indian tribes and even a place of leadership among the Crow. While he spent most of his life in the West, he returned often to St. Louis to trade his furs and to visit his family. Added fame came with his discovery of a new pass through the Sierra Nevada during the gold-rush days. There in his later life, at his own hotel and store, he told a newspaperman, T. D. Bonner, about his adventures; these stories were later published in a book. Advanced readers will enjoy a more detailed account of these adventures in *Mountain Man: The Life of Jim Beckwourth* by Marian T. Place.

29. Blassingame, Wyatt. *Sacagawea, Indian Guide* (The American Indian Series). Illustrated by Edward Shenton. Champaign, Ill.: Garrard, 1965. 80 pages. (Ages 7–10) *Biography*

Sacagawea's adventures were only beginning when, at the age of twelve, she was stolen from her Shoshone tribe by Minnetaree warriors. Later, as the wife of Charbonneau, the French trapper and guide for Lewis and Clark, she and her newborn son, "Little Pomp," went west with the expedition. Sacagawea was invaluable to the explorers: She helped to keep peace with the Indians they met, she helped the men to find food and horses, and she protected their precious supplies. After the expedition was over, she made her home in St. Louis for a while, and her son grew up under the guardianship of Capt. William C. Clark.

Written in simplified style, this fictionalized account adheres to the historical facts while providing action and dialogue appealing to young readers. Two introductory pages give factual information about the Shoshone Indians along with a map showing the route of the expedition and highlighting locations important in Sacagawea's story.

30. Borland, Kathryn, and Helen Ross Speicher. *Eugene Field: Young Poet* (Childhood of Famous Americans). Illustrated by William Moyers. New York: Bobbs-Merrill, 1964. 200 pages. (Ages 8–12) *Biography*

In keeping with the formula for this series, the conversations, thoughts, feelings, and actions of the young Eugene Field suggest his accomplishments in adult life. The story of the leprechaun introduces the mischievous boy who was to become an equally cheerful man who left a heritage of imaginative poetry. Most of the book is devoted to Field's childhood, his fun-loving pranks, his appealing manner, and his increasingly creative nature. Episodes in the story highlight his growing up in St. Louis and Amherst with anecdotes about his education at the University of Missouri–Columbia, his trip to Europe followed by his marriage to Julia Comstock of St. Joseph, and his work as a newspaper reporter. Some of his poems included in the closing chapter are "Jest 'fore Christmas," "Wynken, Blynken, and Nod," and "The Duel." Lists of facts about the period when Field lived, review questions, related topics for study, things to do, books to read, and a glossary make up the final sections of the book.

31. Botkin, Benjamin A., editor. *A Treasury of Mississippi River Folklore: Stories, Ballads, Traditions and Folkways of*

Mid-American River Country. New York: Crown, 1955.
620 pages. (Ages 10 and up) *Fiction*

This scholarly anthology covers a wide range of folklore within the vast region of the Mississippi. As with most
folklore, Missouri folklore defies documentation, but Botkin has gathered an interesting and valuable collection of
Missouri tales and has identified numerous authentic
sources that include works by several Missourians. The
volume is divided into nine sections and contains an index
of authors, titles, and first lines of songs, as well as an index of subjects, names, and places. While many of these
stories are suitable for children and youth, teachers, librarians, and parents could use this volume to select stories for reading or for telling to young children or as a
reference for older children. Botkin's *A Treasury of American Folklore* (Crown, 1944) and *A Treasury of Western Folklore*
(Crown, 1951) are also valuable references for Missouri
folklore.

32. Bowman, James Cloyd. *Mike Fink.* Illustrated by Leon-
     ard Everett Fisher. Boston: Little, Brown, 1957. 147
     pages. (Ages 9–12) *Fiction*

This version of the story of Mike Fink, the legendary
riverboatman, is one of the best of the traditional American tall tales. Bowman's scholarly research and the tales of
his own pioneer ancestors provided authentic background
for his stories. His heroes were real people whose amazing
feats won them a place in history and legend. The adventures of Mike Fink are filled with excitement, courage,
laughter, and loyalty. Fink became known as the king of
the keelboatmen—"the snapping turtle of the O-hi-oo and
snag of the Mississippi." Wherever rivermen gathered
along the Ohio, Mississippi, and Missouri rivers, the tale of
Fink's huge strength, his unfailing aim with Bang All, and
his undaunted courage, tempered only by his sense of humor and his softheartedness, was sure to be heard. His
name and fame soon spread throughout the frontier.
One of his daring encounters resulted in his arrest at the

Louisville dock and a strange courtroom trial. When Mike and the *Light Foot* crewmen outwitted the bandits at Cave-in-Rock (Illinois), they won more than the battle. A truly frightening experience arose when they were navigating the *Light Foot* on the Mississippi near New Madrid, Missouri, during the 1811 earthquake. As time went on and the frontier surged forward, Fink set out for further adventures on the Missouri and in the Far West where his legendary fame continued to grow.

33. Bratton, Helen. *It's Morning Again.* Illustrated by Ray Abel. New York: McKay, 1964. 215 pages. (Ages 12 and up) *Fiction*

In this book, Ruth Ashley faced the problems of growing up and becoming independent when she decided to finish her senior year at Jefferson City High School. While she was happy in her beautiful, old Missouri farm home and knew everyone at the Moniteau Consolidated High School, her interest in art and in the attractive social life in her grandmother's gracious home promised a challenging year. Ruth's lovable, considerate parents, domineering Grandmother Barton, ambitious cousin Richard Clarke, friend and neighbor Jubah Dalton, along with other teen-aged youngsters were part of the pattern that made up Ruth's new life. The book describes the fun of the dances, school games, picnics, and Christmas in the country as well as disappointments such as losing the art scholarship. Chapter headings highlight major episodes filled with local color in this novel set in the 1960s.

34. Breihan, Carl W. *The Escapades of Frank and Jesse James.* Illustrated with photographs. New York: Frederick Fell, 1974. 288 pages. (Ages 13 and up) *Nonfiction*

A native Missourian and an authority on the legendary bandits of the Old West has added another chapter to the lore of the notorious James brothers and their band of outlaws. This volume contains detailed accounts of the

James gang's numerous bank and train robberies and gives the reader a broad outline of the character and atmosphere of the period. Frank and Jesse James grew up during the decade prior to the end of the Civil War—years often referred to as a training ground for outlaws. Although much of their activity occurred in Missouri, these daring bandits rampaged throughout the West, into the Deep South, and even into Mexico. Boldness characterized their manner, and destruction marked their pathway. The narrative is supported with newspaper accounts, letters, and testimonies. One particularly interesting document is from George Caleb Bingham, the adjutant general at that time, to the governor of Missouri, reporting on the bombing of the James home in February 1875. The outlaws' actions were dramatized by the publication of Jesse's own impudent communications to the newspapers. Two such letters (1876) concerned the holdup of the Missouri Pacific express train at the Lamine River bridge, east of Sedalia near Otterville, Missouri. The author perpetuates the myth of the man who was feared and hated as a robber and killer yet went into folklore as a hero. A bibliography is included, and chapter divisions are especially attractive for random reading.

35. Briggs, Ernestine Bennett, and Claude Anderson Phillips. *Missouri Stories for Young People.* Illustrated with photographs. Columbia, Mo.: Lucas Brothers, 1934, 1936, 1938. 349 pages. (Ages 9–12) OP. *Nonfiction*

Although outdated, this textbook contains useful material dealing with the early history of Missouri. The format includes clear, easy-to-read content and helpful study guides. The book is divided into two major parts with chapter and topic subdivisions. Part 1 includes fourteen chapters dealing with such aspects as physical features, industries, and government (limited to the copyright date). Twenty-one chapters in part 2 emphasize the early history of Missouri and present brief biographical sketches of famous Missourians.

While the word "stories" in the title may seem misleading, each chapter does contain mini-essays on specified topics. Each topic is identified in bold type. Study questions are posed at the beginning of each chapter. An objective test and a list of suggested activities are given at the end of each chapter. A list of teacher references is included as well as a word list with meanings and pronunciations. The book is fully indexed and contains a table of contents and numerous pictures and maps that are listed for easy reference.

36. Brookins, Dana. *Rico's Cat*. Drawings by Michael Eagle. New York: Seabury, 1976. 135 pages. (Ages 8–12) *Fiction*

Brookins has captured the atmosphere of a tenement neighborhood near Washington University in St. Louis during World War II and has vividly portrayed a variety of memorable characters. Twelve-year-old Dee Haymacher, the story's narrator, tells how her nine-year-old brother Rico's determination to keep a stray cat not only created some frustrating problems but also led to a series of surprising adventures. Rico knew that the landlord in their four-apartment building did not permit pets, so he attempted to hide the cat and her kittens, which soon arrived, in the basement. When the hardhearted Mr. Frisbie discovered the cats, Rico's only course was to move them to the alley where rodents and mystery lurked. As the plot unfolded, Rico and his friends, the school, and the entire neighborhood became involved in the cat's activities as well as with the children's war efforts. They also encountered some unforeseen problems and solved the mystery of the "mad scientist" and his laboratory. Rico's calico cat, Molly, brought about a completely surprising end to the story.

37. Brown, Billye Walker, and Walter R. Brown. *Historical Catastrophes: Earthquakes*. Illustrated with photographs. Reading, Mass.: Addison-Wesley, 1974. 191 pages. (Ages 10–16) *Nonfiction*

In chapter 3, "New Madrid, Missouri—December 1811–March 1812," the authors present some fascinating information about the pattern of earthquakes around the world and vividly describe the disastrous earthquake that almost totally destroyed the pioneer town of New Madrid, Missouri, in 1811. This earthquake is particularly interesting since the New Madrid area is an unlikely place for an earthquake to occur. Even more unusual is the fact that this quake was felt over such a wide area; it is estimated that people felt the earth tremble over a million miles of the earth's surface. The authors also point out that today's scientists believe that the town must have stood at the epicenter of the earthquake; the tremors were so strong that nearly all the log houses, which are rarely damaged by earthquakes, were either completely destroyed or badly damaged. These quakes also changed the countryside for miles around the town. Many of the high bluffs along the waterfront slipped into the muddy water; the Mississippi and several tributaries were whipped into heavy waves by the shaking of the river bed and the collapsing banks. More than two hundred square miles of forests were uprooted, and thick deposits of sand made farming in these areas almost impossible for years afterward. The book also has chapters describing three other earthquakes in the United States (in San Francisco; in Hebgen Lake, Montana; and in Alaska) as well as other major earthquakes throughout the world. Terms peculiar to the subject are clearly explained in conjunction with their use. An index, photographs, maps, and diagrams also provide helpful information.

38. Brownlee, Richard S. *Gray Ghosts of the Confederacy: Guerrilla Warfare in the West, 1861–1865.* Illustrated with maps and photographs. Baton Rouge: Louisiana State University Press, 1958. 274 pages. (YA) *Nonfiction*

While *Gray Ghosts of the Confederacy* is based on scholarly research and is designed for the general reader of military history, the book could provide a substantial reference source for discerning readers in the upper grades. Since the literature for young people includes several pieces of fiction set in Missouri during the Civil War period as well as a number of factual books dealing with the subject, this volume is a convenient source for verifying facts, for establishing authenticity, and for deepening understanding of the subject. The detailed and documented content is divided into fourteen chapters covering the complex issues, the campaigns and raids, and the people involved. The reader is given a clear but sobering picture of the conflict centered in Missouri as "the Civil War West of the Mississippi River degenerated into widespread insurrection and almost complete military tyranny" (pp. vii–viii). The narrative points out how using Union forces to deal with insurrection in the area not only lessened needed strength elsewhere but also added to the complexity and ruthlessness of the turbulent situation. The events, along with portrayals of their leading participants, are discussed under the following topics: "The Missouri–Kansas Storm Center," "Sterling Price's Guerrillas," "The Union Military Occupation of Missouri," "William Quantrill's Guerrillas," "Porter Raids in North Missouri," "From Independence to Arkansas," "Lawrence Is Destroyed," "Quantrill and the Confederacy," "Martial Law," "Control of the Populace," "'Bloody Bill' Anderson and George Todd," "The Last Campaign," "The Final Struggle," and "Surrender." Photographs of some of the important people involved; maps showing the Union military districts and the Confederate guerrilla theater of war; a selected bibliography; an appendix listing information about known members of Quantrill's, Anderson's, and Todd's guerrillas; and an extensive index add usefulness to the book.

39. Buchheimer, Naomi. *Let's Go down the Mississippi with La Salle* (Let's Go Series). Illustrated by Albert Micale. New York: Putnam's, 1962. 47 pages. (Ages 8 and up) *Nonfiction*

The author gives a brief but straightforward account of La Salle's expedition down the Mississippi in 1681. Beginning in Montreal where the settlers talk about the great river, the story takes the reader to Fort Frontenac on the Niagara River where La Salle gathers supplies for the dangerous journey to the unexplored mouth of the Mississippi. Almost two months passed before the party reached the confluence of the Missouri and Mississippi rivers, and more than three-and-a-half months passed before the groups reached their destination at the Gulf of Mexico. Many Indian tribes who lived along the banks of the Mississippi are introduced as well as information about the river's larger tributaries. The easy-to-read text of this book would also have appeal for older readers needing high-interest, low-vocabulary material for social studies. A map, appropriate illustrations, and a glossary are other useful features.

40. Bulla, Clyde Robert. *Down the Mississippi*. Illustrated by Erwin Hoffman. New York: Crowell, 1954. 113 pages. (Ages 9–12) *Fiction*

Erik Lind lived on a farm in Minnesota, but he had always dreamed of being a river boy. In 1850, when he was thirteen years old, he got his chance to travel down the Mississippi with his cousin Gunder. Erik worked as a cook's assistant on a log raft bound for St. Louis. He began to think that he had had enough of the Mississippi; the kitchen duties were endless, and a rainstorm and an Indian raid made the journey frightening and dangerous. But then he found out how he really felt about the big river. The book's high-interest and low-vocabulary levels would appeal to reluctant readers.

41. Bulla, Clyde Robert. *Riding the Pony Express*. Illustrated by Grace Paull. New York: Crowell, 1948. 95 pages. (Ages 8–12) *Fiction*

Bulla's dramatic story of the early days of the West is told through the eyes of young Dick Park, the son of a Pony Express rider. The familiar cry, "Here comes the Express," always brought together a watchful crowd of people in St. Joseph, Missouri, when Dick arrived there in October 1860. He had come by train all the way from New York City, and seeing the frontier town of St. Joseph and learning about how the mail was being carried between Missouri and California was just the beginning of his many exciting adventures. Dick continued his journey by stage-coach into Nebraska where he joined his father at the Owl Creek way station. There he made friends with Katy Kelly, the daughter of the station keepers, and Little Bear, an Indian boy, and eventually helped to keep the mail moving. Having made one fast and dangerous dash as a rider for the Pony Express, Dick knew the true feeling of security in the words, "All's well along the road." Bulla composed the words and music for a song using these words and for three other songs that accompany some of the episodes. According to biographical notes, Bulla grew up in Missouri, and his grandfather was a Pony Express rider. While this story is written for eight- to ten-year-olds, it has appeal for a wide age-range. Bulla's writing style, which combines simplicity of language with substantial content, makes a good story for older children with reading difficulties; the story is also appropriate for reading aloud to younger children.

42. Burchard, Peter. *The Deserter: A Spy Story of the Civil War.* New York: Coward-McCann, 1973. 95 pages. (Ages 11–16) *Fiction*

The story takes place during February and March 1862 on the Mississippi River between St. Louis and New Madrid, Missouri, with Island Number Ten as the focus of interest. Since control of the Mississippi was vital to the control of the West, Island Number Ten was important to both the North and the South. As the story opens, the Union was in control of Cairo, Illinois, but the Confederate troops occupied every town south of Columbus, Kentucky. (A map providing a clear picture of the area is included in the opening pages of the book.) Levi Blair, a sailor attached to the *Essex*, flagship of the Union's western flotilla, decided to become a spy and made his way down the Mississippi into enemy territory. Facing freezing weather, treacherous river currents, and gunfire from both sides, he posed as a Confederate soldier and traveled to Island Number Ten. There, working with enemy soldiers, he gathered important information that he personally delivered to General Pope, who was encamped on the outskirts of New Madrid. On 13 March, within a few days after the close of this story, Pope captured the town, and on 7 April, Island Number Ten surrendered. While this concise, absorbing story is valuable for its authentic historical detail, it also provides insight into personal feelings and conflicting emotions. An interesting comparison of the same incident can be drawn from the factual report in Orrmont's biography, *James Buchanan Eads*, chapter 4, "Gunboats for the Mississippi."

43. Burress, John. *Bugle in the Wilderness*. New York: Vanguard, 1958. 222 pages. (Ages 12 and up) *Fiction*

The bootheel of southeast Missouri is the setting for this novel dealing with a boy's haunting experience during the Civil War. Dunklin County was on the line between the Union and the Confederacy, and while the bugles of both armies sounded in the surrounding wilderness, twelve-year-old Billy Goforth and his father lived in the shadow of their own family tragedy. What had happened to Billy's mother affected their lives and blurred their happiness, but release of their conflicts came with Nancy Goforth's death as Billy resolved the ominous and recurring dreams that had obsessed his memory. He also came to understand the meaning of growing into manhood when his father chose to join the Union army.

The story is told in the first person, but Billy's unschooled dialect is often overwhelming and seems inconsistent with the story's depth and range.

44. Burress, John. *Little Mule*. New York: Vanguard, 1952. 314 pages. (Ages 11 and up) *Fiction*

The community of Zenith, Missouri, is the rural setting for a story about a poor but hardworking family. Jefferson Randell Singleton, the youngest of the five children, wanted to be called Jeff but was nicknamed "Little Mule" because of his stubborn manner and "mule-headed" mischievousness. The death of his father, a Baptist minister, left the family, for the most part, at the mercy of the townspeople, but Ider Singleton managed to keep her family together. She and the older children took advantage of all available work, menial as it was during those depression years. Little Mule encountered several difficulties on his own, but he also learned the meaning of real work. Along with his siblings—Bud, Arnola, Ladybird, and Irene—he finally proved that he was growing up.

All the characters are realistically portrayed, and the accounts of their adventures are humorous and touching. However, some of the characters' language and attitudes reflect prevailing racial overtones of the period.

45. Burress, John. *Punkin Summer.* Illustrated by Roberta Moynihan. New York: Vanguard, 1957. 202 pages. (Ages 9–12)   *Fiction*

The bootheel of southeast Missouri during the summer of 1955 provides a colorful setting for a realistic story about a young boy beginning to grow up. Punkin Bradley's family and neighbors in the small town of Cordwood shared the summertime excitement. Wild geese returned along Muddy River, the children learned to weave on grandmother's loom, and Punkin got his bicycle. But, more important, James Edward "Punkin" Bradley began to grow up and to assume responsibility.

While the characterization of the one black family in the story is positively portrayed, an occasional use of the terms "colored" and "Negro" dates the story. Chapter headings and a glossary with generous explanations of terms used in connection with handloom weaving enhance the readability of this book.

46. Burris, Letty. *Azaleas for the Doctor's Bride*. New York: Vantage Press, 1971. 207 pages. (Ages 14 and up) *Fiction*

The setting for this melodramatic novel is the foothills of the Ozarks in southeast Missouri, probably during the early part of the nineteenth century. As part of his training, young Dr. Amel Jargas was sent to Mocking Bird Village for six months to conduct a medical practice. While life in the small village was considerably different from that in the large cities with which he was familiar, his dedication to his work and his accomplishments in his new and special project soon helped him to adjust to the change. When he first came to the little village, he was confronted with local mannerisms, with the stubborn philosophy of the people, and even with small-town gossip. But Dr. Jargas gradually won the respect of the people, as well as their warmth and welcome. His influence on the young people in the community and his love for Amy Trend were bound together with his achievements as a physician. However, the author's excessive sentimentality and a contrived reliance on the deity diminish the effectiveness of the plot.

47. Calhoun, Mary. *Depend on Katie John*. Illustrated by Paul Frame. New York: Harper, 1961. 181 pages. (Ages 9–12) *Fiction*

In this second book about Katie John Tucker, the author has continued the tale of the lively heroine and her family who live in the small Missouri town described in *Katie John*. Having decided to keep the old three-story house that was built in the 1860s, the Tuckers rented their extra rooms as a means of meeting expenses. Much as Katie John loved the old house, she found that her family's great plans had some unforeseen drawbacks: The boarders were demanding, and the work was never-ending. Her problems were all very real and her adventures were realistic and believable. Although Sue was still her best friend, Katie was a new girl and an outsider at school. Eleven-year-old Katie thought boys were impossible until Valentine's Day came along and she became interested in a certain shining knight. Katie John's imagination often got her into trouble, but it also brought her many joys. The story is told with humor and is filled with the kind of details about everyday life that appeal to nine- to twelve-year-olds.

48. Calhoun, Mary. *High Wind for Kansas*. Illustrated by W. T. Mars. New York: Morrow, 1965. 48 pages. (Ages 7–10) *Fiction*

Down the main street of Westport, Missouri, came a strange-looking wagon. It was like any other wagon except that it had tall masts with big white sails, and it was steered with a rudder. John Jones, the man who owned it, had the ingenious idea that a whole fleet of these wagons could revolutionize western migration. Jones proposed "to harness the wind," but the men who saw the windwagon were from Missouri and had to be shown. How they were shown is revealed in the story of the newly formed Overland Navigation Company. Calhoun's lively and humorous tale is complemented by equally appropriate illustrations. The author cites authentic sources on which the story is based. Other versions of this same story include Ennis Rees's *Windwagon Smith*, Edna Shapiro's *Windwagon Smith*, and Ramona Maher's *When Windwagon Smith Came to Westport*.

49. Calhoun, Mary. *Honestly, Katie John!* Illustrated by Paul Frame. New York: Harper, 1963. 214 pages. (Ages 9–12) *Fiction*

In this book, the third one about the heroine of *Katie John* and *Depend on Katie John*, twelve-year-old Katie John accustomed herself to the idea of becoming a teenager. Katie John and the rest of the Tucker family were settled comfortably in the old house at Barton's Bluff that Katie John's great-grandfather had built in the Missouri hills by the Mississippi River. There were no more quarrels with the tenants, Dad's writing was going well, and around her

From *Honestly, Katie John!* (Calhoun)

were all the people she loved. All together, life was pleasant and uncomplicated until one of her sixth-grade classmates implied that Katie John was boy-crazy. Katie loudly declared that she hated boys, and, in an effort to prove it, she formed a boy-haters' club. As could be expected, things went from bad to worse for Katie John. Her friend Edwin Jones turned rudely against her, and her friends who had enthusiastically become boy haters quickly withdrew from the club to pursue new activities such as experimenting with lipstick and telephoning boys. Even her loyal friend Sue continued her longtime association with Bob, leaving Katie John to brood alone about growing up. During this uneasy time, she found comfort by moving into Aunt Emily's old room and by pursuing the imaginary Netta Calkin who "lived" at the old farmhouse in Wildcat Glen. Katie John could get herself into some ridiculous predicaments, but her sense of humor and fair-mindedness enabled her to regain her classmates' respect and Edwin's cherished friendship.

50. Calhoun, Mary. *Katie John*. Illustrated by Paul Frame. New York: Harper, 1960. 134 pages. (Ages 9–12) *Fiction*

Ten-year-old Katie John Tucker had not looked forward to spending the summer in Barton's Bluff, Missouri, a quiet little town overlooking the Mississippi just north of St. Louis. The Tuckers had just moved into an enormous old house inherited from Aunt Emily so that Katie John's father could finish writing his book. They intended to sell the house and to move on to New York; instead, they grew to love it and decided to stay.

Katie John had not wanted to leave her home and friends in California, but she soon discovered new friends, became fond of the old house, and had a wonderful summer. By fall she was hoping that her parents would decide to stay there always. While the old house wasn't haunted as Katie John's new friend, Sue Halsey, had said, it was full of exciting surprises. The girls' discovery of the old system of speaking tubes and the dumbwaiter cleared away

some of the mysteries about voices and the sudden disap-
pearance of the cat. A bicycle trip to the ancient covered
bridge along the old road linking Barton's Bluff and John's
Landing, the society for improving people (especially
older sisters), and Aunt Emily's story were all a part of that
eventful summer. Preteenagers are sure to welcome this
credible story that effectively characterizes their fictional
counterparts.

51. Calhoun, Mary. *Ownself*. Jacket painting by Eros Keith.
    New York: Harper, 1975. 149 pages. (Ages 9–14)   *Fic-
    tion*

Laurabelle Morgan, middle child of a large family living in northeast Missouri during the early 1900s, felt alone
and unwanted because she lacked any real role in the
family. Each of her two brothers and four sisters was
needed or had a place of importance, but all Laurabelle
seemed to have were her fears and fantasies. More than
anything else she wanted the approval of her father who
had sung delightful songs and told wonderful tales of
Welsh faerie folk. But now that her father had become a
"shouting Methodist" and a pious follower of Preacher
Jenkins's fire-and-brimstone religion, there was no room in
his mind for those fun-loving times of the past; in fact, he
harshly rejected Laurabelle's interest in the old folklore as
well as her efforts to win his affection. Her resolution of
this conflict with her father and her learning what "ownself" means are woven into a sensitive and unusual story.
All the characters are sympathetically portrayed, and the
realistic plot evokes a strong feeling for the time and place
as well as an understanding of the family relationship.
Vivid scenes reflect the influence of religion on the sense
of right and wrong and the way that society determines
parents' expectations of their children. The author portrays the weariness of the mother burdened with responsibility and the discouragement of the father, a poor carpenter, with no work to provide for his family. But there is
also humor in the antics of the children and occasionally

From *Three Kinds of Stubborn* (Calhoun)

in the behavior of the adults as well. The story has social as well as entertainment value.

52. Calhoun, Mary. *Three Kinds of Stubborn* (A Reading Shelf Book). Illustrated by Edward Malsberg. Champaign, Ill.: Garrard, 1972. 48 pages. (Ages 8–12) *Fiction*

The three folktales included in this book share a common theme, but each reflects a different kind of Missouri stubbornness. These humorous yarns make good reading, as well as good listening, when Uncle Peeler, Mister Bob, and Hawk Jones stop arguing and start topping each other's stories. As these old fellows would say, just wait till you hear about "The Time Cousin Emmett Out-Stubborned His Mules," "The Time Lightning Struck Little Ida's Umbrella," or "The Time Blue Louisey Put a Hex on the House." Distinctive color illustrations match the easy-to-read text.

53. Campion, Nardi Reeder. *Kit Carson, Pathfinder of the West* (A Discovery Book). Illustrated by Shannon Stirnweis. Champaign, Ill.: Garrard, 1963. 80 pages. (Ages 7–10) *Biography*

An ad in the Franklin, Missouri, newspaper on 6 October 1826 read: "Notice: Christopher Carson, a boy about 16, small for his age, but thickset and light haired, ran

away about September 1st" (p. 29). Kit Carson had been
bound out for seven years as an apprentice to a saddlemaker, but he longed to join the mountain men who often
stopped at the shop on their way west in their wagon
trains. He finally made his way to Santa Fe with Capt.
Charles Bent. Carson's skill as a trapper, his bravery in the
face of danger, and his knowledge of the Indians earned
him a place of leadership throughout the Rocky Mountain
area. He helped John Charles Frémont to map the Oregon
Trail and later served as U.S. Indian agent.

While this story is highly fictionalized by its use of dialogue and thoughts of the characters, the basic content,
though limited in depth, is historically accurate. Written in
simple style for young readers, the fast-moving adventures
of the frontier hero from Missouri should have appeal for
all ages getting started in reading on their own.

54. Carpenter, Allan. *Missouri: From Its Glorious Past to the
    Present* (Enchantment of America Series). Illustrated
    by Roger Herrington. Chicago: Childrens Press, 1966.
    95 pages. (Ages 10 and up) *Nonfiction*

The true story of the founding of St. Louis sets the
scene for Carpenter's history of the state of Missouri. The
book deals with the state's geography, prehistoric times, an
account of the Missouri and Osage Indians, and early ex-
plorations in the area. One section provides a survey in
which many interesting facts are given about the history of
the state. There are discussions of the natural resources—
plants, animals, minerals, and water—and manufacturing,
agriculture, transportation, and communication are identified with the people's use of their goods and services.
Highlights from the lives of several distinguished Missourians emphasize Missouri's place in American history. The
large number of colleges and universities reflects the state's
leadership in the field of education. Missouri has the distinction of having been the first state west of the Mississippi to establish a state university, and in 1908 the University of Missouri opened the first school of journalism in the
world to grant a degree. St. Louis University, a Catholic

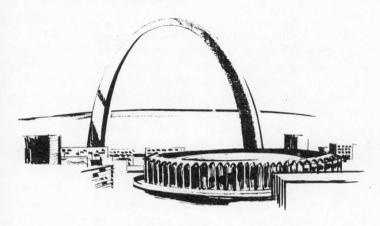

From *Missouri: From Its Glorious Past to the Present* (Carpenter)

institution founded in 1818 as an academy, is the oldest private university west of the Mississippi. The book concludes with information about selected regions and specific cities including St. Louis, Kansas City, Ste. Genevieve, Jefferson City, and many others. A handy reference section provides a chronology and lists of miscellaneous facts, famous people associated with Missouri, and the governors of the state. A comprehensive index and a map are other useful features.

55. Carrière, Joseph Mèdard. *Tales from the French Folk-Lore of Missouri*, Northwestern University Studies in the Humanities Number 1. Menasha, Wis.: George Banta, 1937. 354 pages. (Adult) OP. *Nonfiction*

This scholarly monograph presents a collection of folktales told by French descendants living within a ten-mile radius of Old Mines in southeastern Missouri. As the author states in the preface, his purpose was to save "from oblivion this rather valuable group of stories which I believe to be a representative cross-section of the oral material once so popular among the French of Old Kaskaskia and other villages founded in Southern Illinois and Southeastern Missouri between 1699 and 1760" (p. vii).

The seventy-three stories are presented in both English and French with "greatest caution [taken] to reproduce the language and style of [the] informants" (p. vii). The stories are arranged in three groups (based on the Aanti Aarne and Stith Thompson classification of folktales): "Animal Tales"; "Ordinary Folk Tales"; and "Farces, Anecdotes, and Cumulative Stories." A comprehensive introduction contains specific notes and information about the historical background of the French-speaking population of Old Mines, local customs and traditions, and the scope of the study including sources, subject matter, and language. The monograph also contains a glossary, a list of the tale types, a list of motifs, and a map of the district of Ste. Genevieve. This volume will be of interest to teachers and students of folklore. While only brief English translations of the texts are given, some of the stories, along with their background, would be appropriate for telling to children and youth.

56. Castor, Henry. *America's First World War: General Pershing and the Yanks* (Landmark Books). Illustrated with photographs. New York: Random House, 1957. 182 pages. (Ages 10–15) *Nonfiction*

As indicated by the title and subtitle, this book is a historical narrative and a biography. Castor has woven together the threads of the historical events during John Joseph Pershing's long and active life with emphasis on the important role that he played in shaping history. The first part of the story covers Pershing's early childhood in Laclede (Linn County), Missouri; his training at West Point; his service as an officer during the Indian uprisings in the West; his victory in the Spanish-American War; his subduing the Moro rebellion in the Philippines; his pursuit of Pancho Villa into Mexico; and his marriage, his family, and their tragedy. Most of the book, however, deals with the history of World War I and with Pershing's distinguished service as commander in chief of the American Expeditionary Forces in Europe. There are passages reflecting on his likeness to another famous general, Ulysses S. Grant, from whom he borrowed the tactics of his steady, powerful, and relentless attacks. Also of interest is the account of the men from Missouri in the Thirty-fifth Division of the AEF, especially that of an artillery captain, Harry S. Truman. Throughout his exploits, Pershing's strength of character and his special abilities are strikingly revealed. Numerous photographs lend understanding to the descriptions of important people and to the significant events recounted in the text. An index also adds to the book's usefulness. Although this book is one of the few that deals with the subject at a level appropriate for ten- to fifteen-year-olds, the poor quality of the writing, particularly Castor's use of crude and inappropriate expressions to characterize important personalities of history, mars an otherwise worthy story.

57. Cavanna, Betty. *Jenny Kemura*. Jacket and endpapers by Evaline Ness. New York: Morrow, 1964. 217 pages. (Ages 12 and up) *Fiction*

Readers are given an opportunity to see Kansas City and other parts of their country through another's eyes as Jenny Kemura Smith compares her experiences in the United States with her life in Japan. Sixteen-year-old Jenny, whose mother was Japanese, came to Kansas City to spend the summer with her paternal grandmother. Jenny's visit to Grandmother Smith's upper-middle-class surroundings proved difficult at times, not so much because of differences in language and customs as because of her American grandmother's domineering manner and biased viewpoints; after twenty years, Mrs. Smith still resented her son's marriage to Japanese Midore Kemura. Even so, the summer was filled with many enjoyable activities as Jenny's socialite grandmother arranged for her to become acquainted with other teenagers. Alan Carlisle liked Jenny's thoroughly Japanese appearance and began showering her with flattery and attention. When his mother's intolerant attitude toward foreigners became offensive to Jenny's grandmother, Mrs. Smith whisked Jenny away for a vacation outing on Cape Cod. The summer flew by all too quickly, and in following her father's advice to be herself, however difficult it might be, Jenny gained some lasting friendships as well as an understanding grandmother.

58. Chapman, Carl H., and Eleanor F. Chapman. *Indians and Archaeology of Missouri* (Missouri Handbooks). Illustrated with photographs and drawings. Columbia: University of Missouri Press, 1964, 1978 (paperback). 161 pages. (Ages 12 and up) *Nonfiction*

The authors, who are authorities on the archaeology of Missouri, have designed this book for the mature reader, but it does contain a great deal of information that young people can understand and appreciate. It is an excellent source to which they can turn for more comprehensive answers than those supplied by textbooks or storybooks. Chapman and Chapman have appropriately set their revealing account of Indians and the archaeology of Missouri within a historical background that reflects the cultural development of the American Indian. The entirely factual information is interestingly presented with vivid descriptions and careful explanations. Each page is filled with authentic details that are illuminated with fascinating drawings, and the discussion in each chapter is followed by a list of books for suggested reading. The material is organized around seventeen major topics, with an emphasis on the chronological periods of cultural development. Those topics most suitable for young people include "Our Heritage from the American Indian"; "Indians of Missouri"; "The Missouri and Osage: Indians of History"; and "The Remnants: Tribes Passing through Missouri." Several pictorial maps that afford provocative viewing include "Cultural Areas: Typical Houses"; "Migration Routes"; "Old Map Showing Missouri and Osage Villages"; and "Archaeological Regions." A glossary of specialized terms adds to the usefulness of the book.

59. Chidsey, Donald Barr. *Louisiana Purchase: The Story of the Biggest Real Estate Deal in History.* Illustrated with photographs. New York: Crown, 1972. 231 pages. (Ages 12 and up) *Nonfiction*

The author of several popular history books presents an interesting and chronological account of the critical years (1513–1815) before and after the acquisition of the Louisiana Territory. The fast-moving, detailed narrative vividly re-creates essential episodes affecting the thoughts and actions of the people involved: Thomas Jefferson, the Virginia gentleman and intellectual who was elected president during this period of internal dissent; Robert Livingston and James Monroe, who were sent on a special mission to Paris to negotiate with Napoleon Bonaparte; and Napoleon himself who surprised everyone with the suggestion that the United States purchase not only New Orleans but the entire Louisiana Territory. These and other characterizations highlight the political intrigue and maneuvering involved in the purchase of the Louisiana Territory. Of particular interest is the running account of the role of the less prominent but active Gen. James Wilkinson, who became the first governor of the Louisiana Territory and was stationed at St. Louis. A table of contents, chapter headings, and a chronology help to clarify the book's organization and scope, but Chidsey's material is loosely organized and his style is mediocre with some poorly chosen expressions and irrelevant comments that are confusing. (Mary Kay Phelan's *The Story of the Louisiana Purchase*, written on a lower level of difficulty, is well organized and more clearly presented.) Collective footnotes, a substantial bibliography, and an index are also included.

60. Chittum, Ida. *Tales of Terror.* Illustrated by Franz Altshuler. Chicago: Rand McNally, 1975. 123 pages. (Ages 10 and up) *Fiction*

Chittum, a native of the hills of Missouri and southern Illinois, believes that writing about the darker side of life in the hills is as important as writing humorous tales about mountain life. This collection of short stories set in the Ozark Mountains deals with natural and supernatural events. The people who lived their lives in the hills shared these stories only among themselves, but, as Chittum says, "These are tales that need telling before they are lost or forgotten" (p. 12), and she offers them as "a memorial to those other days and other ways." There are frightening tales of monsters washed up from underground rivers, creatures that appeared by night and vanished by day, and a beast of darkness known to lure people to their doom with a low, provocative whistle. While most of the stories identify no actual places, the back hills of Pike County are the setting for "The Haunted Well," and Iron County is the locale for "Courtland Wethers and the Pit." The reader would need to have a sound understanding of the background for these tales, as well as a strong sense of what is real and what is imagined.

61. Churchill, Winston. *The Crisis*. New York: Macmillan, 1901, 1929. 434 pages. (YA)   *Fiction*

St. Louis, Missouri, is the locale for Churchill's novel set in the Civil War period. *The Crisis* remains a classic combination of history and romance. The lives of Sherman, Grant, and Lincoln, all of whom came from St. Louis or from the neighboring state of Illinois, are shown in remarkable contrast. Likewise, the two streams of emigrations from the North and South brought into focus the northern and southern cultures. Historical characters and events blend naturally with those that are fictional. The experiences of the fighting men are pictured graphically as the author tells a dramatic story of an idealistic young New England lawyer and an aristocratic southern beauty.

When the guns of Fort Sumter reverberated in 1861, St. Louis became a city divided between proslavery southerners and antislavery northerners. Friends and families found themselves at odds over whether Missouri should side with the Union or with the Confederacy. When war was declared, Missouri was caught in a campaign of its own as the governor attempted to use the militia to seize the state. During these engagements, the young lawyer, Stephen Brice, first made the acquaintance of an ex-army officer named Sherman and of another man, Ulysses S. Grant, who claimed that he should be given a regiment. From then on to the close of the war, their concerns and activities were interwoven. During a final audience with President Lincoln, Stephen and Virginia Carvel both realized that there was much to be forgiven and forgotten in the struggle that was drawing to a close. This novel will be of interest to able readers in the upper grades who are exploring this historical period.

62. Clayton, LaReine Warden. *Now Be a Little Lady.* Illustrated by the author. New York: Exposition Press, 1967. 338 pages. (YA) *Fiction*

" 'Now be a little lady,' said mother, looking very lady-like. She smiled pleasantly, seeming to indicate that pleasantness was a part of ladylikeness. I followed her example as nearly as I could" (p. iii). But for a little redhead growing up in the waning Victorian years, it was not always easy or convenient to follow her mother's dictum.

In a highly readable account of proprieties, customs, and personalities, Clayton brings to life a small Missouri town (Mexico, Missouri) during the decade from 1900 to 1910. The story is told from the point of view of a child who regarded her elders as heroes and heroines. Reminiscences of incidents about childhood friends, pets, and gracious ancestors reveal scenes and values of turn-of-the-century culture. Numerous pen-and-ink sketches add authenticity to the verbal descriptions of societal mores and manners. While the narrative sometimes lengthens into recitations of genealogy, many of the episodes are filled with warmth, charm, and local color. The nighttime ride across Indian Territory, Father's history books, Hu and the fur neckpiece, Bessie, Old Biddy, and the first automobiles in town are sure to bring interest, excitement, and laughter to the younger reader or listener as well as to the adult.

63. Clements, Bruce. *I Tell a Lie Every So Often*. Jacket illustration by Charles Robinson. New York: Farrar, 1974. 149 pages. (Ages 10–14)   *Fiction*

Every so often, fourteen-year-old Henry Desant had told lies that were of little consequence. But one lie that he told led him on a five-hundred-mile adventure that he would never forget. It all started over a friendly feud with Clytemnestra "Clemmy" Burke and her twin sister Caroline who lived next door to the Desants. To distract his brother Clayton from the situation with the Burke twins, Henry made up a story about their cousin Hanna who had disappeared nine years ago from her farm home near Kanesville, Iowa. Now Henry and his brother were traveling up the Missouri River by steamboat from St. Louis to St. Joseph and beyond to Kanesville, where they were supposed to spend the summer learning about farming from their cousins. The hazards encountered on the ten-day-long river trip were only the beginning of the danger and excitement that lay ahead as Henry and Clayton sought to rescue Hanna from the Indians. The fast-moving story, narrated by Henry, is full of humor and honest expression. While he admits that telling lies is wrong, he does not regret anything about the summer except the sinking of the *Jane Sure*. Vivid descriptions of scenes and events present a convincing picture of the Midwest in 1848. A hand-drawn map helps to clarify the journey.

64. Clifford, Eth. *Show Me Missouri: A History of Missouri and the World around It*. Illustrated by George Armstrong, Russell E. Hollenbeck, and Gene Jarvis. Indianapolis: Unified College Press, 1975. 192 pages. (Ages 9–14)   *Nonfiction*

The format is the striking feature of this easy-to-read book that has appeal beyond its use as a textbook. The text of this large-sized book is presented in two columns and is accompanied by numerous photographs and colorful drawings, charts, and maps. One particularly interesting chart presents good information about the North American Indians. Another chart gives a clear chronology of industry from village crafts to the space age. The content is divided into twenty-four chapters interspersed with fifteen culture units. Each short chapter is subdivided into brief topics identified by bold type, and the culture units stand out in color-contrasting paging. The content covers a wide range of information beginning with a brief look at that historical and geographical background that includes explanations about America's first people and about the Indians of Missouri. The Missouri story (chapters 8–13) begins with the early exploration and settlement periods, pioneer days, and transportation then and now. Chapters 14–16 deal with Missouri's early statehood, the gateway to the West, and the Civil War period. The remaining chapters give attention to Missouri's educational progress, industry, government, and natural resources and introduce the people who have left an impact on the nation as well as on the state. The culture units, appropriately placed, are interesting vignettes featuring the work of archaeologists, selected myths, outstanding events, famous people, and a salute to the women of Missouri. A glossary and an index are provided. Unfortunately, the front-page Missouri map shows St. Louis as located north of the Missouri River.

65. Clifford, Georgia McAdams. *Indian Legends of the Piasa Country.* Drawings by Gurnsey LePelley. St. Louis: Clark-Sprague, 1932. 114 pages. (Ages 10 and up) OP. *Fiction*

This volume contains twelve stories about the American Indians who lived in the legendary Piasa country. Piasa country, as indicated in the stories and as shown on the endpaper map, is that geographical area located along both sides of the Mississippi and within that point of land between the Mississippi and Missouri rivers where the Mississippi makes the great bend flowing eastward and on to the confluence of the Missouri. It was here in this region that the Osage and other American Indian tribes left indelible traces that are more than enchanting legends; their culture is part of America's history. While all the themes are closely related, several of the stories are connected with the Missouri setting and with the Osage Indians in particular. These include "The Peace Conference"; "The Battle of Blue Lake, a Legend of Missouri Point"; "The Story of Lovers' Leap"; "The Origin of the Harp"; and "La Portage des Sioux." Each of these interesting and well-written stories is preceded by author's notes drawn from history and legend. This attractive book is a collector's item since it contains important and valuable legendary material about the American Indian; it is unfortunate that it has been allowed to go out of print.

66. Collins, Arthur Loyd, and Georgia I. Collins. *Hero Stories from Missouri History.* Kansas City: Burton, 1956. 335 pages. (All Ages) OP. *Nonfiction*

The authors have written a collection of fifty-four short essays on Missouri history that deal "with stories of heroism, of outstanding personalities, and of noted achievement" (p. 9). The anecdotal style makes reading about the important facts in the development of the state of Missouri interesting. The stories are arranged in chronological order. While there is no index, the title of each story clearly indicates what it is about. Some of the titles are "Famous Scouts of the Plains"; "Frontier Justice"; "General LaFayette Visits Missouri"; "An Historic Old Missouri Tavern"; "In and around Historic Lexington"; "The Indian Attack on St. Louis"; "Is Daniel Boone Still Buried in Missouri?"; "Pioneer Women"; "The Pony Express Goes West from Missouri"; "President for a Day"; "Ste. Genevieve Today, First Permanent Missouri Settlement"; and "Women of the Pen." The book also contains a table of contents, endpapers, a list of important dates in Missouri history, a list of books on Missouri for students and teachers, and a list of suggested topics for reports.

67. Collins, David R. *Charles Lindbergh: Hero Pilot* (A Discovery Book). Illustrated by Victor Mays. Champaign, Ill.: Garrard, 1978. 80 pages. (Ages 7–10) *Biography*

In this easy-to-read story of the dramatic life of Charles A. Lindbergh, the young reader learns about the pioneer aviator who made the first solo transatlantic flight. Collins realistically portrays Lindbergh's courageous and fearless involvement in many daring and often dangerous activities—from his early barnstorming days to his heroic adventure that won the hearts of people all over the world—but the skill of flying was always his foremost challenge. Shortly after he became an air force reserve officer, he took a job with a St. Louis company carrying airmail from St. Louis to Chicago. This experience led him to enter the Orteig contest, which offered a reward to the first pilot to fly nonstop from America to France. The name of his plane, *The Spirit of St. Louis*, honored the people who supported him financially as well as with their belief in him.

The book provides young children with informative reading at a suitable level of difficulty and offers them an interesting adventure with an especially appealing hero. The illustrations are an asset to the book; they picture the types of planes used in the early part of this century as well as the clothing styles of the times.

68. Collins, David R. *Harry S. Truman, People's President* (A Discovery Book). Illustrated by Paul Frame. Champaign, Ill.: Garrard, 1975. 80 pages. (Ages 7–10) *Biography*

This fictional biography covers the life of the "man from Missouri" from the time he was eight years old and living on the farm at the edge of Independence, through his years of public service, to his final years in Independence where he died in 1972. Early in the story, the reader is introduced to Bess Wallace whom Truman married after his return from service in World War I. Only brief attention is given to his early childhood except to underscore his love for reading history and for playing the piano. His interest in politics was heightened when he worked as an errand boy at the Democratic National Convention held in

Kansas City in 1900. Then, after his return from the war, he began to participate seriously in local politics, which led him to Washington, D.C., as U.S. senator, vice-president, and finally president during World War II. While the story omits his business failures and only sketches his achievements, he is portrayed as a hero among his war veterans, as an able leader of people, and as a support to the war-torn countries of Europe.

This easy-to-read story is designed to introduce young children to the lives of famous people. The informative content should also make the book useful for older, retarded children as encouragement for reading.

69. Collins, Earl A. *Folk Tales of Missouri*. Boston: Christopher Publishing House, 1935. 133 pages. (Ages 10 and up) OP. *Fiction*

According to Collins, this group of tales was collected wholly within the boundary lines of Missouri and portrays the state's pioneers as honest, hardworking, and imaginative people. Some of the stories have been told many times and printed in many different forms, but others are Collins's own anecdotes. The stories are grouped into five divisions: tall tales, heroes and heroines, current expressions, origin of names and places, and supernatural tales. The chapter entitled "Legendary Sayings" provides an interesting account of the probable origins of the familiar expression, "I'm from Missouri, you've got to show me." While some stories have employed that expression as a term of reproach and ridicule, Missourians more readily accept the entirely different versions that use it to indicate the stalwart, conservative, noncredulous character of the people of the state. Specific locales can be identified in several stories such as "The Footprints on the Rocks," "All the Way from Pike," "Calamity Jane," "The Fountain of Speaking Waters," "Breadtray Mountain," "The Legend of Knobnoster," "The Muir Mansion," and "The Seven Year Light on Bone Hill."

70. Collins, Earl A. *Legends and Lore of Missouri*. Photographs by Garland Fronabarger. San Antonio: Naylor, 1951. 115 pages. (Ages 10 and up) OP. *Fiction*

Missouri's location and place in history, as well as the ancestry of its early inhabitants, have provided their share of legends and folk stories to the history of the nation. Collins has presented an interesting and informative collection arranged according to the following nine groups: "Our Heritage," "Beliefs and Traditions," "Scenes from Life," "'True' Ghost Stories," "Witchcraft and Magic," "Tall Tales," "Legends from Another Race," "Ballads," and "Other Legends." The Indian legends are noteworthy, particularly "The Legend of Taum Sauk." Taum Sauk, the highest mountain in the Missouri Ozarks, was named in honor of a great chief of the Piankishaw tribe; the legend concerns his daughter, Mina-Sauk, and the Osage tribe.

An index and a table of contents that indicates specific stories as well as chapter headings contribute to the usefulness of the information for reference purposes as well as for entertainment.

71. Collins, Earl A., and Felix Eugene Snider. *Missouri Midland State*. Illustrated with photographs and maps. Cape Girardeau, Mo.: Ramfre Press, 1961. 440 pages. (Ages 14 and up) *Nonfiction*

While this history of Missouri is designed for use as a high-school textbook, it could provide useful reference material for elementary and junior-high-school students. The extensive selected bibliographies at the end of each chapter are invaluable. These lists provide not only an abundance of titles conveniently arranged by topics but also a rich historical collection of which many of the titles are available only in libraries; there are also several references of particular interest to certain local communities and geographical areas. In addition to the twenty bibliographies that accompany the chapters, there is a four-page general bibliography. The volume contains more than one hundred illustrations including photographs and maps. Endpapers; table of contents with subtopics, a listing of illustrations, and chapter headings; and an index add to the book's usefulness.

72. Connor, Dick. *Kansas City Chiefs* (A National Football League Book). Illustrated with photographs. New York: Macmillan, 1974. 192 pages. (Ages 14 and up) *Nonfiction*

Kansas City Chiefs, one of the National Football League's Great Teams' Great Years series, tells the story of the team from its beginnings in Dallas as the Texans (1960–1962) to 1974. A discussion of the team's early years is followed by an account of five great games, including Super Bowl IV (1970) when the Chiefs became world champions. Fifty pages are devoted to comments by and about some of the men who have contributed to the greatness of the team, including Lamar Hunt, the founder and owner, and Hank Stram, head coach. The book contains numerous photographs and six pages of statistics. Its appeal would be to the older sports fan and to the able reader. Julian May's *The Kansas City Chiefs: Super Bowl Champions* is more suitable for younger readers and contains material that has obviously been drawn from the same source.

73. Conroy, John C. (Jack), and Arna Bontemps. *The Fast Sooner Hound.* Illustrated by Virginia Burton. Boston: Houghton Mifflin, 1942. 42 pages. (Ages 7–12) *Fiction*

Believe it or not, here is a hound dog that would sooner run than eat, sleep, or fight! This long-legged, flop-eared hound even outran the Cannon Ball Express, the fastest train on wheels and thereby became a legend in American railroad folklore. Burton's illustrations reinforce the humor of the text. While *The Fast Sooner Hound* is a good story for reading aloud to children in the primary grades, it is also highly suitable for independent reading in the intermediate grades and is entertaining to young people in the upper grades. It is an excellent introduction to the Mike Fink and Paul Bunyan stories.

74. Constant, Alberta Wilson. *Paintbox on the Frontier: The Life and Times of George Caleb Bingham.* Illustrated with reproductions. New York: Crowell, 1974. 193 pages. (Ages 11 and up) *Biography*

Paintbox on the Frontier is a vivid record of people and events of the nineteenth century as well as a biography of Bingham. The book is generously illustrated with thirty-four reproductions, many in color. Bingham's early years in Missouri; his political involvement as state representative, state treasurer, and adjutant general; and his participation in the Civil War were all related to his artistic achievements. Although Bingham's larger body of work consists of portraits, his artistic reputation was chiefly derived from his ability to capture the colorful flatboatmen, fur traders, Indians, and electioneering politicians of the West. These popular subjects earned him recognition first as "the Missouri Artist" and later as "an American Artist." Two chapters of the book are devoted to the Civil War and to *Order No. 11*, the painting that was scarcely dry before it became famous and controversial. Constant has carefully authenticated many historical details throughout the story. In addition, the volume includes a selected bibliography, a list of public places where Bingham paintings may be seen, and an index. This beautiful book makes a valuable addition to any library and offers fascinating reading to the eleven-year-old and up.

75. Cook, Olive Rambo. *Coon Holler.* Illustrated by Kathleen Vocite. New York: Longmans, Green, 1958. 178 pages. (Ages 8–14) *Fiction*

Coon Holler, a Junior Literary Guild selection, was chosen as an outstanding book for boys and girls.

While JoAnn and Kenney Brice had enjoyed a happy summer vacation with their grandparents on their farm in northern Missouri, they had looked forward to returning home to Kansas City for the beginning of school and were disappointed and resentful about having to attend the nearby country school where their father had gone when he was a boy. As far as JoAnn was concerned, Coon Holler was an old, shabby, one-room school, and she had no intention of making new friends among the "hillbillies" and "foreigners" who were to be her classmates. But there were many surprises for both children as they learned to know the other children and became involved in the school's activities. They soon realized that they would have to work harder than ever before to keep up with their classes, and their love of music flourished amid even more creative opportunities. Aided by the talented young Joszef Varga with his "Song of Coon Holler," the school group was invited to appear on a TV program in Kansas City. Before the 1956 school year closed, the children were convinced that Coon Holler was a fine place to attend school, and when the school was consolidated the next year, all the children, their teacher, and their parents worked hard to raise the money to buy the Coon Holler schoolhouse to use as a community center.

76. Cook, Olive Rambo. *Locket*. Illustrated by Helen Torrey. New York: McKay, 1963. 149 pages. (Ages 10 and up) *Fiction*

In this sequel to *Serilda's Star*, horses again figure prominently in the continuing story of Serilda Shaw and her family. Serilda now had three horses on her father's farm in northern Missouri: Star and her fillies, two-year-old Locket and six-month-old Teka. Locket won favor as a circus performer and as a show horse at the county fair in Chillicothe. Serilda's hope for a new buggy and harness was finally realized but not before the entire family shared in the efforts to earn the money to buy it. Training Locket as a circus horse and grooming her for the horse show had been a pleasure for Serilda, Katie, and Jeff, but the gathering and marketing of barrels of wild honey was hard work even for Pa and Ma. However, rewards came when crowds cheered as the young circus horse jumped through hoops, marched to music, and answered questions, and a special pride was felt as Serilda's Locket won first place at the county fair.

Chapter headings and authentic illustrations contribute to reading ease and give added interest to this story about rural life in 1870.

77. Cook, Olive Rambo. *Serilda's Star.* Illustrated by Helen Torrey. New York: Longmans, Green, 1959. 176 pages. (Ages 8–12) *Fiction*

In *Serilda's Star*, Cook has drawn on a number of authentic sources as well as on her own memories of growing up on a farm near Chillicothe in northern Missouri. Anecdotes about the covered bridge, the ferry across Grand River, the old mill, the log home, childhood pleasures, and pioneer ways all impart the flavor of the 1866–1868 period.

Up on the high rock overlooking the Grand River valley, ten-year-old Serilda Shaw "always felt as if she were high above the world with a giant colored map spread before her" (p. 3). Very much a part of her everyday world were her older brother Jeff, little sister Bell, Pa and Ma, Grandma, Katie Briggs, the daughter of a family of itinerant travelers, and Star, the horse that turned out to be a thoroughbred. Because Jeff had to help Pa with the timber for the new bridge, Serilda went alone to school on that first day. On her way home, she encountered Katie's stepfather and traded her precious locket for the lame sorrel horse. Her family objected to the transaction, but in the months to come, they were often grateful to have the horse. There was the time that the ferryboat broke loose and the new bridge was threatened, and there was the long drive to get Jeff to the doctor. The loyalty of the gentle horse and the courageous determination of the children accentuated these and many other exciting events throughout the story.

78. Cook, Olive Rambo. *The Sign at Six Corners.* Illustrated by Don Lambo. New York: McKay, 1965. 210 pages. (Ages 12 and up)   *Fiction*

Six Corners where the highway cut through a crossroads was three miles northwest of Fairview, Missouri, on Highway 36. One-quarter of a mile south was the old farm and the vacant house that sheltered Nancy and her family, first as a haven from a storm and then finally as a home. Seventeen-year-old Nancy Adams, her fourteen-year-old brother Joe, and their Aunt Cora put their pluck and ability to work and found happiness in making a living for themselves. Local goodwill and the assistance of kind, elderly Dr. Barney also encouraged them in their determination. Matt Henshaw, the owner of the farm, even included Almiry Davis's clutter of furniture when they traded their camper-trailer for the deteriorated log cabin and thirty-three acres of uncultivated land. But the value of the old walnut handloom and the secret in the hidden drawer of the secretary were revealed in a hexagonal sign at Six Corners that read:

> South—¼ Mile
> SIX CORNERS SHOP
> Weaving—Pottery
> Nancy Adams
> Manager

79. Cortesi, Lawrence. *Jean duSable: Father of Chicago.* Jacket design from a sketch in the Chicago Historical Society. Philadelphia: Chilton, 1972. 177 pages. (Ages 12 and up)   *Biography*

"On this site in 1772, Jean Baptiste Pointe duSable, a Negro from Santo Domingo, built the first cabin at Chicago." This corroded plaque on an old dilapidated building at the corner of Pine and Kenzie streets was the first clue that led to the final proof that Jean duSable was the rightful father of Chicago. For two centuries, the plain that bordered Lake Michigan had been regarded by North American explorers as a strategic portage on the inland water route between the Atlantic and the Gulf of Mexico. However, the Eschikagou [Chicago] plain, named after an Indian warrior, had been a centuries-old battleground among warring Indian tribes who kept each other as well as outsiders from settling in the area. But duSable, a native of Haiti, broke through this barrier and started a settlement and a trading post. This fascinating story covers the period from 1764 when duSable, a black, and his boyhood friend Jacques Clemorgan, a white, set sail to seek their fortunes in New France to duSable's death at St. Charles, Missouri, in 1818. In 1765 the two young men and their newfound Indian friend made their way from New Orleans to St. Louis where they established a trading post. But in 1769 duSable, at the request of Chief Pontiac, visited the Potawatomi on the banks of St. Joseph River and brought about a peace treaty with the Ottawa, Miami, and Illinois tribes. So great was their respect for him that he was not only invited to remain with them but was also granted permission to build a cabin on the Indians' ancient battleground. He soon established his family there and built a successful trading post. While the story continues with emphasis on the beginnings of Chicago during the period from 1772 to 1805, it includes much information about the history and geography of the Midwest. The story also presents an excellent viewpoint of the relationships between Europeans and the Indians during that period and deals with the theme of man's injustice to man. The book contains a bibliography and an index. While the text is geared for senior-high-school readers, the worthy content is appropriate for competent younger readers and listeners.

80. Craz, Alvin. *Getting to Know the Mississippi River* (Getting to Know Series). Illustrated by Nathan Goldstein. New York: Coward-McCann, 1965. 64 pages. (Ages 9–14) *Nonfiction*

Like its companion volume, *Getting to Know the Missouri River*, this book highlights some of the everyday life of the river region and briefly surveys its geography and

From *Getting to Know the Mississippi River* (Craz)

history. Interesting descriptions of the varied modes of boat travel along the river are interspersed with some of the related legends of the past. The discussions of flood control, industries, and recreational facilities are made clear by Craz's personal style of writing and by his frequent explanation of special terms. While the book does not cover the entire length of the river that extends along the eastern boundary of Missouri, there are several specific references to the Missouri scene, especially in regard to the growth of St. Louis. The first reference is to Missouri during the 1830s—the golden age of the steamboat when products were sent downriver to New Orleans and to world markets. The showboat was a part of this age, and several pages describe the *Goldenrod* and the *Admiral*, both showboats that docked at St. Louis. The Douglas Mac-Arthur Bridge, the longest double-span steel bridge in the world, is cited as is the Eads Bridge, the first to span a river with a steel arch. Mention is also made of James Buchanan Eads's other achievements. The famous riverboat pilot and storyteller, Mark Twain, and his home in the river town of Hannibal, Missouri, also have a place in this story. There

are no chapter divisions and only a brief index, but two good maps and numerous illustrations are included.

81. Dalgliesh, Alice. *Ride on the Wind.* Illustrated by Georges Schreiber. New York: Scribner's, 1956. Unpaged. (Ages 7–9) *Biography*

Dalgliesh has used, by permission, Charles A. Lindbergh's *The Spirit of St. Louis* in a brief retelling of the story in simplified language and picture-book format. She has re-created appealing incidents from Lindbergh's early childhood and from his barnstorming days as he traveled around the countryside with other young fliers performing in a flying circus. Accounts of his efforts to get support for his transatlantic flight and for the construction of his plane, as well as a description of his dramatic solo flight, have been included. The book has been designed especially for reading aloud to young listeners but also has value as an introduction to biography for the beginning independent reader.

82. Darby, Ada Claire. *Gay Soeurette*. Illustrated by Grace Gilkison. New York: Frederick A. Stokes, 1933. 312 pages. (Ages 9–12) OP. *Fiction*

Although Soeurette's story is fictional, it may well have happened as narrated in the pages of this book. The characters, for the most part, actually lived, and the events are related against the colorful and authentic backdrop of historic Ste. Genevieve at the beginning of the nineteenth century. The Guibourd-Vallé House stands in all its grandeur today as a reminder of the past and of Soeurette Vallé whose childhood was touched by an array of historical figures and events. She had seen the four flags that had flown over Ste. Genevieve as the territory of Louisiana changed hands among France, Spain, France again, and finally the United States.

Nine-year-old Soeurette was the third daughter of Don François Vallé, the French commandant of Ste. Genevieve. Her friendly, sociable manner and her lively interest in everything that went on in the household and in the village are vehicles for a detailed portrait of many of the French customs that prevailed in everyday life as well as on special holidays. Once her curiosity about a trade that her father was making resulted in her being carried away by some Indians. One of Soeurette's favorite friends and playmates was young Stephen Austin; he often accompanied his father who sought business dealings and political favors from the commandant. Moses Austin hoped to be granted land for a settlement near the port of Nouvelle Orléans through Vallé's friendship with Governor De Lassus. The story comes to a dramatic close for Soeurette and her family as the Spanish and French flags are lowered and replaced by the flag of the United States. Becoming American citizens was the start of a new kind of life for the people of Ste. Genevieve.

83. Darby, Ada Claire. *Hickory-Goody*. Illustrated by Grace Gilkison. New York: Frederick A. Stokes, 1930. 277 pages. (Ages 10–14) OP. *Fiction*

In 1816 Franklin was the most thriving town on Missouri's frontier. Many travelers from the south and east who followed the famous trace from St. Louis westward were on their way to Boonslick country. Years afterward, Martha Reeves recalled with special interest the great pageant along that rough, irregular highway during the early days when Missouri was still a territory, when there were no railroads and few steamboats.

When Martha was eight years old, her family left their wilderness home at Fort Hempstead and made the day-long wagon drive to Franklin to make their home "in a place of wonderful advantages" (p. 37) that already boasted a tavern, a couple of horse-drawn mills, a saddlery shop, a newspaper, and any number of good log houses. Details of daily life in the bustling settlement are woven into a picturesque story as the characters deal with the problems, hardships, and unforeseen challenges of frontier life. Daniel Boone, Capt. William Becknell, the marquis de Lafayette, and the Chouteaus are among the historical personages involved in events that depict the story's authentic background. Young Kit Carson taught Martha and her brother Benji to chew the sweet gum from the hickory tree, which he called "hickory-goody."

While particularly important to historical collections, this book also could be useful, with reservations concerning style, for specialized assignments.

84. Darby, Ada Claire. *"Jump Lively, Jeff."* Illustrated by Grace Paull. New York: Frederick A. Stokes (Lippincott), 1942. 280 pages. (Ages 9–12) OP. *Fiction*

While the story belongs to the imaginary character Jefferson Davis Hickman, St. Joseph, Missouri, during the early 1870s and the historical figure of Eugene Field provide realistic and colorful background. In creating her story, Darby has particularly drawn on events and anecdotes surrounding the wedding of Field and Julia Comstock. (Friends of Field have recalled that he really did stop on his way to his wedding to separate two small boys in a fight and that he gave his bride a French poodle brought from Europe.)

It was Jeff's good fortune that Mister Eugene Field stopped to rescue him from an attack by some town bullies. Following this encounter, Mr. Field paid Jeff to take care of his French poodle while he and his bride went on their honeymoon. The orphaned Jeff made his home with the Bledsoes, a large family struggling to make ends meet in their newly found freedom from slavery. The care of the dog Tootles brought added hardships because Jeff lost the money that Mr. Field had given him. Then the dog mysteriously disappeared and wasn't found until some time after Mr. Field's return home.

There is extensive use of black dialect and a great deal of conversation among the many black characters. The story inoffensively depicts the attitudes and feelings that were common among blacks and whites in the period immediately following the Civil War. Readers might find it interesting to compare and contrast this book with Mildred D. Taylor's Newberry Award–winning *Roll of Thunder, Hear My Cry* (Dial, 1976), which is set in Mississippi at the height of the depression.

85. Darby, Ada Claire. *Peace-Pipes at Portage, a Story of Old Saint Louis.* Illustrated by Grace Gilkison. New York: Frederick A. Stokes, 1938. 263 pages. (Ages 10 and up) OP. *Fiction*

The peace council at Portage des Sioux held a special meaning for ten-year-old Jean Baptiste. During this historic event, he learned about his heritage and came to realize his profound appreciation for his good friend and guardian, Captain Billy. In the waning period of the War of 1812, the Indian situation in the Northwest was still critical as uprisings reached into the Missouri Territory. "Within the limits of St. Louis, now a thriving town of 2600 people [in 1815], there was nothing to fear, but the Wilderness pressed so close that no one save Governor Clark ventured to live beyond the stockade" (p. 9). Some settlers were especially victimized by Chief Black Hawk of the

Rock River Fox tribe. But through the efforts of Gov. William C. Clark, a peace agreement was concluded at the council of Indian tribes that met in the little village north of St. Louis.

Important background is provided through Darby's details covering the ceremony of the peace pipes. The reader is given a realistic insight into the appearance and customs of the great Indian tribes of the north and west including the Illini, Osage, Sioux, Potawatomi, Sac and Fox, Ojibway, Shawnee, and Crow. While the story of young Baptiste is fictitious, Darby's picture of life in old St. Louis during the early 1800s is authentic. In addition to Clark, the gallery of historical characters features such notables as the Chouteaus, Manuel Lisa, William Ashley, George Sibley, and Sacagawea. (History records that the children of Sacagawea grew up under Clark's guardianship.) The book may be found in libraries that have maintained a Missouri historical collection of children's literature.

86. Darby, Ada Claire. *Pinafores and Pantalettes; or, The Big Brick House.* Illustrated by Billy Chapman. Boston: L. C. Page, 1927. 270 pages. (Ages 8–12) OP. *Fiction*

Oakwood, a large home at the edge of Fayette, Missouri, is the antebellum setting for a story about the large family of Leverett children ranging from baby Willy to sixteen-year-old Mary. While they did not have many amusing things to entertain them, these lively children managed to have great fun among themselves and with other young friends and relatives who came to visit. Especially enjoyable were those young aunts from Kentucky and the cousins from Ravenswood across the river in Cooper County. Ada and Kate, the two mischievous little middle children, and their two little aunts about the same age often met with their comeuppances during some of their adventures. One time when Kate followed Ada's example of sliding backward down the roof of the icehouse, she found herself hanging from the edge by one leg, the ruffle of her pantalette damaged beyond repair. Even though platitudes and proverbs reminded them of proper behavior, the young people of this family seemed never short of opportunities for mischief-making. The family name, Leverett, is fictional, but the story envisages a historical parallel since there is in fact an antebellum home called Oakwood, built in 1830 in Howard County, and Ravenswood was built in 1880 on the exact foundation of the older home in Cooper County.

The story of the Leonard family, who may be the historical antecedents of the Leveretts, characterized pioneer living in Missouri. The two Leonard brothers came to central Missouri in 1825. Abiel the lawyer, like the father in this story, was a judge living at Oakwood, and Nathaniel, Uncle Nat in this story, the farmer, did live across the river at Ravenswood. Moreover, as in this story, the two brothers seldom missed a weekend visit with each other. (See "*Show Me" Missouri* by the same author.)

87. Darby, Ada Claire. *Pull Away, Boatman*. Illustrated by Millard McGee. New York: Lippincott, 1953. 247 pages. (Ages 12 and up) OP. *Fiction*

The locale is New Madrid, Missouri, in 1811—the time of the great earthquake and flood. The story is particularly interesting as period fiction as it depicts cultural details as well as the devastating earthquake. Disaster had threatened the people of New Madrid all during the summer of 1811 in the form of drought, sickness, and finally the earthquake that came in early December. Sixteen-year-old Roseanne Murrell, an orphan living with her Uncle Ot and his family, not only shared the family problems but also her own personal worry concerning the whereabouts of her cousin Randy. A young boatman, Guyon Gibson, helped her to deal with these problems and also won her love. Their courtship was marked with uncertainty because of his reluctance to leave his rough and dangerous river life, but the story closes with the final promise of a future together in which Guyon would leave the river and would settle down in the territory. Since the earthquake had destroyed Uncle Ot's house and land, his family decided to move to new territory in the northwest. They planned to take the boat as far as St. Louis and then to follow the Boonslick Trail to a suitable location.

Teachers and other adults, as well as children and youth seeking a factual account of this subject, can turn to *The New Madrid Earthquakes of 1811–1812* by James Penick, Jr. (University of Missouri Press, 1976).

88. Darby, Ada Claire. *"Scally" Alden* (Junior Press Books). Illustrated by Gaye Woodring. Chicago: Albert Whitman, 1939; Laidlaw Brothers, 1929. 241 pages. (Ages 9–12) OP. *Fiction*

Scally was the youngest of five children living in Columbia, Missouri, during the early 1900s. Ever since the father's illness, the Alden family had come to know more than they liked about making ends meet. Scally soon discovered that the lack of money interfered with every pleasant thing that she wanted to do. Her oldest brother Bob was now in Japan with the battleship *Mississippi*, her sister Anne was working while attending the university, and the two middle brothers (who were twelve and fourteen) had found several ways of earning money. But what could a ten-year-old girl do to earn thirty-five dollars? That's what this story is all about. Scally's accomplishments enabled her to realize her dream of going to Devil's Lake in Wisconsin, traveling by train and boat, to visit her best friend, Sally Lacy. Scally's trip, the visit in Chicago, the Treasure Box back home, and the Portrait Tea Party are only a few of the highlights in this warm family story.

While the size of the book appears thick and the paper heavy, the large type, wide margins, several color illustrations, and chapter headings all facilitate reading.

89. Darby, Ada Claire. *"Show Me" Missouri*. Illustrated by Ellen Word Carter. Kansas City: Burton, 1938. 157 pages. (Ages 10 and up) OP. *Nonfiction*

This book is a travelogue intended as a guide to Missourians as well as for other people interested in learning about the state. Geography and history are intermingled to extend the reader's horizons and to provide renewed knowledge of Missouri's past and present (to 1938). The value of the book lies in its interesting information about less commonly known places, people, and events. As Darby points out, "Missouri is full of these mute reminders of our forbears who . . . , recorded history as they lived their daily lives" (p. 15). To mention a few, there is the "Golden Spike" marker located a few miles east of Chillicothe, a town called Far West south of Bethany in Caldwell County, Conception Abbey and Chapel of Perpetual Adoration near King City, Ravenswood and Oakwood in central Missouri, Julia Dent's home in St. Louis, Fort Ancient near Springfield, and Fort Osage near Sibley.

An introductory section giving a brief historical and geographical background of the state is followed by nine other sections detailing the author's tour. An automobile map of the state shows the pilgrimage's progress as it crosses the state from the Platte Purchase in the northwest to Hannibal in the northeast. Parallel with the Mississippi, the journey goes southward to the oldest settlements of the state and into the bootheel. Descriptive paragraphs extol the Ozark region before the route turns north at Carthage and goes through the Old Plains region and eastward along the Boonslick Trail. The last sections of the book are devoted to the three largest cities—St. Louis, Kansas City, and St. Joseph—and to the capital at Jefferson City. Title headings for each section, pen-and-ink drawings of authentic places, and a comprehensive index add to the worth of this volume as a reference tool. There are ten titled illustrations and eleven pages of approximately five hundred indexed items.

90. Darby, Ada Claire. *Skip-Come-a-Lou* (A Stokes Book). With frontispiece in color by M. L. Kirk. New York: Lippincott, 1928. 243 pages. (Ages 9–12) OP. *Fiction*

Can't get a redbird, a bluebird'll do,
Skip-Come-a-Lou, Skip-Come-a-Lou, my Darlin' . . . (p. 241).

In October 1830, eight-year-old Medora Mehitable

Green took a long journey riding behind her father on horseback all the way from St. Louis to Arrowrock (written as one word throughout this book). Stories of quick fortunes to be had in the new state of Missouri had brought Nathaniel Green from Massachusetts to this western frontier of the United States. When he decided to join a caravan of traders going west to Santa Fe, he left his young motherless daughter at Arrowrock in the care of the good and kindly tavern owners, Mr. and Mrs. Zadock Sevier. While she was very often lonely during her father's absence, Medora readily endeared herself to her newly found family and friends, including Malinda, Rily Sevier, and little Jenny who was near Medora's own age. In spite of her "lady-like" ways, Medora was lively, mischievous, and frequently disobedient and troublesome. She had much to learn about frontier living, especially since each member of the tavern family was responsible for certain chores, and Medora was no exception. "Skip-Come-a-Lou" was a popular play-party song and dance of the period. Medora taught her father how to dance it at the Christmas celebration during their final stay in Arrowrock. This book is a quaint period story mainly valuable to historical collections.

91. Darby, Ada Claire. *Sometimes Jenny Wren.* Illustrated by Grace Gilkison. New York: Frederick A. Stokes, 1931. 294 pages. (Ages 9–12) OP. *Fiction*

In 1843 the tempo of life in the river town of Boonville was quickened with the arrival of steamboats and Santa Fe caravans. A familiar sight on the cobbled streets of this bustling town was Leverett Adair, owner of Thornwood, one of the richest farms in Cooper County. An indulgent father, he was often accompanied by his family, especially his daughter and one or more of his five sons. Eight-year-old Jeannette (sometimes called Jenny Wren) was endowed with a lively imagination and with a great deal of curiosity. During one unintended trip by steamboat from Boonville to Arrowrock (written as one word throughout this book), she made friends with the famous

naturalist John James Audubon, whom she was to visit
later in his own home. Jenny also became acquainted with
Sen. Thomas Hart Benton when her family went to Roche-
port to hear him speak against the annexation of the Re-
public of Texas and on the question of paper currency.
While the children found political speechmaking dull,
there were more interesting sights for them at this meeting. The next best thing to having a sister happened when
Capt. Joel Prewitt brought seven-year-old Sylvia Peyton,
an orphan, to live with the Adairs. While the two little girls
were opposites in many ways, they became close companions and often doubled the mischief-making about the
household. They had their portraits painted by George
Caleb Bingham and made the long journey to New York
City when the whereabouts of Sylvia's grandfather were
revealed.

92. Daugherty, James. *Daniel Boone.* Illustrated by the au-
    thor. New York: Viking, 1939. 95 pages. (Ages 10–14)
    Biography

Daugherty's distinguished biography of Daniel Boone
presents a challenge to good readers seeking a more satis-
fying account of the courageous pioneer than those provided by more oversimplified biographies. Both the text
and the illustrations reflect Daugherty's enthusiastic interpretation of the drama and hardships of wilderness life.
Daugherty actually followed the trail that Boone took
when he left his comfortable home in Pennsylvania to
blaze a wilderness road into Kentucky and finally traveled
on to the Missouri Territory, where his long and vigorous
life ended. The introductory letters to Boone, as well as
the appeal to the "lanky sons of democracy" (p. 7), take the
reader beyond the confines of geography; each inspires a
kinship with the wilderness scout that continues throughout the story. The main text is divided into five sections.
Daugherty's device for including some of the episodes is
sometimes confusing and tends to break the thread of the
narrative, although these episodes do provide an extended

portrayal of the wide range of Boone's illustrious encounters. The entire last section of this impressive story depicts Boone's life in Missouri. When the news of Boone's death reached St. Louis in September 1820, the constitutional convention, which was preparing for Missouri's statehood, adjourned for the day "to remember Boone—of Missouri, of Kentucky, of Carolina, of Virginia and Pennsylvania. / Boone—Trail-breaker for destiny for a free people marching on" (p. 95). The book's format with its profusion of Daugherty's original lithographs in color is in keeping with the excellent content.

93. Davis, Julia. *Ride with the Eagle: The Expedition of The First Missouri in the War with Mexico, 1846.* Maps by Jean Paul Tremblay; jacket design by Karolina Kniel. New York: Harcourt, 1962. 191 pages. (Ages 12 and up) *Nonfiction*

In an informal style using fictionalized dialogue, Davis has written a vivid and dramatic account of a little-known but impressive segment of American history. When Mexico declared war on the United States in 1846, President Polk called for fifty thousand volunteers to serve as the Army of the West commanded by Brig. Gen. Stephen Watts Kearny. Among the thousands of volunteers from Missouri was a special group of young men known as The First Missouri under the command of its elected colonel, Alexander William Doniphan of Liberty. Their remarkable expedition covered nearly four thousand miles before they returned home a year later. They traveled on horseback and on foot to conquer Santa Fe, El Paso, and Chihuahua. They fought battles against armies four times their size, they had no supply line and little communication with their government in Washington, and they received no pay during the entire year that they were in service. Their worst enemies were not the Mexicans but cold, heat, hunger, thirst, and distance. In spite of all their suffering, The First Missouri managed to survive and to secure the southwest for their country. They were led on by the good omen soaring above their lines—the legendary image of an eagle on the setting sun. On their return to Missouri, they received national attention and heroes' welcomes all the way from New Orleans to St. Louis. Six of the men kept diaries, which Davis has used to reconstruct their true adventures. In addition to the maps that illuminate the story, the book includes a bibliography of sources and a calendar of events.

94. DeGering, Etta. *Wilderness Wife: The Story of Rebecca Bryan Boone*. Illustrated by Ursula Koering. New York: McKay, 1966. 138 pages. (Ages 11–15) *Biography*

DeGering's story of Rebecca Boone is a tribute to this courageous frontierswoman. From the time of her girlhood marriage while living on the forks of the Yadkin River in North Carolina to her death at the new frontier settlement in Missouri, Rebecca's life was a continuous wilderness adventure. Pioneer life was difficult for all women, but her life was harder than most because she was married to the famous frontiersman, Daniel Boone. As her husband pushed westward founding new settlements in the untamed wilderness, Rebecca went along, assuming an unbelievable share of the responsibility for establishing each new home. She was determined not to "hopple her traipsin' man" (p. 21) who was seldom at home with his family. Rebecca faced many hardships as she reared her nine children as well as six others in the strange, rough land inhabited by Indians and wild animals. She learned to manage with bare necessities; she had to weave cloth from nettles, to mold bullets, and to handle firearms. She heard the scream of a daughter kidnapped by Indians, she saw a tomahawk raised above her husband's head, and she worked along with her husband to pay off excessive debts. The story presents a good picture of the entire period as well as a fine account of the life of this pioneer family, particularly the last years of Daniel and Rebecca and the founding of the Boone family settlement along the Missouri River west of St. Charles. A bibliography, documentation, and maps add to the value of the book.

95. Devaney, John. *The Greatest Cardinals of Them All.* Illustrated with photographs. New York: Putnam's, 1968. 223 pages. (Ages 12 and up) *Biography*

Throughout the years, the St. Louis Cardinals have been one of the greatest and most exciting teams in the major leagues, and Devaney's biographical sketches of some of the great Cardinal players are generously touched with human-interest stories. While the account contains enough of the usual statistics to satisfy the most avid sports fan, the many anecdotal comments about the performances and personalities of the players keep the casual reader turning the pages with increasing interest. Included among these outstanding players are Stan Musial, Ken Boyer, Mort Cooper, and Walker Cooper. Musial has made his home in St. Louis throughout his career. When he retired in 1963, he held a lifetime batting average of .330, and in seven of his twenty-three years on the Cardinal team, he had led the National League in hitting, making a total of 3,629. Boyer was born in 1931 on a farm near Alba, Missouri. There were seven boys and six girls in the family. All seven of the boys signed to play professional baseball, and three became big-league stars. The Boyer family watched the 1964 World Series with mixed emotions: Ken Boyer was playing third base for the Cardinals, and Clete Boyer was the third baseman for the Yankees; one of the Boyer boys had to lose. Mort Cooper, a pitcher, and his younger brother Walker, a catcher, were the heart of the 1942 Cardinal team. The brothers, who were born in Atherton, Missouri, had a brilliant record of performance together. An index adds to this book's usefulness.

96. Dick, Trella Lamson. *The Island on the Border: A Civil War Story.* New York: Abelard-Schuman, 1963. 169 pages. (Ages 11 and up) *Fiction*

When the conflicts of the Civil War pressed heavily on the people living in the extreme area of southeastern Missouri, an area beset with rampant sectional hatreds, David Clark had to assume responsibilities far beyond his thirteen years. Since his father was fighting with General Sherman's Union army, the family was dangerously unpopular with local residents who were Confederate sympathizers. Even the Wades, their closest longtime friends, had turned against them. So Mrs. Clark moved her family to a small piece of land across a swift channel of the Mississippi—Spook Island—which was deserted except for ghosts that supposedly lived on it. During their brief but difficult stay there, David grew up fast as he did a man's work providing food for the family and guarding their safety. Through Pete Wade, Cousin Sam, old Caleb, and others, he learned the meaning of friendship and loyalty. His experiences gave him a clear understanding of the real meaning of war. Some children today may not quite understand why the family didn't go immediately to Grandmother Waring who lived just across the river in Tennessee, but they will appreciate the many adventure-filled episodes in the story.

97. Dines, Glen. *Bull Wagon, Strong Wheels for Rugged Men—the Frontier Freighters*. Illustrated by the author. New York: Macmillan, 1963. Unpaged. (Ages 9–14) *Nonfiction*

Bull Wagon tells the story of frontier freighting across Missouri. After Capt. William Becknell of Franklin, Missouri, blazed the Santa Fe Trail in 1821 and began trading with Mexican merchants, thousands of freight wagons lumbered westward from supply points across Missouri and along the eastern fringe of the Great Plains. In these wagons were supplies for frontier ranchers, army outposts, and stagecoach stations as well as tons of goods to be exchanged for silver, mules, and furs in Santa Fe and at western trading posts. Thousands of these wagons were made in St. Louis by Joseph Murphy whose factory was located at 362 Broadway. As many as thirty carpenters, wainwrights, wheelwrights, blacksmiths, and painters worked under the same roof in his factory. (A picture of his Conestoga wagon appeared as a trademark in a wagonmaker's advertisement, a copy of which is included among *Bull Wagon*'s illustrations.) In *Bull Wagon*, the author-illustrator provides interesting, clear, and detailed explanations of wagon construction; lucid descriptions of the animals that pulled the wagons (oxen, mules, and horses); and remarkable characterizations of the men who operated the wagon trains—the wagon bosses (townsmen and frontiersmen), the teamsters (bullwhackers and mule skinners), and other "hirelings." Many owner-bosses or hired teamsters were Missourians. The use of exact terms, which are fully explained in text and pictures, gives the reader a clear and complete understanding, as well as a great appreciation, of the intricate details involved in taking freight wagons across the frontier wilderness. Fascinating drawings, diagrams, maps, copies of advertisements, and photographs illuminate the text. A glossary of special definitions, suggested readings, a bibliography of sources, and acknowledgments are also included.

The book makes an interesting supplement for readers acquainted with stories about the wagon trains that moved west along the historical trails. Such readers are familiar with the names of Missouri gathering spots and jumping-off places for wagon trains heading for the Santa Fe and Oregon trails. They know the names of famous mountain men who played a part in winning the West, and they are sensitive to the adjectives describing the challenges faced by those journeyers. Now, *Bull Wagon* furnishes those readers with details about the skills and equipment undergirding the stories.

98. Dooley, Thomas A., M.D. *Doctor Tom Dooley, My Story.* Illustrated with photographs. New York: Farrar, Straus, 1962. 160 pages. (Ages 12–16) *Autobiography*

This volume, prepared especially for young people in the upper elementary grades and beyond, is an abridgement of three of Dr. Dooley's books telling about his work in Southeast Asia—*Deliver Us from Evil*, *The Edge of Tomorrow*, and *The Night They Burned the Mountain* (Collected ed., Farrar, Straus & Giroux, 1960). His story began in 1954. Thousands of people were seeking freedom from the Communists who, according to the Geneva Treaty, were

scheduled to assume control of North Vietnam in May
1955. Dooley, a young naval medical officer attached to the
Preventative Medical Unit, was placed in charge of the U.S.
Navy rescue operation for these refugees migrating to
South Vietnam. The suffering, hardships, hunger, and disease that he saw during his ten months at Camp de la Pa-
gode so impressed him that he decided to return to Indo-
china following the completion of his tour of duty. His
story continued with Operation Laos, which marked the
establishment of a hospital and a clinic in Vang Vieng and
concluded with the foundation of MEDICO—a nonprofit
organization that contributes medical aid to underdevel-
oped countries. In telling his story, Dooley included interesting background information about the culture, political
struggles, and living conditions of Southeast Asia. Although his life was one of serious purpose, some of his
experiences—his own doubts about his mission in Vietnam, the mandarin's tale of how a village escaped communism, his own encounter with the witch doctors—are
not without humor. Throughout the pages of the book,
Dooley's activities reflected sacrifice and humanitarianism.
The publishers have added an epilogue describing the final tragic months of Dooley's life. His funeral and burial
were in St. Louis, Missouri, his hometown. Among the
worldwide tributes was a statement issued by the American
Medical Association saying that Dr. Dooley had "won the
reputation of 'the good American' for his dedication to the
art of healing and constructive work for peace" (p. 157).

99. Dorian, Edith. *Trails West and Men Who Made Them.* Il-
    lustrated by W. N. Wilson. New York: McGraw-Hill,
    1955. 92 pages. (Ages 10–14) *Nonfiction*

Dorian and Wilson have created a fascinating factual
book about the historic trails by which America moved
west. Following a brief introduction, Dorian discusses
eight famous trails and the trailmakers, calling attention to
familiar terms from the old trail days that color our speech
today just as they did when America was young. While all
these trails were important to American history, the three

that held particular impact for Missouri were the Water
Trail, the Santa Fe Trail, and the Oregon Trail. A realistic
description of each trail is woven into true accounts of exciting events and of people whose courage, endurance,
and adventurous spirit helped to create the nation that was
yet to come. Along the Water Trail, down the Mississippi
and up the Missouri, appeared the trappers, traders, explorers, voyageurs, and missionaries bearing such familiar
names as Joliet, Marquette, Lewis and Clark, and Sacagawea. It took 150 years to open the Water Trail, but both
the Santa Fe Trail and the Oregon Trail opened more rapidly. The Santa Fe Trail, our first transcontinental trail, was
old before white men came to America; it was the trail of
the buffalo and the Indians and later the trail of Spanish,
French, and Yankee trappers, traders, and soldiers. But in
1821 William Becknell of Franklin, Missouri, inaugurated
the trail's greatest days. From St. Louis, Independence,
Westport, and other places in Missouri came Jim Bridger,
Tom Fitzpatrick, Kit Carson, the Sublette and Bent brothers, and even the aging Daniel Boone pointing the way
westward. The Oregon Trail, over which the Pony Express
raced, was depicted as the symbol of pioneer America.
Settlers and gold seekers trekked across Missouri to journey over one of the three branches of the trail to Oregon,
California, and the Great Salt Lake (the Mormon Trail).
An index, detailed black-and-white drawings, and maps
enrich the informational content of the book.

100. Draper, Cena Christopher. *Dandy and the Mystery of
the Locked Room.* Illustrated by Pat Minnis. Independence, Mo.: Independence Press, 1974. 224 pages.
(Ages 10–14) *Fiction*

The sprawling Minnewawa Hotel with its twisting hall-
ways, forgotten attics, and barricaded east wing provides
the ideal setting for a mystery that keeps the reader turning the pages until the secret is unlocked. Following the
death of his parents in 1898, young Dandy Delaney arrived at his grandfather's famous resort, Pertle Springs,
near Warrensburg, Missouri. Fifteen years earlier, his

From *Dandy and the Mystery of the Locked Room* (Draper)

mother had eloped with his father, a Shakespearean actor. The colonel had never forgiven his daughter and viewed his namesake as "the devil . . . come to plague me" (p. 23). Conflicts between the proud old man and the equally spirited boy continued to mount until a series of incidents turned the tide to forge a lasting bond between them. Dandy's determination to locate his mother's letters led him to his mother's old room, which had been kept locked and boarded up since she left. The sinister housekeeper, Hannah, the aunts T'any and Terza, the handyman and trusted friend Nippy, Cousin Owsly, and the confident servant Walker are all skillfully interwoven into the scenes that complete this dramatic story.

101. Draper, Cena Christopher. *Ridge Willoughby*. Illustrated by Elizabeth Rice. Austin: Seck-Vaughan, 1952. 119 pages. (Ages 8–12) *Fiction*

The Ozark foothills of Missouri are the setting for the adventures of Henry Clay Hale. He got the name of Willoughby because of his insistent question, "Will I be late for school? Will I be?" Willoughby seemed to get himself into an unusual amount of trouble with his five younger sisters, forever chanting "You're gonna get it," with his Aunt Jennie, Uncle Jim, Mom Po, Pa Ham, and even Pa Hale always somewhere on hand to chastise him. However, he found satisfaction in many of his escapades such as being allowed to keep a pet skunk named Pew. One of his most exciting adventures was his discovery of a buried treasure near an old tree that had been uprooted during a violent storm.

102. Draper, Cena Christopher. *Rim of the Ridge*. Illustrated by Emil Weiss. New York: Criterion, 1965. 157 pages. (Ages 10–14) *Fiction*

This story from the Missouri ridgeland is set in Boone County in 1902 and is dedicated to the "memory of those who have passed along the winding banks of Postoak, Bearcreek, and Clearfork" (p. v). Among these real and imagined people was William Wallace Bunn, nicknamed Punk, who was raised "Bible-wise" by his stepgranny. In addition to his conflicts with Granny, which continually created a mounting war within himself, he was further tormented by the grudge-carrying Hood brothers. But Granny's old friend, Hummy Humphreys, the best coon hunter in the whole county, persuaded her to let the boy "run wild with the winds" for a while. So Hummy and Punk, both sensitive to the beauty and wonders of the

From *Rim of the Ridge* (Draper)

countryside, tramped the woods with the coon dogs at their heels. A mature Punk returned home with the courage to deal with the horrible Hood brothers and with a strong realization of his true love for Granny. While the background abounds with strong feelings about nature, the theme of love transcends the setting as the plot develops around the warm humanity of unforgettable characters who conjure up both humor and pathos.

Rim of the Ridge was chosen as one of the American Ambassador Books to interpret the lives, background, and interests of American young people to readers in Great Britain.

103. Draper, Cena Christopher. *The Worst Hound Around.*
Philadelphia: Westminster, 1979. 116 pages. (Ages
9–14) *Fiction*

Draper's feeling for nature and for the Missouri locale, an engaging plot, and apt characterizations combine
to make a lively and rewarding story. Set in the ridgeland
of Johnson County, the tale abounds with folk history. Men
and dogs alike knew that hounds on the ridgeland were
for trailing coons, except for Blue Dog who was considered the worst hound around by everyone except Jorie
and Boone Clayton. Jorie was worried enough with all the
neighborhood hunters joking about his dumb hound.
Then a wagonload of cousins, Seth Sullins and his three
daughters, arrived from Arkansas to create further com-
plications during their long visit. Eighteen-year-old Sue
Ellen was to become an immediate threat since Jorie's
father was a widower; with so many visitors without a "y'all
come" (p. 13), Jorie had to sleep in the barn; and Cousin
Sully's mean-looking, high-spirited hounds sent Blue Dog
scurrying to safety. But Cousin Lou Ann, the middle girl,
was different. She not only understood Jorie's loneliness
but also knew a great deal about training coonhounds.
How she and Jorie's longtime friend, the Duke, helped to
train Blue Dog for the fall raccoon hunt led to many exciting and enjoyable adventures. Praise came from every
member of the hunt as they stood spellbound at the final
confrontation between Old Timer and Blue Dog. The
Crittensons' lodge just beyond Devil's Trail and their acquaintance with the hill folks marked the changing scene
of the ridgeland. The Crittensons, owners of coal land in
the area, came there from St. Louis each year to spend a
few weeks hunting and to oversee the mines. While Jorie
didn't care much for young Francis Crittenson III, he did
puzzle over the impression that the lad's city ways had on
Cousin Lou Ann.

104. Dunham, Montrew. *Langston Hughes: Young Black Poet*
(Childhood of Famous Americans). Illustrated by

Robert Doremus. New York: Bobbs-Merrill, 1972. 200 pages. (Ages 8–12) *Biography*

I dream a world where man
no other man will scorn
where love will bless the earth
and Peace its path adorn.

—from "Troubled Island" by Langston Hughes

With an easy-to-read vocabulary, using a great deal of conversation and verbalizations of the characters' thoughts, Dunham introduces young readers to Langston Hughes. The story only mentions his birthplace (Joplin, Missouri) and moves quickly into the poverty years spent in Topeka and Lawrence, Kansas, with his mother and grandmother. His acquaintance with his father, a lawyer in Mexico City, was meager, and his impressions of him were far from favorable; Grandma Langston gave him pride in his heritage. His father finally did agree to pay Hughes's expenses so that he could attend Columbia University, but Hughes found the university unsuitable and took a job on a ship sailing to Africa, where he gathered ideas that he later put into his poems and other writings. Hughes graduated from Lincoln University in Pennsylvania and became well known throughout the world as a lecturer and poet.

In addition to a table of contents, the book contains a list of facts about the time when Langston Hughes lived, a set of review questions, questions for further discussion, a list of interesting things to do, a list of other books to read, and a glossary of interesting words used in the story.

105. Eaton, Jeanette. *America's Own Mark Twain.* Illustrated by Leonard Everett Fisher. New York: Morrow, 1958. 251 pages (Ages 12–16) *Biography*

Eaton's biography is notable for the picture that it gives of the period in which Mark Twain lived—the Mississippi steamboat days, the western mining camps, and the rapidly growing American frontier. The story is filled with interesting details that characterize the man and his kinship to his country. He knew America, and he wrote about that part of America that he knew best; his stories, original and of lasting value, were inspired by his own experiences. Many humorous escapades included in this biography reveal Twain's natural wit. The story also shows the serious nature of the man as he faced personal sorrow and coped with financial difficulties. This spirited and well-rounded story should give readers an increasing appreciation of the heritage that one of America's most gifted authors left to future generations. They may also find it interesting to compare this biography with any one of the many other books about Mark Twain.

106. Eliot, T. S. *Old Possum's Book of Practical Cats*. Designed by Robert Josephy. New York: Harcourt, 1939. 46 pages. (Ages 10 and up) OP. *Poetry*

Eliot's book belongs to cat lovers of all ages, but some of these cats have been longtime favorites of younger generations in particular. Eliot, winner of a Nobel Prize for his contributions to poetry, signed his dedication for this book with the initials, O. P. [Old Possum]. The publishers' notice states, "Mr. T. S. Eliot's intimate friends receive from time to time typewritten verses which are always identifiable. The poems which concern cats are presented here." Eliot not only gave his cats impressive names but also characterized them with descriptive adjectives and unforgettable actions. These cats were as equally ridiculous as the famous calico cat, the cat with the fiddle, or Pussy-Cat who went to sea. Old Possum's cats had some other qualities, too. There was that "terrible bore, the Rum Tum Tugger" (p. 17), who was a curious beast, and "Macavity: The Mystery Cat" who was also "a ginger cat . . . a fiend in feline shape" (pp. 32–33). In addition to the verses about Rum Tum Tugger and Macavity, there are twelve other poems in this collection. These and other poems suitable for children and youth can also be found in Eliot's *Collected Poems, 1909–1962* (Harcourt, 1964) as well as in anthologies. These poems are fun to hear when read by the teacher or by the poet himself on a recording. Children can enjoy reading them, too, by forming choral speaking groups and turning an otherwise dull or frustrating part of the school day into relaxation and pleasure.

107. Erdman, Loula Grace. *Another Spring*. New York: Dodd, Mead, 1966. 305 pages. (Ages 13 and up) *Fiction*

"That was nature's gift to mankind, the gift of time. Always another year. Always, another spring" (p. 300). So ends the story of a group of exiles bound together in their struggle for survival. The book deals with people driven from their homes in four western counties of Missouri by General Order No. 11. Writing with authority about the period and the place, Erdman gives a clear picture of the historical and political backgrounds for this dramatic novel. In the author's notes, she states, "This is not a Civil War novel, although that period is the background. It is, rather, a story about displaced people . . . who were the victims of these tragic events and their reaction to what happened. It is a story of their endurance under stress, of their courage and dignity and compassion, of the triumph of the human spirit over great adversity" (pp. 301, 305).

By federal edict—Order No. 11—thousands of people were banished from their homes in 1863. Harried by desperate raiders, their homes burned, people fled the proscribed area. Taking with them only the bare necessities, the Weatherly and Nichols families joined the crowds of refugees that jammed the roads. They were rich landowners and friends despite their conflict in loyalties. The bond between them was strengthened by the engagement of Richard Nichols and the Weatherlys' niece, Betty. The Carroways, also neighbors, had heretofore been separated from the Weatherlys and the Nicholses by their lesser station in society, but Pete Carroway played a decisive role in the future of the three families. Being able to survive—to accept being uprooted, to live off the land, to cope with hunger and danger—depended on their ability to change and to forget the old ways. As the war ends, they return home, not to their antebellum world of balls and parties, but to the shadows of tragedy balanced by the stronger light of hope.

108. Erdman, Loula Grace. *Life Was Simpler Then.* New York: Dodd, Mead, 1963. 186 pages. (Ages 12 and up) *Fiction*

Growing up in the rural area of western Missouri during the early 1900s may have been simpler, but according to Erdman's reminiscences of her own childhood, it was no less exciting than growing up today. Her sixteen stories are grouped under the headings of the four seasons. Her lively discourses cover a variety of subjects ranging from accounts of the hired hands called "Heroes in Overalls," to the events at Christmastime that occurred "But Once a Year." Chapters such as "Hello Central," "Not a Speck of Dirt," and "The Ice Cream Supper" could provide excellent dramatizations as well as entertaining and informative reading. Many details of household and community life along with sensitive and often humorous vignettes about a child's development of a sense of values are effectively woven into these stories. Education was recounted in "Feet That Went to School." "The House Will Come to Order" and "We Did It for the Town" reflect further cultural opportunities through the literary society and the chautauqua, and the joy of reading is eloquently expressed in "Reading Aloud." *Tom Sawyer* was one of the books read aloud by the author's family, and every child growing up in that part of Missouri read Caroline Abbot Stanley's *Order No. 11.* Concerning the latter, Erdman gives a brief discussion of its theme and historical background, as well as a reference to Missouri's George Caleb Bingham.

109. Erdman, Loula Grace. *Lonely Passage.* New York: Dodd, Mead, 1948. 234 pages. (YA) *Fiction*

The texture of Thurley Renfro's life was made up of the house in which she lived, of the town in which the house was set, and of the family of which she was a part.

Thurley had been born in the house, which had been built in the late nineties, and had never been very far away from it. To the west was Kansas City, to the east St. Louis, to the north the Missouri River, and to the south the foothills of the Ozarks. In her family, "everyone seemed to reach out to the others, bound together in a tenuous web of kinship, a tie as intricate and as well defined as the roads that criss-crossed across the countryside" (p. 181). To her, all roads led to the homes of her relatives in the town of Helton and beyond. Yet Thurley came to feel that she had been alone all her life. As in the book that Chris had read aloud to her, "his life must always walk down lonely passages" (p. 181). Until she was fifteen, her family was all her world. The details of everyday activities were treated with utmost importance by the self-sufficient, sure Pembertons—her mother and father, aunts and uncles, and cousins. Then church, music lessons, and school began to fit into the pattern of her life, creating a mixture of adultness and immaturity, until, at eighteen, Thurley grew up. Unrequited romance entered her life as did the sad and shocking realities of human behavior. But in the end, love and marriage promised to continue her circle of security. As the novel proceeds, the unfolding situations and a parade of people are characterized with the author's usual skill.

110. Erdman, Loula Grace. *Save Weeping for the Night.* Jacket illustration by Kerry Gavin. New York: Dodd, Mead, 1975. 205 pages. (Ages 13 and up) *Fiction*

This historical novel provides one of the few accounts of Bettie Shelby, the wife of Gen. Joseph O. Shelby. While much has been written about the Confederate hero from Missouri who led the famed Lafayette County Cavalry, little mention has been made of his wife. As the basis for this novel, Erdman used *Reminiscences of the Women of Missouri during the Civil War* (State Historical Society, 192?), which contained a brief account that Bettie Shelby wrote of her own life. Set against the background of turbulent times in a locale familiar to the author, the book is historically accurate with vividly described scenes and faithfully drawn characters. Bettie Shelby's steadfastness and devotion to her husband and children won the love and respect of those who knew her. She and her children dared to follow her husband from Waverly, Missouri, to the battlefields of Arkansas. Then back in Missouri, she defied the bushwhackers and looters as violence spread throughout the Missouri–Kansas border. As a refugee from General Order No. 11, she fled to Kentucky, the home of her husband's parents. From there she made a perilous journey to Clarksville, Texas, located near the seat of Missouri's government-in-exile. When Jo Shelby refused to surrender after the war ended, she followed him to Mexico. Despite having known only the luxuries of a comfortable way of life, she faced difficulties and hardships with unusual courage and endurance. The book provides a clear picture of the Civil War period through the historical figures and events that were an integral part of Bettie's story. Missouri had been divided on the issues of slavery and secession for years, and civil war raged there in its worst sense. The hostility between friends and even families is sensitively depicted as is the dilemma of many of the slaves in the area. The loyalty and respect between slaves and their owners are effectively revealed through the characterization of Billy Hunter and other blacks as well as through detailed descriptions of the various activities of their owners.

111. Erdman, Loula Grace. *Separate Star*. Decorations by Janice Holland. New York: Longmans, Green, 1944. 200 pages. (Ages 13 and up)   *Fiction*

> And each, in his separate star
> Will paint the thing as he sees it
> For the God of things as they are. (p. 104)

The author of *Separate Star* has painted a picture of the way things were for a young teacher in a small town probably during the early 1940s. Although Missouri is not specifically mentioned, it could well be the setting of the story, since it is likely that Erdman has drawn on her own experience as a beginning teacher in Missouri.

Gail Warren was confronted with many of the same trials that beset most young people starting their first teaching positions. Although not entirely prepared for the complexities of the problems, her skills and ideals enabled her to prove her ability as well as the value of her chosen profession. As Gail became adjusted to the small town of Clayton, population 1,014, with its poor school facilities, she also succeeded in creating a community spirit and cooperation among the townspeople. When she had discovered an almost total lack of interest in learning on the part of her seventh- and eighth-grade pupils, she gathered books for them to read. Then she began to plan engaging programs to suit individual interests, arranged for playground equipment, and finally managed to convince the school board of the need for home economics and shop classes. The story climaxes on a romantic note as her friendship with the promising young principal, Dave Patterson, leads to his proposal of marriage.

112. Erdman, Loula Grace. *The Far Journey*. New York: Dodd, Mead, 1955. 282 pages. (YA)   *Fiction*

Young adolescents reaching upward for longer, more adult novels will find adventure and romance in *The Far Journey*. Set during the latter part of the nineteenth century when homesteading was a way to go west, the plot shifts from Missouri to Texas through a series of dramatic episodes.

From her upstairs room in the Old Montgomery House overlooking the little town of Grafton in west-central Missouri, Catherine could see the outward dimensions of the world in which she had spent most of her nineteen years. Her life might have taken an entirely different direction if her aristocratic, Virginia-born mother's plans had succeeded, but Catherine had met the twenty-two-year-old Yankee, Edward Delaney, who, with dreams of his own, soon captivated her love. For several years, their married life followed the pattern of domesticity in the peaceful little town where Edward managed his uncle's general store. Following the death of his uncle, he sold the business and went to Texas, promising to return for Catherine and their son as soon as he could establish a claim and build a dugout. After almost a year had passed, Catherine, her five-year-old son, and Uncle Willie set forth in a supply-filled covered wagon to travel more than four hundred miles overland from west Missouri to the Texas Panhandle.

Full details not only give a picture of domestic life in western Missouri during the period but also present a day-by-day account of the harsh conditions faced by overland travelers and a panoramic view of the countryside.

113. Erdman, Loula Grace. *The Years of the Locust.* New York: Dodd, Mead, 1947. 234 pages. (YA) *Fiction*

Set against a background of the rich bottomlands and rolling hills of central Missouri, the story of "Old Dade" Kenzie and the relatives and friends who knew him makes a warm and understanding novel. The entire story takes place over a three-day period beginning when Old Dade died on the morning of 26 May. "It was a most inconvenient time" (p. 3).

All the people whose stories fill the pages of the book knew Dade, and none would forget the important part that he played in their lives. As the story unfolds, each of these people—Beulah Fulton Kenzie, Laura Meeks, Barry Kenzie, and a host of others—took a portion of the past, examined it, and recalled things that they had not thought of for years. Like life itself, the story becomes more complex through the richness and diversity of those men and women of the neighboring farms and villages. While interwoven with each other, their lives had been changed because they had known and respected this man who was wise and prosperous yet uncommonly simple in manner. Through the atmosphere of a small community, Erdman has skillfully expressed the feelings of home and kinship and the need for security lying deep within each individual.

Excellent characterization, authentic background, and lively narrative distinguish this award-winning novel. While only secondary components of the story, the time will be recognized as the 1940s; Missouri towns and cities such as Columbia, Excelsior Springs, and Kansas City are mentioned.

114. Ernst, John. *Jesse James*. Jacket by Arvid Kneedsen; maps by Theodore R. Miller. Englewood Cliffs, N.J.: Prentice-Hall, 1976. 76 pages. (Ages 8–14) *Biography*

"He [Jesse James] became in legend what he never was in life" (p. 72). In *Jesse James*, Ernst examines the life of the notorious outlaw in the light of nineteenth-century society and politics. Born in 1847, Jesse grew up on a farm near the Missouri–Kansas border where trouble and violence were a way of life. Yet there was a peaceful side to growing up for the three James children as their family maintained firm religious beliefs and held a place of respectability in their community.

This biography explores the impact of the Civil War on Jesse's life as he came to accept violence and revenge as inevitable. The book covers the various exploits of the James gang that created national news throughout their strikingly wide geographical range. The reader is given a clear image of Jesse's methods of robbery, of his skill as a horseman, of his ability to lead his accomplices, and of his characteristic way with words. In this factual account, Jesse James emerges as less of a hero than many legends have portrayed him. Several maps help in the interpretation of details. The book contains an index, but there is no documentation of sources.

115. Evans, Mark. *Scott Joplin and the Ragtime Years*. Illustrated with photographs. New York: Dodd, Mead, 1976. 120 pages. (Ages 10 and up) *Biography*

Evans's knowledge and feeling for his subject come through so clearly that the reader almost hears the familiar strains of "Maple Leaf Rag" or "The Entertainer." In this biography, Evans writes enthusiastically about the rediscovery and revival of ragtime as well as about the 1890 period when Scott Joplin was the king of ragtime, a highly syncopated rhythm played over the steady bass rhythm of black folk music. Evans points out that many pianists like Joplin played ragtime, but, unlike most rag musicians of his time, Joplin knew music and captured the beautiful rhythms in writing for others to enjoy in the years ahead.

As a young, black, itinerant musician, Joplin traveled from the Mississippi riverboats, gambling houses, and cafés to the World's Columbia Exposition in Chicago. Always eager to learn and to improve his performance, he absorbed the sounds and rhythms that he heard. In 1885, at the age of seventeen, he arrived in St. Louis for the first time. He worked there for the next eight years, but he composed "Maple Leaf Rag," which brought him fame and fortune, in Sedalia, Missouri. The song was an immediate success and marked the beginning of a new era in black music. Before it faded out in the early 1900s, ragtime became internationally popular. While Joplin enjoyed the success of his publications, his teaching, and his performances, he never gave up his dream of writing classical music. However, the operas that he composed were not critically successful during his lifetime. Now, more than sixty years after his death, recent performances of his opera *Treemonisha* have been highly acclaimed. Two museums, one in Nashville and one in Texarkana, have collections honoring him. A marble monument has been placed on the site of the Maple Leaf Club, where he was working as a piano player when his "Maple Leaf Rag" was published; and a Scott Joplin Festival was recently held in Sedalia, the town called the cradle of classical ragtime.

116. Evarts, Hal G. *Jedediah Smith: Trail Blazer of the West* (A Westerners Book). Illustrated by Bernard Krigstein. New York: Putnam's, 1958. 192 pages. (Ages 10–16) *Biography*

In this fictionalized biography, the fabulous life of Jedediah Strong Smith is seen clearly against the glamorous background of the early days of Missouri and the nation. At the age of twenty-three, Smith arrived in the frontier town of St. Louis and became associated with the Rocky Mountain Fur Company owned by Gen. William H. Ashley and Maj. Andrew Henry. During the ten years that followed, his feats of endurance and courage as a fur trader and explorer became legendary even in his own time. In the spring of 1822, he was among the adventurous crew on the maiden voyage of the keelboat *Enterprise* as it ascended the Missouri River.

Among those illustrious Missourians engaged in this venture were rugged farmers, experienced mountain men, shrewd businessmen, and tough riverboatmen such as David Jackson, William and Melton Sublette, Tom Fitzpatrick, Hugh Glass, Jim Bridger, Moses "Black" Harris, Mike Fink, and his troublemaking friends Talbot and Carpenter. Slender, soft-spoken, and religious, Smith seemed unlikely to survive the river trip, much less succeed as a fur trapper, but within a few years his boundless energy and his bravery made him an acknowledged leader. While he left a personal fortune to his family in St. Louis, his legacy to the nation was beyond measure. He was more than an explorer and trader; his reports hastened the day of American control of the vast western wilderness, which had been unexplored prior to the efforts of Smith and his fellow trappers. By 1826 he had led a party of men from Great Salt Lake to California and entered the territory from the Mojave Desert. He made his way back to Utah by finding a pass in the Sierra Nevada. By 1828 he had blazed much of what later became the Oregon Trail, having opened the end of the trail to Fort Vancouver. In his footsteps followed the Oregon settlers, the California forty-niners, the army troops, and the surveyors and mapmakers. Legend has characterized the man with his Bible, his rifle, and a sack full of traps, and history has recorded his contributions to the nation.

117. Farnsworth, Frances Joyce. *Winged Moccasins: The Story of Sacajawea.* Illustrated by Lorence F. Bjorklund. New York: Messner, 1954. 189 pages. (Ages 10 and up) *Biography*

According to the preface, the framework for *Winged Moccasins* was based on detailed research on the Shoshone Indian woman, Sacajawea, who made such an important contribution to American history. Farnsworth has given the reader a remarkable insight into the life of this noble woman in a dramatic and moving story set against a historical background that includes the actual characters and authentic customs of the times.

Sacajawea was only twelve or thirteen years old when she was captured by a hostile tribe and sold into slavery. During the next several years, she was traded from tribe to tribe until she married Toussaint Charbonneau, a French fur trapper and trader. When the Lewis and Clark expedition arrived at the Mandan camp along the headwaters of the Missouri, both Lewis and Clark were so impressed with Sacajawea's bearing and with her knowledge of the region and of Indian dialects that they decided to take her and Charbonneau along with them. She proved to be an excellent guide who was loyal and dependable. With her little son Baptiste, she endured the hardships of the journey and gained the respect of every member of the party. When the expedition was over, Sacajawea settled in St. Louis so that Baptiste could attend school. There she herself learned both French and English, which proved valuable in later life when she returned to her own people and became active in Indian affairs.

Throughout the story she is characterized by her determination and by her spirit of adventure (her name means "motion"). Although she encountered suffering and tragedy, each experience led to new and interesting horizons. She proved herself to be a brave, proud, and intelligent woman who was highly honored by the white men as well as by the Indians. According to Clark's own reports, the expedition owed its success to Sacajawea who persuaded the Shoshone to give the explorers information and other necessary help. As Indian hunting and camping grounds grew smaller, she gave advice and counsel to both the white men and her own people at a time when an Indian squaw had no voice in the Council of the Chiefs. The book is indexed and contains a bibliography and a memorial page.

118. Felton, Harold W. *Mike Fink: Best of the Keelboatmen.*
Illustrated by Aldren A. Watson. New York: Dodd,
Mead, 1960. 159 pages. (Ages 10 and up) *Fiction*

Mike Fink, the best of the keelboatmen, was a legend
even in his own time. According to his own boasting, he
"was chock-full of fight" and could outrun any man along
the river from Pittsburgh to New Orleans. He had plenty
of chances to prove his prowess, according to legend, including challenges with Davy Crockett and other historical
figures. Fink was as real as the age in which he lived; he
was born at Fort Pitt in 1770. He was a keelboatman, carrying goods and passengers from Pittsburgh to St. Louis
and on to New Orleans. As he matched wits and might
with the rough and dangerous frontier, he represented the
hardworking, tough, strong, boisterous boatmen who kept
the rivers clear and reasonably safe for travel. There were
stories everywhere about his skill with his rifle and his fists,
his tall tales, and his practical jokes. Some, no doubt, were
based on truth that grew in the telling. While Felton's story
deals mostly with Fink on the Ohio and on the lower Mississippi, the last chapter takes Fink west on the Missouri
with Gen. William H. Ashley's crew of fur trappers and
traders, who included Jedediah Strong Smith, Jim Bridger,
and Hugh Glass.

119. Field, Eugene. *Poems of Childhood: The Poems of Eugene Field*, complete ed. New York: Scribner's, 1889,
1932. 553 pages. (All Ages) *Poetry*

Children continue to respond to the comic humor and
to the lively meter of Field's narrative poems as well as to
the sensitive imagery of his lullabies and his lyrical fantasies. Among their favorites are "The Duel" of the gingham
dog and the calico cat, "Wynken, Blynken, and Nod"
(Dutch lullaby), "The Sugar-Plum Tree," "The Rock-a-By
Lady," "The Dinkey-Bird," and "Cradle Song." "Seein'
Things," and "Jest 'fore Christmas" (both dialect poems)
and "Song" (Why do bells on Christmas ring?) make fre-

quent appearances at Halloween and Christmastime. There are more than 120 poems classified in the "Poems of Childhood" section of this complete edition (pp. 214–49), and appropriate selection is tedious; many of Field's poems are about children rather than for them. Scribner's 1932 publication of Field's *Poems of Childhood*, illustrated by Maxfield Parrish, and anthologies are more convenient sources for his poems that are suitable for children. His poems for children also can be found in his other books published by Scribner's—*Love-Songs of Childhood* (1894), *With Trumpet and Drum* (1892), *A Little Book of Western Verse* (1890), *Second Book of Verse* (1893), and *Lullaby Land* (1897). Field, who was the father of eight children, was unsurpassed as an author of charming lullabies, and his retrospective verse has had wide appeal among adults through such poems as "Little Boy Blue," "Ashes on the Slide," "The Bells of Notre Dame," "Lover's Lane, Saint Jo," and "The St. Jo 'Gazette.'"

120. Fisher, Aileen. *In the Woods, in the Meadow, in the Sky.* Illustrated by Margot Tomes. New York: Scribner's, 1965. 64 pages. (Ages 5–10) *Poetry*

Fisher's forty-eight nature poems in this volume reflect children's interest in the outdoors. She sees the world of small creatures with an inquiring eye, and her verses invite the young reader to explore the woods and fields and to share their wonders. In "Snail's Pace" and "Daddy Longlegs," children may discover why the snail is so slow or whether the daddy longlegs has any fun. Fisher's poems all express a pleasant feeling, and most of them have a free, rhythmic pattern. Two of her longer poems, "Once We Went on a Picnic" and "Listen Rabbit," have been individually published as picture books. The realistic illustrations for her collections of poetry capture the spirit of her poems and bring added meaning as well as pleasure to the young reader. Other titles of her collected works are *Cricket in a Thicket* (Scribner's, 1963) and *Out in the Dark and Daylight* (Harper, 1980).

121. Fitzgerald, John D. *Brave Buffalo Fighter*. Illustrated by John Livesay. Independence, Mo.: Independence Press, 1973. 188 pages. (Ages 10–14) *Fiction*

This historical novel is based on the actual diary of Susan Parker, a ten-year-old who traveled by wagon train from St. Joseph, Missouri, to Fort Laramie, Wyoming, in 1860. During this period, wagon trains and paddlewheel steamboats were bringing prosperity to the little Missouri River village of St. Joseph. Susan's mother Ellen was proud of her home and of her family's social position and was content with the security of life there. But one day, her husband Stephen quit his job as a bookkeeper at the trading post and announced that his family was going west. He was determined to stake a government claim and to raise livestock. At first, Ellen refused to go, and it was decided that she and Susan would remain in St. Joseph with her parents until Stephen and twelve-year-old Jerry were settled and could send for them. But by the time that the prairie schooner was equipped, the entire family joined a wagon train and began their trek westward across the prairies through hostile Indian country toward Fort Laramie. Interwoven with illness, death, and frustrations were strands of bravery and sacrifice as these pioneers overcame the endless hardships. After one devastating Indian attack, they escaped complete massacre only through the courage of Jerry Parker. Near Chimney Rock, he earned the Sioux title, Waditaka Tatanka Kisisohitika, Brave Buffalo Fighter. With this honor came a demand that saved the wagon train but that brought the story of the Parker family to an unforgettable conclusion.

Readers will find this a well-paced and interesting story with insight into Indian ways of justice as well as into a family's need for adjustment to unforeseen challenges.

122. Fleischman, Sid. *Jim Bridger's Alarm Clock and Other Tall Tales*. Illustrated by Eric von Schmidt. New York: Dutton, 1978. 56 pages. (Ages 10 and up) *Fiction*

The real mountain men of the Old West were well

known for the tall tales that they told about their adventures, and Jim Bridger was no exception. But without doubt, even he couldn't have topped Fleischman's three entertaining tales that are sure to please a wide audience. Biographies of Bridger reflect seriously on his accomplishments and discoveries, but these new exaggerations provoke laughter as Bridger discovers a flattop mountain that returns an echo. In the first tale, for example, Jim used the mountain as an alarm clock to awaken him after eight hours of sleep during a blizzard. That mountain also helped him to outwit the fiddler who refused to play for a barn dance. (Never let it be said that Jingle-Bob Earl back in Missouri could outfiddle Buryin' John Potter!) Finally the mountain and Jim saved Blue Horizon from bank robbers on the fifth of July after the townspeople had shot off all their gunpowder celebrating Independence Day. Schmidt's caricature drawings match the tone of these tall tales.

123. Fleming, Alice. *General's Lady: The Life of Julia Grant.* Illustrated by Richard Lebenson. New York: Lippincott, 1971. 155 pages. (Ages 10 and up) *Biography*

This story of Julia Dent Grant is highlighted with dramatic episodes and dialogue. While the people and events bearing on Julia's life are interestingly related, Fleming adheres closely to the title theme by showing again and again how the courage and devotion of a loving wife sustained one of history's great men. Julia Dent, pretty St. Louis belle, exchanged her carefree existence at White Haven, the country home of her prominent family, for a rugged army life and a series of long hardships as the wife of Ulysses S. Grant. Julia shared the many successes scored by Grant, the soldier, statesman, and eighteenth president of the United States. She also shared his business and financial failures and the political scandals that marred his second administration, but throughout the story, Julia is characterized as serene, gracious, warmhearted, and loyal. In accordance with her husband's last wishes, she was buried beside him within the imposing monument on Riverside Drive in New York City.

124. Flory, Jane. *The Golden Venture*. Illustrated by the author. Boston: Houghton Mifflin, 1976. 232 pages. (Ages 10 and up) *Fiction*

For eleven-year-old Minnie Weldon, home was a sturdy, comfortable house in St. Joseph, Missouri. But then her father, Pierce Weldon, got the gold fever and suddenly decided to set out for California to claim his share. Determined to go along with him, Minnie stowed away behind the flour barrels in the big covered wagon. Pa nearly turned back when he discovered her several days later, but she finally convinced him that she could be a help on the way as she shared his dream to be free of spinster Aunt Addie's commands. After the long trip across the prairies and over the Rockies, they at last made the descent into the wild, rough town of San Francisco at the height of the gold rush. Here, a whole new life opened for Minnie. She often survived by her wits alone and even managed to amass her own crock of gold. In the meantime, back in St. Joseph Aunt Addie made a decision that helped to solve the problem of freedom for both Minnie and her father.

125. Fogel, Julianna A. *Wesley Paul, Marathon Runner*. Photographs by Mary S. Watkins. New York: Lippincott, 1979. 39 pages. (Ages 8–12) *Biography*

This book is classified as biography even though it is written in first person as if Wesley Paul were telling his own story. It is a portrait of the young Chinese-American boy who held a national record for long-distance running and who had participated in several marathons by the time that he was nine years old. When the story was written, Wesley was living in Columbia, Missouri, where, at the age of three, he had begun running for fun with his father. He tells what it is like to spend many months training to be a marathon runner; he also explains the importance of regular exercise and discusses some of the races in which he has participated. The story highlights his record-breaking performance in the 1978 New York City Marathon— twenty-six miles, three hundred eighty-five yards, in two hours and fifty-nine minutes. Many large photographs accompany the text and furnish interesting and realistic details. According to a notation on the copyright page, a portion of the proceeds from this book supports a running program for children sponsored by the Columbia, Missouri, Track Club.

126. Foster, John. *John J. Pershing: World War I Hero* (Defenders of Freedom Series). Illustrated by Herman B. Vestal. Champaign, Ill.: Garrard, 1970. 112 pages. (Ages 12–15) *Biography*

The clear, effective format suitable for easy reading lends immediate appeal to this impressive story of the only American other than George Washington to receive the title General of the Army of the United States. John Joseph Pershing, born in Linn County, Missouri, in 1860, graduated from West Point in 1886. The story highlights Pershing's unparalleled career as a professional soldier. During a period of more than thirty years, he experienced more kinds of warfare than any American military officer, fighting on battlefields throughout the world. He served in the frontier army with the U.S. Cavalry during the last of the Indian troubles and in the Spanish-American War; he distinguished himself by subduing the Moro rebellion in the Philippines and led a patrol force against Pancho Villa's Mexican rebels. As commander in chief of the American Expeditionary Forces during World War I, he displayed a tremendous capacity for organization, brilliant leadership, and a determination that his soldiers fight as an American unit, not as replacements in the British and French armies. Pershing suffered a deep personal tragedy with the death of his wife and three daughters, but throughout his life, he remained close to his only son. Young readers will be interested especially in the account of Warren Pershing who, at the age of ten, joined his father in Europe at the close of the war. Warren spent a great deal of his vacation time with his father, and, though not a career soldier, he enlisted and saw active duty on the European battlefields of World War II. Photographs, maps, and drawings complement the text, and an index adds to the value of the book.

127. Franklin, H. Bruce. *Robert A. Heinlein: America as Science Fiction* (Science Fiction Writers Series). Illustrated with photographs. New York: Oxford University Press, 1980. 232 pages. (YA) *Biography*

Franklin's *Robert A. Heinlein: America as Science Fiction* is designed for the general reader of science fiction and contains much information of interest to science-fiction fans in the upper elementary grades and beyond. The book is a particularly valuable contribution to Missouri's literary heritage for young people since Heinlein is a native Missourian (Butler and Kansas City), and his works frequently reflect memories of his early years as well as the influences of his background. In this full-length study of the life and work of the dean of science-fiction writers, Franklin treats Heinlein as a major literary figure, showing the importance of his background to an understanding of his work. This book is a combination of biography, cultural history, and literary criticism. As Franklin surveys Heinlein's entire career and its place in modern American history, he provides a detailed examination of Heinlein's stories and novels. He cites Heinlein as a popular, influential, and controversial author and explains his key role in spreading science fiction throughout American culture in the form of movies, television, comic books, and games. The first chapter, "Robert A. Heinlein: His Time and Place," covers biographical information; the remainder of the book is divided into five sections representing distinct periods of his career as an author. The works of each period are identified with major historical events including the depression era, the Truman–Eisenhower years, the 1960s, and the 1970s with projections into the 1980s. The section entitled "New Frontiers: 1947–59" examines fables for youth and the juvenile novels such as *Rocket Ship Gali-*

leo, Space Cadet, and *Have Space Suit—Will Travel,* and the section called "The Voice of the 1960's" contains a discussion of *Podkayne of Mars: Her Life and Times.* These and many other Heinlein stories about interspace travel appeal to young people; the stories are well told with reasonable themes, convincing episodes, and well-drawn characters. While young readers are not likely to be interested in the detailed literary criticism, the material would be helpful to teachers for discussion purposes. The author's notes at the close of each chapter, his wide use of quotations from Heinlein's books, a chronology, a checklist of Heinlein's works, and an index add to the book's value.

128. Frazier, Neta Lohnes. *Sacajawea: The Girl Nobody Knows.* New York: McKay, 1967. 182 pages. (Ages 12 and up) *Biography*

The style of writing, the selection of subject matter, and the organization of the material make Frazier's story different from other biographies of Sacajawea. A unique feature is an account of the author's research on what happened to Sacajawea and her son after the Lewis and Clark expedition ended. She divides the highly dramatic story into three parts: "The Preparation," "The Journey," and "Afterwards." She uses frequent quotations taken from the explorers' journals to support her narrative and her own impressions of characters and happenings, but the material is interesting and reads easily. In the first pages, the main characters are assembled and the stage is set for a realistic portrayal of Sacajawea. "The year is 1789 . . . Six persons, except for Washington and Jefferson as unrelated as humans can be. Their chances of ever being drawn together in any significant way, only a computer could estimate. Even a computer might balk at the possibility that the Indian baby will become the heroine in one of the greatest dramas of American history and that she will be, for a few ticklish moments, the pivot on which the future of that history will swing" (pp. 1–2). The background for the famed expedition is established during those years (1789–1805) described in "The Preparation." The drama unfolds slowly and the threads begin to interweave as the plot begins to move. Lewis and Clark, having progressed sixteen hundred miles up the Missouri, encounter Sacajawea, already living at the Mandan village. The journey between there and the Pacific is recounted with vivid and fascinating details. In the concluding part, the author offers provocative conjectures about the remainder of Sacajawea's life, mostly by tracing the activities of her husband and son through various reports and official records. This is the only book reviewed in this bibliography that gives a final account of her son's life. A bibliography and an index add to the usefulness of the book.

129. Friermood, Elizabeth Hamilton. *Jo Allen's Predicament*. Garden City, N.Y.: Doubleday, 1959. 238 pages. (Ages 12–15) *Fiction*

The book is worthwhile for the part depicting the St. Louis World's Fair in 1904, although most of the story is set in the Mississippi River town of Larson, somewhere north of St. Louis. When the two Allen girls were suddenly orphaned, they were determined to stay together. So instead of returning to Moreland Academy fifty miles away where she had been studying to become a teacher, eighteen-year-old Josephine found work at nearby Orchard Farm; there she could keep little Cindy, her ten-year-old sister, with her. Mrs. Abigail Snow's orchards were the best in Missouri and her home was big and imposing, but life there wasn't easy for the girls. Mrs. Snow herself was a stern-looking, gruff-voiced woman who operated her business and ran her household with exacting precision. In spite of Jo's hard work, her steady and dependable nature, and her great effort to please, one self-willed mistake lost her the job. Leaving Cindy with friends, Jo went by steamboat to St. Louis where she expected to find suitable employment. While her work experience there was something less than desired, she cherished the memorable sights and sounds of the big world's fair that celebrated the centennial of the Louisiana Purchase. By the end of the summer, she was back with Cindy at Orchard Farm in

good standing with Mrs. Snow and in the company of devoted friends, especially Hugh McAllister. An underlying
theme of the story is woven around the prize apples and
involves the two young McAllister men as well as a visit by
the famous Luther Burbank.

130. Garst, Doris Shannon. *Buffalo Bill [1846–1917]*. Illus-
      trated by Elton C. Fax. New York: Messner, 1948. 224
      pages. (Ages 12 and up) *Biography*

Garst's biography of Buffalo Bill is more than a story
of the famous plainsman who grew up during the gold-
rush days to become a scout, Pony Express rider, and creator of Wild West shows; it is also the story of the changing
frontier and of the growing nation. The author has realistically portrayed the vigor and action that marked this hero
of the American West. William Frederick Cody was born
in Scott County, Iowa, and grew up in the vicinity of Fort
Leavenworth, Kansas, a lawless area at that time. The
family lived in the frontier town of Weston, Missouri, before moving into the Kansas Territory where Isaac Cody
set up trade with the Kickapoo Indians and later operated
a sawmill. Young Bill did not attend school but learned to
shoot, hunt, and ride expertly since a frontier boy had to
be able to take care of himself. He also learned the games
and languages of the Indians and listened eagerly to the
tales of buffalo hunts and Indian fights told by travelers
passing along the Oregon Trail. When he was fourteen, his
father died, leaving him to support his mother and two
sisters. He then returned to Missouri and became a rider
for the Pony Express. His reputation for courage and endurance soon led to assignments on some of the most dangerous stretches of the Pony Express's route. His knowledge of the Indians proved valuable during the Civil War
when, as a Union soldier, Cody was able to keep Indians
from interfering with military operations. The name "Buffalo Bill" resulted from his skill as a buffalo hunter for the
railroads. In another challenge during the Sioux war of
1876, he killed the great Cheyenne chief, Yellow Hand, in
a duel. Cody's friends among the great western frontiers-

men included Kit Carson, Jim Bridger, and Wild Bill Hickok. Buffalo Bill outlived these men as well as the Indian fights, buffalo hunts, and the Pony Express of his youthful fame, but, as the creator of the Wild West show, he made these exciting days live again and, for forty years, delighted audiences throughout the world with his troupe of cowboys and Indians. A number of biographies of Cody are available for young children, including those by d'Aulaire, Stevens, and Stevenson. It is fortunate that these stories of national heroes have been told at different levels of difficulty so that readers of all ages and stages of maturity may know and appreciate them.

131. Garst, Doris Shannon. *Cowboy-Artist: Charles M. Russell (1864–1926)*. New York: Messner, 1960. 192 pages. (Ages 10 and up)　*Biography*

The St. Louis waterfront was a favorite spot for young Charlie Russell. He could stroll there for hours watching the bustling activities and listening eagerly to the colorful talk of a fascinating assortment of people. Stories about Manuel Lisa, Kit Carson, Jim Bridger, and Joe Meek, as well as the heroic deeds of Charlie's great-uncles George and Charles Bent, made a deep impression on him and he longed to seek his own fame and fortune in the Wild West.

Born in St. Louis, Missouri, in 1864, Charles Marion Russell's artistic talent was evident in early childhood. While his parents had expected him to get a college education and to enter the prosperous family business, Russell's dream for his own destiny overshadowed his formal education. Seeing the West became a reality at the age of sixteen when, with a supply of paints and sketchbooks, he traveled to Montana. For years he worked as a sheepherder, horse wrangler, and cowhand. He loved the open ranges, the great sky, the Indian ways, and the freedom of the West. Drawing and painting the scenes that he saw and felt always occupied most of his spare time, and he soon became known as "the Cowboy Artist." With his natural talent, coupled with a romantic love for adventure, he recorded great living pictures of the West that has passed.

His famous mural, *The Meeting of Lewis and Clark with the Flathead Indians in Ross's Hole*, is regarded as the finest historical work of art in existence. Russell won international acclaim, and, in spite of the reckless scattering of his early works, hundreds of his paintings and drawings along with several of his bronze figures are proudly displayed in numerous museums.

Garst's well-written biography is fully indexed and contains bibliographic sources, but it includes no reproductions of Russell's artwork. Several of these can be found in Shirley Glubok's *The Art of the Old West* and in *America's Great Outdoors: The Story of the Eternal Romance between Man and Nature* (Crowell, 1976) by The Outdoor Writers Association of America.

132. Garwood, Darrell. *Crossroads of America: The Story of Kansas City*. Illustrated with photographs and maps. New York: Norton, 1948. 331 pages. (Ages 13 and up) *Nonfiction*

This volume contains a series of stories about selected events and personalities representing different influences on the development of Kansas City. The underlying theme centers on the history of the nation. The character of Kansas City's past is depicted in light of the city's geographic position—two historic borderlines cross one another where Kansas City is located—as well as in light of the currents of change and conflicts within the nation as a whole. Garwood points out that as the American frontier pushed beyond the Mississippi, Kansas City became the jumping-off place for westward migration. It was also on the border between the North and South during the slave versus free-state controversy.

The book is divided into twenty chapters whose content includes topics dealing with the founding fathers of 1838; the border war and Order No. 11; George Caleb Bingham; the Frank and Jesse James story as well as that of Jesse, Jr.; the coming of the railroads; the cattlemen and the stockyards; multimillion-dollar real-estate and the Swope case; the William Rockhill Nelson Art Gallery and the *Kansas*

City Star; the two Thomas Hart Bentons; and the Pender-
gast era and Harry S. Truman. The book contains photographs, maps (including those on the endpapers), sources,
and an index. The material could be useful for reference
purposes as well as for supplementary reading on selected
topics in social studies.

A more comprehensive reference suitable for the advanced reader is volume 2 in the Western Urban History
series, *K.C.: A History of Kansas City, Missouri,* by A. Theodore Brown and Lyle W. Dorsett (Pruett, 1978).

133. Gibson, Bob, with Phil Pepe. *From Ghetto to Glory: The
Story of Bob Gibson.* Illustrated with photographs. En-
glewood Cliffs, N.J.: Prentice-Hall, 1968. 200 pages.
(Ages 12 and up) *Autobiography*

Bob Gibson, famous pitcher for the St. Louis Cardinals, has told in his own words the story of how his athletic
ability helped him to escape the ghetto through baseball.
This autobiography describes his disadvantaged childhood, his high-school and college years, and his professional career with the Cardinals. Although he was poor,
fatherless, and black, he had two gifts in his favor: his
ability to throw a baseball and his older brother Josh, who
started him in organized sports. There were many disappointments and difficulties to overcome in those years between the Urban League and the National League. But the
day that Gibson signed as a pitcher-outfielder with the
Cardinals, he was on his way to becoming one of the great
heroes of the World Series. While the book includes plenty
of baseball action with enough games, scores, and statistics
to satisfy the most avid sports fan, the story also provides
an excellent reflection of Gibson's character as he participated in those games and grew into responsible manhood.
Gibson explains his pitching techniques and the strategies
that made him an exceptional player; he discusses the importance of team relationships and pays tribute to numerous other players including Clete and Ken Boyer, Lou
Brock, and Stan Musial. He speaks frankly about racism,
reporters, fans, umpires, and managers. His wife and two

daughters hold an esteemed place in his life, and his deep concern for civil rights is ever present.

134. Giffen, Jerena East. *First Ladies of Missouri: Their Homes and Their Families.* Illustrated with photographs by Wright Studio; jacket design by Jay Bob Estes. Jefferson City, Mo.: Von Hoffman Press, 1970. 296 pages. (Ages 12 and up) *Biography*

First Ladies of Missouri highlights important aspects of the state's history as well as providing entertaining biographical sketches of the women who have reigned over the governor's mansion. The material is arranged thematically under fifteen chronological periods of history from the early 1700s when the French and the Indians controlled the lower Missouri River valley to 1970 on the eve of the state's sesquicentennial. "An Indian princess, daughter of the great chief of the Missouris, . . . returned to her faraway village on the banks of the Missouri River and started her reign as the first, first lady of a New World area later to bear the name of her Indian tribe" (p. 1). (On the second floor of the state capitol is a painting entitled *Lunette*, showing the Missouri princess returning to her Indian village with her French husband.) Thus begins a fascinating account of the first ladies of Missouri. While the Indian princess reigned in her thatched roof "mansion" at Fort Orleans long ago in 1725, somewhere on the banks of the Missouri River in what is now Carroll County, it was nearly a century later that her title was passed to American first ladies, and even another century before Missouri's first ladies acquired their own public identity. Among these forty-three ennobled ladies, none had their loyalty to their husbands tested more severely than Ann Biddle Wilkinson, wife of the first permanent governor to serve in the Territory of Louisiana (1805–1807), and no name was more illustrious than that of Panthea Grant Boone Boggs, a granddaughter of Daniel Boone and the second hostess of the new mansion built in 1834. The book contains a chart of the floor plans of the mansion, a biographical chart of first ladies, a bibliography, and an index.

135. Glubok, Shirley. *The Art of America from Jackson to Lincoln.* Designed by Gerard Nook. New York: Macmillan, 1973. 48 pages. (Ages 10 and up) *Nonfiction*

This third volume of the Art of America series presents American art from the 1820s to the 1860s as the eyes and hands of American artists record the young country on its way to power and prosperity. Among the artists whose paintings reflected the excitement of the frontier, were Seth Eastman, George Catlin, and George Caleb Bingham. Eastman painted outdoor scenes of Indian life, and Catlin recorded the appearance and customs of the Plains Indians before the coming of the eastern settlers. He journeyed up the Missouri River from St. Louis, visiting Indian settlements that had never been seen by white men; his paintings of Indians have dignity and beauty. A group of early pioneers is the subject of a painting by George Caleb Bingham, a Missouri artist. Even before the Revolutionary War, Daniel Boone had blazed the Wilderness Trail through the Appalachians; Bingham's painting, *Daniel Boone Escorting Settlers through the Cumberland Gap*, shows the frontiersman leading the settlers into Kentucky. With simple text and sumptuous photographs, the author integrates sufficient background information to make the selected works of art meaningful.

136. Glubok, Shirley. *The Art of America in the Early Twentieth Century.* Designed by Gerard Nook. New York: Macmillan, 1974. 48 pages. (Ages 10 and up) *Nonfiction*

The fifth book of the Art of America series presents a collection of paintings, drawings, architecture, sculpture, and photographs created in the years from 1900 to 1939. Glubok's text captures the major art trends of the period. Her writing is exceptionally readable, and her choice of prints represents the thrust of each artist's efforts. The works of Missouri's Thomas Hart Benton and Walt Disney are included. While Disney created worlds of fantasy, Benton recorded real-life rural Americans at work. Both have made outstanding contributions to the cultural life of the state and nation.

137. Glubok, Shirley. *The Art of the Old West*. Designed by Gerard Nook. New York: Macmillan, 1971. 40 pages. (Ages 10 and up) *Nonfiction*

The Old West still lives in the drawings created by Missouri artists George Caleb Bingham, Charles M. Russell, and others who carried their paints into the unknown country a century ago. In the early 1860s the Old West was a world of spectacular landscapes and abundant animal life. It was a world of Indians, trappers, and settlers, of cavalrymen, cowboys, and prospectors. But by the early 1900s their world of freedom, adventure, hard work, and danger had vanished—the frontier had been settled. The Old West was gone except for the rich variety of paintings, sculpture, and old photographs that re-create this exciting era. Bingham painted scenes along the Mississippi and Missouri rivers. His sketches of people in various poses, which he used to compose his large oil paintings, are now a treasured collection. *The Jolly Flatboatmen in Port* shows people who worked on the river enjoying themselves along the waterfront. Bingham's painting, *Fur Traders Descending the Missouri*, shows a fur trader and his son easily paddling down the Missouri River in a dugout canoe. Russell, born in St. Louis, became known as "the Cowboy Artist." His paintings show how cowboys really lived. *Cowboy Camp during a Roundup*, *The Wild Horse Hunters*, and *In without Knocking* depict the open ranges, the life, and the freedom of the West that he loved and understood.

138. Glubok, Shirley. *The Art of the Plains Indians*. Designed by Gerard Nook. New York: Macmillan, 1975. 48 pages. (Ages 8 and up) *Nonfiction*

Indian tribes roamed the Great Plains hunting buffalo on the vast ranges that stretched from the Mississippi to the Rockies and from Texas far into Canada. With skillful integration of text and pictures, Glubok presents a comprehensive view of this important segment of American culture. The special art of the Plains Indians reflects their daily life, their traditions, and their experiences. The variety of art forms represented within the pages of this book include buffalo-hide paintings, splendid warbonnets made of eagle feathers, elaborate horse trappings, and carved medicine pipes. This companion volume of the Art of the American Indian series makes a valuable contribution toward a clear picture and an accurate understanding of the different Indian tribes.

139. Grant, Bruce. *American Forts Yesterday and Today*. Illustrated by Lorence F. Bjorklund. New York: Dutton, 1965. 381 pages. (Ages 10 and up) *Nonfiction*

The forts of America have a significant place in the history of the country. These romantic and historic fortifications have included structures ranging from a single log cabin with loopholes for rifles to trading posts with strong stockades and army posts with elaborate military garrisons. Many towns and cities today carry the names of these forts that grew into settlements. Many important forts have become national historical monuments and state parks. Among the most notable and picturesque forts that have been reconstructed is Fort Osage at Old Sibley, Missouri. Grant's book contains ten sections representing eight regions within the United States. Each region is divided into states, and a discussion of each fort therein provides interesting information about its location and history as well as about unusual incidents and events connected with it. Missouri is included in "The South Central States" section along with Arkansas, Oklahoma, Kansas, and Texas. The thirty Missouri forts identified and discussed were typical of American frontier forts established between 1778 and 1865. Fort Zumwalt State Park west of St. Charles, Jefferson Barracks near St. Louis, Fort D preserved as a public park in Cape Girardeau, Fort Leonard Wood near Rolla, and the Fort Osage Restoration have been set aside and designated as historic areas. A bronze plaque on the south facade of the Old Courthouse in St. Louis commemorates the site of Fort San Carlos, erected in 1778, and a marker at Main and State streets in Troy identifies the site of Wood's Fort, erected in 1812. An excellent introduction and well-drawn regional maps preceding each section, as well as a glossary, a bibliography, and an index, add value to the book.

140. Hagen, Harry M. *This Is Our . . . SAINT LOUIS*. Illustrated with reproductions and photographs. St. Louis: Knight, 1970. 632 pages. (Ages 10 and up) *Nonfiction*

Hagen's personal collection of old photographs, books, and stories gave inspiration to the production of a pictorial review of St. Louis, one of America's most richly historic cities. In 1763 Pierre Laclede ordered, "you will come here as soon as navigation opens, and will cause this place to be cleared in order to form our settlement after the plan which I shall give you." He had blazed a spot, which is now the foot of Walnut Street, and predicted the future importance of the town to which he gave the name of St. Louis.

In this extralarge volume, Hagen has put together a fascinating collection of pictures and information portraying the story of St. Louis in historical sequence. The book is intended for general readers interested in St. Louis. The broad picture of the founding and growth of the city is based on old photographs, histories, and information from specialized scholars. This reference is fully indexed and contains a selected bibliography.

141. Hagler, Margaret. *Larry and the Freedom Man*. Illustrated by Harold Berson. New York: Lathrop, 1959. 175 pages. (Ages 9–12) *Fiction*

Ever since the wagon train had left Illinois, Larry Phillips and his friends, Karl Groelinger and Will Saunders, had planned how they would ride over the border into Kansas together. But much to Larry's disappointment and anger, instead of going straight into Kansas, Larry's father took the south fork of the trail going down into Missouri.

The year was 1854, and the travelers were bound for homesteads in Kansas Territory. However, as Mrs. Phillips explained, Larry's father and his Uncle Jim were selected to buy supplies for the settlement since they knew the storekeepers in Hazelhurst. Before the end of the first day there, Larry had met Daniel, the slave boy owned by their host, Mr. Beesley. During the next week, their friendship led to an adventure that proved much more exciting than Larry would have had just crossing the border with Karl and Will. He soon discovered that the mysterious "Freedom Man" known by Daniel and other slaves was none other than his Uncle Jim who was operating a station on the Underground Railroad. While the plot of the story is mediocre, the characters of Daniel and the other slaves are realistically portrayed and are seen as individuals rather than as stereotypes.

142. Hammontree, Marie. *Walt Disney: Young Movie Maker* (Childhood of Famous Americans). Illustrated by Fred Irvin. Indianapolis: Bobbs-Merrill, 1969. 200 pages. (Ages 9–12) *Biography*

Hammontree, who has written several other books for the Childhood of Famous Americans series, uses the familiar pattern that reconstructs Walt Disney's childhood with emphasis on early characteristics that led to his later success and fame. His drawing and painting, love of animals, imaginative mind, active nature, and sense of the dramatic characterized the child who was to become world famous for his cartoons, creative movie productions, and the fabulous Disneyland. Most of the book is devoted to his childhood and growing-up years, which were spent in Missouri on the farm near Marceline and in Kansas City. Only the last two chapters deal with his adult life and the Hollywood years. Hammontree portrays Disney's life through a series of events, from his drawing of his pet pig on the side of the house to his creation of Mickey Mouse, as his special talents and abilities led him toward his goal. His direction was not always clear, and his eventual success was not without struggles. While he held odd jobs as a boy and served as an ambulance driver in France during World War I, he began his adult career as a commercial artist. He soon became a film cartoonist, created and produced animated films on a variety of subjects, and finally established his Magic Kingdom. Among the hundreds of honors bestowed on him was an honorary high-school diploma, given to him by his old school at Marceline, Missouri. Pres. Lyndon B. Johnson awarded him the Presidential Medal of Freedom, the highest honor that the U.S. government can bestow on a civilian.

143. Heuman, William. *Missouri River Boy*. Illustrated by Robert Handville. New York: Dodd, Mead, 1959. 153 pages. (Ages 11 and up) *Fiction*

Fifteen-year-old Matt Harris signed on as a cub pilot aboard a sternwheeler bound for a remote army post on the upper Missouri River in the year 1868. His first view of the *River Queen* and of the St. Louis wharves was one of wonderment as he had never seen a river packet, much less blocks and blocks of boats tied up along the wharves. The *River Queen* was a two-stack steamboat, a sternwheeler with a main deck and a texas deck with the pilothouse perched on top. Matt studied the pilothouse with interest as he would be spending most of his time there. According to Uncle Toby, whose persuasion had convinced James Braxton to take on a cub pilot, Mr. Braxton was the finest of the Missouri River pilots. During the course of the long journey to the Red Rock Indian Agency post where the valuable cargo would be delivered, Matt met the challenge of the treacherous Missouri River. He learned to get along with the coldly aloof and stern pilot whose instructions were exacting. But Braxton taught him the skills necessary for piloting a steamboat as well as the importance of remembering a thousand landmarks along the thousand miles of river. Matt helped to navigate the *River Queen* through a herd of stampeding buffalo so numerous that it took four hours for them to move across the river. Holding the *River Queen* steady in midstream was about all the pilot and crew could do until the herd began to thin out. Matt

From *Missouri River Boy* (Heuman)

faced even greater excitement when he entered a hostile Indian camp to rescue a captured white girl.

The story provides a good description of the steamboat, each member of the crew, the cargo, the purpose of the trip, and especially the hazards of traveling on Old Muddy, reputed to be the most changeable river in the world. The book was a winner of the Boys' Life–Dodd, Mead Prize Competition.

144. Holbrook, Stewart H. *Wild Bill Hickok Tames the West* (Landmark Books). Illustrated by Ernest Richardson. New York: Random House, 1952. 179 pages. (Ages 9–14) *Biography*

The adventures of Wild Bill Hickok will lure reluctant readers as well as hold the interest of those who are more able. In a realistic manner, Holbrook has presented authentic information about the life of the American scout and U.S. marshal who helped to bring law and order to the "wild and woolly" West. When the story begins, Hickock is a ten-year-old boy living in Illinois; when it ends, he is a thirty-nine-year-old frontiersman in Dakota Territory. In between those years, the colorful exploits of James Butler Hickok as soldier, scout, peace officer, and U.S. marshal became known throughout the West; his skill and bravery in dealing with the violent and lawless elements of the old frontier were unsurpassed. At the beginning of the Civil War, he recaptured a Union wagon train of supplies from Confederate guerrillas and accompanied it safely to Independence, Missouri. In Independence he was given the name "Wild Bill" after an exciting demonstration in which he quelled a murderous mob. During the remainder of the war, he served as a scout and a spy for Union forces stationed in Missouri. At the end of the war, he took part in an affair in Springfield, Missouri, that added to his growing reputation. Following a brief tour of the East with Buffalo Bill's Wild West Show (1872–1873), Hickok married and settled in St. Louis. But with the news of a new gold strike in 1876, he joined the fortune seekers in the Black Hills region of the Dakota Territory. The tragic end of his short life came at Deadwood only twenty days after his arrival in Dakota. While he is a controversial figure in history, the memory of this fancy dresser and enthusiastic gambler is cherished in folklore as a hero of frontier law and order. The book contains a short bibliography.

145. Hubbard, Margaret Ann. *Dear Philippine: The Mission of Mother Duchesne* (Vision Books). Illustrated by John Lawn. New York: Farrar, 1964. 177 pages. (Ages 10 and up) OP. *Biography*

The author's note alerts the reader to the fact that in the Jefferson Memorial building in St. Louis, Missouri, there is a Pioneer Roll of Fame bearing the inscription, "Some names must not wither." The first name on that roll is that of Rose Philippine Duchesne, religious of the Sacred Heart, 1769–1852. Hubbard has provided a compelling account of the life of this courageous woman who founded the first convent of the Religious of the Sacred Heart in 1818 at St. Charles, Missouri. From the time she was twelve years old and attending a convent school near Grenoble, France, Philippine was determined to become a missionary to the North American Indians. At the age of seventy-two, she was to realize her lifelong ambition when

she left St. Louis to brave the hazards of river and overland travel with the group who founded the Potawatomi
Sugar Creek Mission in Kansas in 1841.

Philippine Duchesne had survived the horrors of the
Reign of Terror in France and had been a strong support
in founding the Society of the Sacred Heart in Europe
when, as a forty-year-old nun, she and four associates left
France for the New World. After a brief stay in New Orleans, she arrived in St. Louis on 22 August 1818. From
there, she went to St. Charles where she opened her first
school. From 1818 to 1827, she established five successful
convents and schools for white and Indian children in the
St. Louis area. Her life was not without disappointments,
deprivations, and severe illness, but her devotion, resolution, and physical endurance marked her memorable career. Ninety-eight years after her death, many thousands
gathered near her burial place at St. Charles, Missouri, to
hear a pontifical mass celebrated in honor of her beatifi-
cation, which Pope Pius XII proclaimed in 1940.

146. Hudson, Wilma J. *Harry S. Truman: Missouri Farm Boy*
(Childhood of Famous Americans). Illustrated by
Robert Doremus. Indianapolis: Bobbs-Merrill, 1973.
200 pages. (Ages 8–12) *Biography*

This easy-to-read fictional biography relates many incidents from the childhood of the Missouri farm boy who
grew up to become the thirty-third president of the United
States. The last two chapters deal briefly with Truman's life
from the time he graduated from Independence High
School at the age of seventeen until his death in a Kansas
City hospital on 26 December 1972 at the age of eighty-
eight. Appendix material contains chronological data re-
lating to Truman's life and times as well as suggested activities such as questions, things to do, selected books to read,
and a glossary of words used in the book. This book offers
a step beyond the See and Read biography, *Harry Truman*,
by Gloria Miklowitz.

147. Hudson, Wilma J. *J. C. Penney: Golden Rule Boy* (Childhood of Famous Americans). Illustrated by Robert Doremus. Indianapolis: Bobbs-Merrill, 1972. 200 pages. (Ages 8–12) *Biography*

As with other biographies in the series, this one deals mostly with the subject's childhood and highlights selected incidents that point to his adult career as a successful merchant. James Cash Penney's life story is fitted to the golden-rule theme that served as the basis for his mighty business enterprise. Penney was born on a farm near Hamilton, Missouri, in 1875. Soon afterward, the family moved into town where the children could have better schooling. Penney worked in a dry-goods store in Hamilton for several years but later moved to Colorado for his health. After working for a short time as a clerk for the Golden Rule Mercantile Company in Longmont, Colorado, he opened his own store and later founded a chain of Golden Rule stores. In 1913 he founded the J. C. Penney Company, which grew rapidly over the years; in 1924 he opened the five-hundredth J. C. Penney store in his hometown of Hamilton. While he had chosen merchandising as a career, he had continued his early interest in farming. As time permitted, he began to purchase farms in several parts of the country and to engage in various aspects of experimental farming, exclusive of the J. C. Penney Company. In addition to his successful business and his contributions to better farming, Penney has also been recognized for his involvement in several philanthropic projects including the Penney Retirement Home in Florida and the *Christian Herald*, a religious magazine. The book contains a chronology, questions to be answered, a list of books to read, and a glossary.

148. Hughes, Dean. *Under the Same Stars*. Salt Lake City: Deseret, 1979. 143 pages. (Ages 10 and up) *Fiction*

The story of the tribulations of the Mormon settlers in Jackson County during the early 1830s is told through the experiences of young Joseph Williams and his family. The family had come to the rugged wilderness of frontier Missouri along with a group of other Mormons from Colesville, New York. Prophet Joseph Smith, who had arrived the previous year, had decreed that Missouri was the land of Zion and that the Colesville Saints were to pave the way for the gathering of the members of the church here on earth. Soon after their arrival, nine-year-old Joseph was "called to a special mission" in life. He and his brother Matthew, almost three years older, were very close and shared many activities, but Joseph led the battle for an understanding between his family and his neighbors. The story is a solemn account depicting the explosive events that characterized the birth of the Mormon church.

While the Williams family is fictitious, as are Ollie Markley and his father and some of the minor characters, most of the characters are drawn from actual people. Likewise, the dates, places, and major incidents of the story are based on actual historical information. Although Hughes states in the preface of the book that he has attempted to represent the points of view of both the Mormons and of the old settlers of Independence, some of the main issues underlying their struggle for religious tolerance are never mentioned. An acknowledgment identifies sources used in researching the background for the story.

149. Hughes, Langston. *Selected Poems of Langston Hughes*. Drawings by E. McKnight Kauffer; jacket photograph by Henri Cartier Bresson. New York: Knopf, 1959. 297 pages. (All Ages) *Poetry*

The poems in this volume are those that Langston Hughes himself wished to be preserved and reprinted. Included are previously unpublished verses as well as poems from his widely published works. These poems represent a wide range of titles organized under thirteen themes. Hughes's poetry is serious and humorous, and while many of his poems reflect a spirit of racial pride and protest, his poetry also speaks for people everywhere. Above all, his poems are intense expressions of things that were important to him; he wrote about life as he saw it and understood it. Although his lyric verses were designed for adults, children have claimed many as their own. Among their choices included in this volume are "Snail," "In Time of Silver Rain," "Joy," "Heaven," "Winter Moon," "Island," "Dream Variations," "My People," "Danse Africaine," "Mexican Market Woman," "Harlem at Night," and "I, Too, Sing America." These and other favorite poems can also be found in anthologies of literature for children and youth as well as in smaller collections of selected poetry.

150. Hughes, Langston. *The Dream Keeper and Other Poems.* Illustrated by Helen Sewell. New York: Knopf, 1932. 77 pages. (All Ages) *Poetry*

Generations of children continue to rediscover Langston Hughes's distinctive verse. The directness of his rhymes provides thoughtful reading and listening and carries quiet but potent messages as well as portraits in words and studies in rhythm. Several of his best-loved poems included in *The Dream Keeper* are "April Rain Song," "Dreams," "Mother to Son," "Mexican Market Woman," and "African Dance." These and other suitable poems can also be found in anthologies of literature for children and youth and in many other smaller collections of selected poems. Hughes's *Fields of Wonder* (Knopf, 1947) contains many favorite selections for children and youth.

151. Kantor, MacKinlay. *The Voice of Bugle Ann.* New York: Coward-McCann, 1935. 128 pages. (Ages 12 and up) *Fiction*

Her voice was something to dream about, on any night when she was running through the hills. . . . Springfield Davis had given her the name she carried so proudly. . . . One of her great grandfathers, many generations removed, had followed Spring Davis away from home when he went off to join Claiborne Jackson and his homespun army . . . , so there was logic in the inheritance which put that trumpet in her throat. (p. 9)

Bugle Ann was a hunting dog who meant more than freedom to her master. For a hundred years, men had bred foxhounds in the green valleys and tangled hill country of Missouri. Like those other men, Springfield Davis was one whose spirit arose and marched when the hounds bayed at night. The cry of Bugle Ann, the greatest voice among all the dogs, led him through the gates of the state prison at Jefferson City and out again! *The Voice of Bugle Ann* is like a page out of folklore. Readers will never be the same after listening to the crack of Spring Davis's rifle, the rattle of Camden Terry's old Ford, and the baying of a white dog who "would come back to those black-dark hills when the bugle called her home" (p. 128).

William Lyon Phelps aptly appraised this compelling story saying, "This is a literary miniature masterpiece. Bugle Ann belongs to the choir invisible of immortal dogs: which includes Homer's Argos, Rab, and Bob, son of Battle. Everyone who loves beauty will love this story" (jacket quotes).

152. Karsch, Robert F., and Gertrude D. May. *Our Home State: Missouri*, 4th ed. Photographs by Gerald Massie, courtesy of Missouri Division of Commerce and Industrial Development. St. Louis: State Publishing Company, 1958, 1967. 176 pages. (Ages 9–12) *Nonfiction*

With an attractive format including large print, color-picture cover, and endpapers, this easy-to-read textbook provides young readers with an impressive portrait of Missouri. Following a brief introduction to the state's geography, the material is divided into five chapters featuring Missouri long ago, communities today, plants and animals of Missouri, government, and recreation in Missouri. Review questions and a list of things to do accompany each chapter; the book also contains an index and a table of contents. Boldfaced topics lend to its particular usefulness as a springboard to fiction, nonfiction, and biography.

153. Karsch, Robert F., and William S. Svoboda. *The Missouri Citizen: History, Government and Features of the State*, 3d ed. Illustrated with maps and photographs. St. Louis: State Publishing Company, 1970. 382 pages. (Ages 12 and up) *Nonfiction*

This textbook treatment of the history, government, and features of the state offers a clear presentation of topics organized into five groups. The first section deals with the state's history and is particularly interesting from the viewpoint of the problems of human relationships encountered in the development of the state. Divided into five chapters, this section presents the chief periods and events in the state's past along with various features that typify the state. The next two sections give attention to the understandings and skills related to ideals and to the concept of government in general, and the fourth section devotes nine chapters to a study of the Missouri constitution. The final four chapters provide some valuable reference material about famous people, physical features, natural resources, and important symbols of Missouri. Each chapter closes with a list of words to understand, a set of review questions, and a list of things to do. The book is fully indexed and contains a generous supply of photographs including endpapers.

154. Keith, Harold. *Rifles for Watie.* Jacket by Peter Burchard. New York: Crowell, 1957. 332 pages. (Ages 12 and up) *Fiction*

Rifles for Watie is a classic in historical fiction, especially among war stories. Keith presents a dramatic story set against the background of the seldom publicized western campaign of the Civil War. Little is known about the savagery of the Civil War and the variety and strangeness of its issues in what is now Missouri, Kansas, Oklahoma, and Arkansas. The book might also be considered a historical sketch of Stand Watie, Cherokee Indian general, who led great numbers of his people into battle for the Confederacy. The story, however, belongs to the book's hero, Jeff Bussey. Sixteen-year-old Jefferson Davis Bussey of Linn County, Kansas, lived three miles from the Missouri border, and the turmoil and violence over slavery raged in his front yard. After bushwhackers attacked his farm home, Jeff volunteered for the Union army. He traveled from Fort Leavenworth on the long march to Springfield, Missouri, and saw action at the battle of Wilson's Creek. He became a Union scout, and as a spy in Watie's camp, he joined the Cherokee Mounted Rifles in order to save his life. Having seen the war from both sides, he learned that all people suffered its devastations while fighting for a cause that they thought was right. The book ends with Jeff returning home in the peaceful summer of 1865, where a letter from Lucy Washbourne awaited him. The story's strong, well-portrayed characters are as unforgettable as its dramatic action and authentic setting.

155. Kennedy, John F. *Profiles in Courage* (Young Readers Memorial Edition). Illustrated by Emil Weiss. New York: Harper, 1961, 1964. 164 pages. (Ages 12 and up) *Nonfiction*

In this remarkable book, Kennedy has paid tribute to eight American statesmen who, at crucial times in history, have displayed a rare kind of courage that resulted in the failure of their political aspirations. But, as in the case of Missouri's Thomas Hart Benton, their courageous acts were of vital importance to the nation's eventual existence, even though political defeat was their reward. Benton had enjoyed political domination in his state for thirty years and was a powerful figure in the U.S. Senate. His accomplishments, particularly in the opening of the West, were outstanding. But the time came when, during the fateful decade before the Civil War, Benton accepted defeat rather than compromise his principles; he chose to stand up for his beliefs at the cost of fierce opposition from his colleagues and waning popularity among his voters. However, his loyalty to the Union was far-reaching; ten years later, in 1861, the key border state of Missouri did not join the Confederacy. A discussion of the time, place, and events surrounding the great senator precedes Benton's profile, which reflects the powerful direction that he gave toward the preservation of the Union.

156. Lane, Carl D. *River Dragon*. Illustrated by Charles Banks Wilson. Boston: Little, Brown, 1948. 106 pages. (Ages 8–12) *Fiction*

Gray Mountain, chief of the Cheyenne, returned from his long, perilous journey over the plains where he had gone to the settlement of the We Hoa (white men) near the Mississippi to trade furs for knives, cloth, and colored beads. But his homecoming, usually greeted with great joy and celebration, was marred by the dreadful news that he brought to his people camped near the banks of the Missouri. He had seen a huge beast walking on the water. To him, this meant even greater danger than the Pawnee enemy who was again on the warpath. While the women and children were hurried to the hills for safety, the warriors gathered to plan their attack on the monster, which they were certain had come to devour them. Young Eagle Feather, who was selected to serve as a messenger for the warriors, proved to be the hero in the story. After he was captured by Many Tongues, a white man who spoke the Indian language, the two became friends, and Eagle Feather was taken aboard the river dragon, a strange boat owned by Stephen Long. In the meantime, the Pawnee had trapped the Cheyenne who were attacking the river dragon from a high bluff overlooking the Missouri. But, with the help of the crew of the river dragon, Eagle Feather's bravery and quick wit rescued the tribe. The steamboat had been built to frighten unfriendly Indians, but Long was making the trip to trade with those who were friendly, and he was especially proud to establish peace and brotherhood with Gray Mountain and his people.

Accounts of the actual existence of such a steamboat on the Missouri have been recorded by several historians including Emma Serl. In *The Story of Kansas City* (pp. 74–75), she gives a similar account of the Indians' fright on seeing the *Western Engineer*, the first steamboat to ascend the Missouri in 1819.

157. Larkin, Lew (Lewis Clark Shepherd). *Missouri Heritage*, vol. 1. Illustrated with photographs. Columbia, Mo.: American Press, reprinted by permission of the *Kansas City Star*, 1968. 172 pages. (Ages 12 and up) *Nonfiction*

158. ———. *Missouri Heritage*, vol. 2. Illustrated with photographs. Lookout Mountain, Mo.: School of the Ozarks Press, 1971. 310 pages. (Ages 12 and up) *Nonfiction*

The dynamic story of the historic role that Missouri and Missourians have played during the past centuries is presented in unique format in these two volumes. Each volume contains one hundred essays that first appeared as single columns in the *Kansas City Star* over a four-year period between 1966 and 1970. Each essay deals with selected aspects of Missouri history and/or with individuals who played a role in the state's history. Included is a wealth of information about customs, traditions, and cultures; significant events and historic landmarks; interesting episodes and fascinating people; and the achievements of famous Missourians. Each volume contains a table of contents, a list of illustrations, credits for photographs, and an index.

Other books by Larkin include *Bingham: Fighting Artist* (Burton, 1954) and *Vanguard of Empire* (State Publishing Company, 1961).

159. Latham, Frank B. *The Dred Scott Decision, March 6, 1857: Slavery and the Supreme Court's "Self-inflicted Wound"* (A Focus Book). Illustrated with contemporary prints. New York: Franklin Watts, 1968. 54 pages. (Ages 10–14) *Nonfiction*

In 1846 Dred Scott, a slave from Missouri, sued for his freedom on the grounds that he had lived in both a free state and territory. While the lower courts of Missouri ruled in Scott's favor, the U.S. Supreme Court overturned the decision in 1857, at the same time declaring that the Missouri Compromise was unconstitutional. The Court's decision further inflamed the controversy between the North and the South and drew America closer to civil war.

Latham's book presents an accurate and effective treatment of this crucial event in our nation's history. The material is organized into thirteen concise and well-written essays providing a thorough study of the events and influences surrounding this historic decision. Scott himself becomes a real person instead of just a name in a renowned court case. The uproar over attempts to free Scott is made dramatically clear as are the efforts of Henry Clay and others who proposed compromises to hold the Union together. These and other interesting accounts give the reader the background to understand the entire period of history in which the event occurred (1827–1868). The book affords an excellent supplement to the social-studies textbook that gives only limited treatment of the topic. A bibliography and an index are included along with several photographic prints.

160. Lipman, David. *Ken Boyer* (Sports Shelf Books). New York: Putnam's, 1967. 221 pages. (Ages 12 and up) *Biography*

Readers who are not already baseball fans will have good reason for increasing their interest in sports after reading this biography of Ken Boyer. Lipman's personal respect for his subject shines throughout the story, giving it immediacy and warmth. He also provides more comprehensive coverage of the hero both on and off the field than other sports biographies in this series do. Baseball statistics abound, and many interesting anecdotes and incidents are included. Boyer, an all-around baseball player, is often regarded as the best third baseman in the history of baseball. He won the National League's Most Valuable Player Award in 1964, the year that the St. Louis Cardinals won the World Series over the New York Yankees. The last game in the 1964 World Series was a special concern to the Boyer family and their friends since Ken and his brother Clete, who had an equally famed reputation as a skillful third baseman, were matched on opposing teams.

Ken Boyer grew up in the southwest Missouri farming community of Alba. He was the fifth of Vernon and Mabel Boyer's thirteen children, six girls and seven boys. The parents encouraged their youngsters to play baseball, and the father often joined in their games. All seven boys played professional baseball, and three—Cloyd, Ken, and Clete—became major-league stars. Ken's baseball skills attracted attention at an early age; he was playing on organized teams by the time that he was seven years old. He signed with the Cardinals when he was seventeen. He was characterized as a quiet, soft-spoken, mild-mannered, and personable individual; he was an assertive leader with a strong determination and a deep sense of civic responsibility. Among the many honors bestowed on him was the Multiple Sclerosis Society's award for his dedicated services in combating that disease. Several incidents reported in this book mention other Missouri-born baseball figures including Yogi Berra and Joe Garagiola (St. Louis), Casey Stengel (Kansas City), and Bill Virdon (West Plains). An index adds to the value of the book.

161. Lipman, David, and Marilyn Lipman. *Jim Hart, Underrated Quarterback* (Sports Shelf Books). Illustrated with photographs by Wayne Crosslin. New York: Putnam's, 1977. 127 pages. (Ages 10 and up) *Biography*

Superstar quarterback Jim Hart of the St. Louis Cardinals did not reach that position easily. While he was a calm, steady, and respected player, he had to surmount injuries, team rifts, coaching problems, and the criticism of fans. But after several seasons and several coaches, he became the number-one quarterback, leading his team to the championship of the Eastern Division of the National Football Conference in 1974. Jim has set several Cardinal career records. He was named the National Football League's Most Valuable Player by *Pro Football Weekly* and the NFC Player of the Year by United Press International and the National Football League Players Association. The story of James Warren Hart, from childhood and early participation in sports to his career in professional football, is told with emphasis on his career with the St. Louis Cardinals. The book is presented in an acceptable format with bold type and readable text and includes an index.

162. Lipman, David, and Ed Wilks. *Bob Gibson: Pitching Ace* (Sports Shelf Books). Jacket illustration by Barbara Higgins Bond. New York: Putnam's, 1975. 191 pages. (Ages 10 and up) *Biography*

"Bob Gibson stood unchallenged as one of the greatest pitchers in baseball history as he neared the end of the long road that had begun when his brother Josh promised him a baseball and glove for getting well in his battle against pneumonia" (p. 186). The St. Louis Cardinals won first place in the National League several times and won the World Series twice during Gibson's outstanding pitching career. Throughout his fifteen seasons with the Cardinals, he earned many victories, records, and awards including the Cy Young Award and the Most Valuable Player Award.

While baseball statistics dominate the story, the chapter headings and the comprehensive index help the reader to relate people and events in Gibson's life. The biographers' interest in their subject does shine through clearly enough to attract avid sports fans. Only brief attention is given to Gibson's family life, his role in civic activities, his work with black youngsters, and other efforts involving civil rights and racial equality.

163. Luce, Willard, and Celia Luce. *Jim Bridger, Man of the Mountains* (A Discovery Book). Illustrated by George I. Parrish, Jr. Champaign, Ill.: Garrard, 1966. 80 pages. (Ages 5–10) *Biography*

Jim Bridger's longing for adventure began in early childhood at his father's inn where he listened to visitors tell tales of the rich wild lands in the West. In 1812, when he was eight years old, his family made the journey by covered wagon from Richmond, Virginia, to St. Louis. Ten years later, he began to realize his dream when he traveled up the Missouri River to Fort Henry on an expedition with the Rocky Mountain Fur Company. With each following year, his fame as a mountain man spread throughout the country. He discovered the Great Salt Lake, explored the Yellowstone region, established Fort Bridger, guided wagon trains west, and acted as a scout for the government. In 1868 he returned to his Missouri farm where he spent his last thirteen years with his family.

The high-interest, low-vocabulary text, typical of the Discovery Book series, provides enjoyable reading for a wide age-range. The fast-moving action and drama will appeal to young readers, and older, reluctant readers should find the content informative.

164. Lyback, Johanna R. M. "The Legend of the Osage Tribe," in *Indian Legends of Eastern America*. Illustrated by Dick West and Alexander Key. Chicago: Lyons and Carnahan, 1963, pp. 105–12. (Ages 8–12)   *Fiction*

This brief legend tells about the origin of the Osage tribe at a place where the Osage River flows into Old Muddy Water (the Missouri). A full-page color painting accompanies the story.

This book is a companion to *Indian Legends of the Great West* (Lyons and Carnahan, 1963). The legends are grouped according to states within geographical regions—Missouri, Arkansas, Louisiana, and Mississippi are identified as the Lower Mississippi Valley States—and the story of the Osage Indians is the only Missouri legend included. While the book's introduction offers inspiring comments about the North American Indians in general, there is no reference to the authenticated source of these stories. Each volume contains maps, table of contents, pronouncing vocabulary, index, and endpapers. According to the publisher's foreword, the paintings that were commissioned expressly for the books are now on permanent exhibit at the Thomas Gilcrease Institute of American History and Art in Tulsa, Oklahoma.

165. McBride, Mary Margaret. *The Growing Up of Mary Elizabeth.* Illustrated by Lorence F. Bjorklund. New York: Dodd, Mead, 1966. 175 pages. (Ages 10–14) *Fiction*

McBride has captured some delightful memories of her own happy childhood on a Missouri farm in the story of Mary Elizabeth McDonald, who is twelve, going on thirteen. The growing up of Mary Elizabeth began at Christmastime 1909 when, for the first time in her twelve years, she was going to choose store-bought Christmas presents for everybody. While Rome, Missouri, looked much like every other little midwestern town, to the McDonald children, it was an exciting place as families for miles around braved the snowy morning to drive into town on sleighs and spring wagons. Mary Elizabeth also had another plan, an exciting "secret" that came uncomfortably close to being ruined. The family had never had a Christmas tree at home, but with necessary help from her brothers Davey and Bruce, she managed to surprise her family on Christmas Eve with a completely decorated tree in their seldom-used best room. Mary Elizabeth's growing up continued on through the new year of 1910 at the Old Home Place when she had to make an important decision. Both she and Davey were outgrowing their education in the country school. But as the family discussed moving into town, Mary Elizabeth realized how much giving up the Old Home Place, which they had all loved, would mean. So she decided to attend boarding school at Fulton, while David would live with Ma and Pa Craig while attending the town school in Rome.

166. McCague, James. *Mississippi Steamboat Days* (How They Lived Series). Illustrated by Paul Frame. Cham-

paign, Ill.: Garrard, 1967. 96 pages. (Ages 9–14) *Nonfiction*

The exciting times along the river during the 1800s are brought to life in this vivid account of the Mississippi steamboat days. The cry, "Steamboat's a-comin'!" brought people flocking to the riverbanks. The steamboats carried cargo up and down the river, some were floating palaces equipped for pleasure cruising, others served as warships, and all stopped frequently at woodyard landings along the banks. But especially welcome was the cry, "Showboat's here!" as these boats brought entertainment to the people.

Frontier settlers long remembered the year 1811 when the *New Orleans*, the first steamboat to sail in western waters, encountered the lingering effects of the earthquakes around New Madrid, Missouri. In 1857 a young man from Hannibal, Missouri (Sam Clemens), won the title "A Lightning Pilot," high praise indeed from passengers and crew on a steamship. The more than twelve-hundred-mile race from New Orleans to St. Louis of the two flash packets, the *Robert E. Lee* and the *Natchez*, two of the fastest, finest boats ever seen on the river, was talked about for years.

The descriptions of the various types of steamboats, the crews, and the passengers provide readers with authentic information and deepen their understanding of the historic era of steamboat travel in this part of the country. A map and an index as well as colorful endpapers and jacket add to the book's attractiveness and utility.

167. McCandless, Perry, and William E. Foley. *Missouri Then and Now*. Illustrated with prints and photographs. Austin: Steck-Vaughan, 1976. 234 pages. (Ages 9–12) *Nonfiction*

A wide range of information about Missouri is presented in simplified language in an easy-to-read text. The textbook format provides for a clear organization of the material within eighteen chapter headings from "A Rich Land" and "Missouri's First People" to "Missouri Today"

From *Mississippi Steamboat Days* (McCague)

and "Fine Arts in Missouri." Each chapter begins with a set of purposeful questions for the reader. Bold type highlights the main topics within each chapter. Words peculiar to the subject are listed, and short exercises for reader evaluation include "Testing Yourself" (questions); "Matching Partners"; "Things to Talk About"; and "Things to Do." "Books You Can Read," a list of books related to the subject, closes most of the chapters. A striking feature of the book, "Famous Missourians," identifies seventeen outstanding citizens in appropriate context within effective color-contrasting paging. The book is generously illustrated and contains an adequate glossary and an index.

Teachers and other adults as well as young people wishing to pursue certain topics beyond the limited information given in *Missouri Then and Now* can turn to these authors' *A History of Missouri*, vol. 1, *1673 to 1820*; vol. 2, *1820 to 1860*, followed by William E. Parrish's *A History of Missouri*, vol. 3, *1860 to 1875* (all University of Missouri Press, 1971, 1972, and 1973, respectively).

168. McGuire, Edna. *Daniel Boone* (The American Adventure Series). Illustrated by Jack Merryweather. Chicago: Wheeler, 1945; New York: Harper, 1961. 252 pages. (Ages 9–12) *Biography*

This story of Daniel Boone is also a story of the sturdy pioneers like him who settled America's frontiers and bravely defended them. As these people moved westward in search of new land and new homes, they endured danger and hardships to make these regions part of the United States. Boone was one of these pioneers whose courageous and daring deeds made America a land of freedom and opportunity. From his early days as a woodsman living at the edge of the wilderness in Pennsylvania until the end of his life as a settler in the new frontier of Missouri, he again and again pushed on to new frontiers. His fame spread nationwide as he led a group of woodsmen that blazed the Wilderness Road into Kentucky, established Boonesborough, fought against Indian sieges, and explored the Missouri frontiers.

While this biography is highly fictionalized, much historical detail about Boone's life and times is included. The high-interest, low-vocabulary text would appeal to reluctant older readers. A table of contents with chapter headings and subtopics highlights sequential events. Review questions at the close of each chapter, a word list of pronunciations, and endpaper maps are also provided.

169. McNeer, May. *America's Mark Twain* (America's Series). Illustrated by Lynd Ward. Boston: Houghton Mifflin, 1962. 159 pages. (Ages 9–14) *Biography*

There are many biographies of Mark Twain for young people, but few, if any, surpass *America's Mark Twain*. McNeer and Ward have combined effective writing and beautiful illustrations, many in full color, along with the publisher's attractive format to make an exceptional book for a wide range of readers. Drama overshadowed the life of Mark Twain: Halley's comet heralded his birth in 1835 and returned from outer space to herald his death in 1910.

McNeer gives a fine portrayal of the man and his devotion to his family. The spirited text highlights incidents reflecting Twain's sense of humor that entertained successive generations here and abroad; it also contains episodes revealing his deep humanity that helped him to bear the financial and personal tragedies of his later life. As a special feature of the book, a preview of one of Twain's books follows each chapter except the last. These excerpts are enticing leads to further reading.

170. Maher, Ramona. *When Windwagon Smith Came to Westport*. Illustrated by Tom Allen. New York: Coward-McCann, 1977. 48 pages. (Ages 6–10) *Fiction*

Maher's version of the Windwagon Smith story is told from the viewpoint of a young boy who saw what adults failed to see on that hot summer day in 1853. When Smith made his startling appearance in Westport, Missouri, and rolled to a standstill right in front of Ericssen's Emporium, young Eric looked at the vehicle and saw what Windwagon saw—a prairie ship that could sail over the waves of tall grasses all the way to Santa Fe. Eric was one of the first aboard when the big windship, *Overland Number One*, set out on its maiden voyage; he was also one of the last to depart the ill-fated contraption. With the failure of his grand illusion, Windwagon gave Eric his compass as a parting gift and "was lost between the blue sky and the rippling grass on the plains" (p. 43). Still loyal, Eric dreamed of setting out for Santa Fe on his own, for as Capt. Windwagon Smith said, "Those who stop at the edge of the sea—be it a sea of water or a sea of grass—never get anywhere" (p. 45). An author's note provides historical background to her story and identifies original sources of the legend.

171. Manber, David. *Wizard of Tuskegee: The Life of George Washington Carver*. Illustrated with photographs. New York: Crowell, 1967. 134 pages. (Ages 12–16) *Biography*

Manber's story is the most comprehensive of the several biographies of George Washington Carver reviewed in this bibliography.

Its coverage ranges from Carver's early childhood, through his relentless struggles for an education and his years of amazing achievements, to his final honors and rewards. The features that make this book different are its depth of content and the inclusion of detailed information and lesser-known facts about Carver's scientific discoveries. A pioneer in agricultural science, Carver's research in his Tuskegee laboratories led to extensive new uses for the native products and the natural resources of the South. Just as his endeavors proved the worth of the peanut plant and the cotton stalk, he also proved that black people were capable not only of independent living but also of distinguished participation in American life. Carver was born a slave but was raised as a son in the Moses Carver household near Diamond Grove, Missouri. The world paid tribute to him as a great scientist and as a wonderful human being. Chapter headings, a bibliography, and an index add to the value of the book.

172. Marriott, Alice, and Carol K. Rachlin. *Plains Indian Mythology*. Illustrated with photographs. New York: Crowell, 1975. 194 pages. (Ages 12–15) *Fiction*

According to the foreword, this collection of thirty-one stories—myths, legends, and folklore—of the Plains Indians is presented "as told by the Indians themselves." The authors further state that they lived, worked, and studied among these Indians. Each story is identified with a particular tribe. Two stories are attributed to the Osage Indians who once inhabited Missouri. The first story, "The People of the Middle Waters and How They Came to Be," is a myth about the origin of the Osage tribe along the banks of the river that now bears their name. Preceding the story is background information about the tribe including a beautiful description of the Osage Indian. A note at the end of the story states that the teller wished to remain anonymous, but the story is fairly common in the literature about Indian myths; a similar story appears in Johanna R. Lyback's *Indian Legends of Eastern America*. The second story, "The Woman General," is folklore about a white child found wandering alone by the Osage who adopted her; she grew up among them and became a leader respected by the white men as well as by the Indians. The authors' note states that the story came from Osage records, teller unknown. Background information preceding the story provides an authentic, historical, and credible setting. The entire book is worthwhile since all the stories are about the Plains Indian tribes, many of whom had similar customs and traditions as well as common concerns. Excellent maps showing the location and movement of the Plains Indian tribes, interesting photographs, and a selected bibliography add to the usefulness of the book.

173. Martin, Patricia Miles. *Daniel Boone* (A See and Read Beginning to Read Biography). Illustrated by Glen Dines. New York: Putnam's, 1965. 62 pages. (Ages 7–9)   *Biography*

This story of a well-known hero provides young children with an introduction to biography that can be read on their own. The book begins with Daniel Boone at the age of nine and leads the reader on through smoothly connected episodes that depict this famous man's way of life. While thoughts, feelings, and incidents are entirely fictionalized, historical facts in this brief account match the authentic background of the time. A list of key words used in the story is included as well as author–illustrator biographical notes.

174. Martin, Ralph G. *President from Missouri: Harry S. Truman*, rev. ed. New York: Messner, 1973. 191 pages. (Ages 12 and up)   *Biography*

Set explicitly against the background of circumstances and the times, this biography is a vivid and mature portrayal of the twentieth century and of the president as a person. The text covers Truman's early years in Missouri, his family background, his financial struggles, his participation in World War I, and his political achievements and success. The text contains authentic facts, clearly identified conjectures, and frequent quotations from Truman. While there is no documentation of sources, the book does contain a list for suggested further reading and a comprehensive index. The first edition was selected as one of the outstanding books of 1964 by the Child Study Association.

175. Mason, Miriam E. *Mark Twain, Boy of Old Missouri* (Childhood of Famous Americans). Illustrated by Paul Laune. Indianapolis: Bobbs-Merrill, 1942. 164 pages. (Ages 8–12) *Biography*

In this easy-to-read story of Mark Twain's boyhood, young readers are introduced to four-year-old Sammy Clemens and his family who live in the pioneer village of Florida in the young state of Missouri; the year was 1839. Sammy's yen for the river was already apparent as he often could be found along the cool banks of the nearby Salt River. His first awareness on nearing his new home at Hannibal was the river landing and the arriving steamboat. In Hannibal, he spent a great deal of time talking to the rivermen and watching the boats being loaded, and he declared that he would be a steamboatman when he grew up. As his father's law practice increased and their store became more prosperous, the family moved into a new house where soon afterward Sammy encountered new acquaintances who would become his best friends. Laura Hawkins was a pretty little girl in ruffled pinafores, and Tom Blankenship was the son of the town's drunkard. The boys' reading of pirate stories led them to explore the cave south of town and to float a raft along the Mississippi to spend exciting days on Pirate's Island. After his father's death, twelve-year-old Samuel quit school to work at the *Missouri Courier*, and a few years later he left Hannibal to work on a newspaper in St. Louis. But the song of the steamboat paddlewheel moving through the safe, deep water of the Mississippi and the pilot's call "Mark Twain, Mark Twain, Mark Twain" continued to echo in his memory. As the years went by, the world came to know Mark Twain as a great American author who wrote about his boyhood in the little Missouri town along the Mississippi in *The Adventures of Tom Sawyer*, *The Adventures of Huckleberry Finn*, and *Life on the Mississippi*.

While this book and others in the series are fictionalized biographies, they do provide a simple story with respectable content appropriate for young readers in the elementary grades.

176. Massey, Ellen Gray, editor. *Bittersweet Country*. Illustrated with photographs. Garden City, N.Y.: Anchor/Doubleday, 1978. 434 pages. (Ages 12 and up) *Nonfiction*

This book is a compilation of articles previously published in *Bittersweet*, a magazine produced for the most part by students of Lebanon High School, Lebanon, Missouri. In addition to an introduction, a prologue, and credits, the contents include five sections dealing with the setting (the origins of early Ozark settlers), the woman, the man (on the farm and in the village), the neighborhood, and the sweet (crafts and musicmaking). Unfortunately there is no index.

"Like the wild bittersweet vine that grew on the bluffs and bushes and covered their rail fences, the early pioneers were hardy people who struggled to survive on their thin rocky soil" (p. xi). But like the bittersweet in fencerows now clean or eliminated, the customs and traditions of a self-sufficient way of life are rapidly disappearing. The stories in *Bittersweet Country* have re-created some of the worth and beauty of this culture established in the Missouri Ozarks. Personalities, institutions, music, and dance are included among the chapters dealing with such diverse topics as the art of rugmaking, the appreciation of mules, and the Ozark fox-trotter.

177. May, Julian. *Ernie Banks: Home Run Slugger*. Illustrated with photographs. Mankato, Minn.: Crestwood House, 1973. 46 pages. (Ages 10–14)   *Biography*

Within a brief text, May scans the life of Ernie Banks, highlighting his sports career and featuring his cheerful disposition. As a youngster serving as a batboy during amateur softball games, he wasn't much interested in sports. But during his high-school days in Dallas, Texas, he excelled in football and basketball as well as in baseball. By the time he was seventeen, he was playing for a semipro club that traveled throughout the Southwest. As soon as he finished high school in 1950, he began his professional baseball career as a player for the top-rated Kansas City Monarchs of the Negro American League. During his years with the Monarchs, he became widely known as an outstanding athlete with an increasing record as a powerhouse slugger. In 1953 he entered the major leagues when he joined the Chicago Cubs of the National League. For the next eighteen years, his spectacular plays led to his climb to super-slugger heights and to many awards and honors. In 1971 he retired as a player to become the Cubs' full-time coach. While the book includes numerous photographs of the baseball star and his associates, only brief mention is made of his family. However, a closing page provides a biographical profile and his baseball statistics.

178. May, Julian. *The Kansas City Chiefs: Super Bowl Champions*. Illustrated with photographs. Mankato, Minn.: Creative Education, 1973. 47 pages. (Ages 9–14) *Nonfiction*

This brief history of the Kansas City Chiefs highlights the team's victory in the last Super Bowl game between the separate American and National Football League teams. When the AFL was founded in 1960, it had eight teams including the Dallas Texans owned by Lamar Hunt. By 1963, after winning the first two AFL championships, the team had moved to Kansas City to become the Chiefs. With Hank Stram as coach, the Chiefs acquired many excellent players such as Len Dawson, Johnny Robinson, Mike Garrett, Buck Buchanan, and Bobby Bell. Although rivalry between the AFL and the NFL continued until the merger of the two leagues in 1970, their war over the player draft subsided in 1966 when the two leagues agreed to share a common player draft as well as to match their top teams in a Super Bowl championship game at the end of each season. In 1969 the Chiefs finished as the top team in the AFL and went on to win Super Bowl IV over the Minnesota Vikings in 1970. Since 1970, the Kansas City Chiefs have belonged to the Western Division of the American Conference of the reorganized National Football League. This book, with its large print and numerous photographs, will be welcome as high-interest, low-vocabulary material for those readers unable to handle the more detailed account in *Kansas City Chiefs* by Dick Connor. A record of achievements (1960–1973) is also provided.

179. Meadowcroft, Enid LaMonte. *By Secret Railway*. Illustrated by Henry C. Pitz. New York: Crowell, 1948. 275 pages. (Ages 9–14) *Fiction*

By Secret Railway is an absorbing adventure story arising out of a loyal friendship between two boys. It is also a vivid picture of a period in history when many Americans concerned about individual freedom faced moral issues beyond the law. Twelve-year-old David Morgan became involved in the work of the Underground Railroad in 1860. One day while seeking a job on Chicago's waterfront, David encountered Jim Clayton, a young ex-slave from Kentucky. Their friendship led David far from home and into some strange and exciting situations. After Jim's freedom papers were destroyed, he was kidnapped and taken to Missouri where he was sold again as a slave. David was determined to find Jim and eventually rescue him. But the long search from St. Louis to Greenfield, Missouri, revealed much about the different attitudes toward slavery: Some people along the way helped slaves to escape to freedom, while others made money dealing in freed or fugitive slaves. The two boys narrowly escaped capture before reaching Illinois where they were passed along homeward by conductors on the Underground Railroad. In the end, Jim decided to stay with the Morgans, and David finally met president-elect Abraham Lincoln whom he had intended to see for a particular reason during his journey to St. Louis.

180. Means, Florence Crannell. *Carver's George, a Biography of George Washington Carver*. Illustrated by Harve Stein. Boston: Houghton Mifflin, 1952. 172 pages. (Ages 9–12) *Biography*

George Washington Carver was born about 1860 in the Missouri Ozarks near the little town of Diamond Grove. While he was born a slave without a family name, his mother Mary belonged to Moses and Susan Carver who were German farmers and breeders of fine horses. One night, border raiders kidnapped Mary, leaving behind the tiny baby George and his brother Jim for the Carvers to look after. So began the appealing story of the humble black child who grew up to be world famous, known for his worthy scientific achievements as well as for his contribution to black education. The inscription on his monument in Tuskegee, Alabama, reads in part, "A life that stood out as a gospel of self-sacrificing service." At Diamond Grove, a tablet and markers proudly show his birthplace, which is set aside as a national monument.

While Means has carefully researched Carver's life and has given attention to the importance of his work, she has been especially skillful in portraying Carver as an individual rather than stressing his accomplishments. A bibliography is included.

181. Meltzer, Milton. *Langston Hughes: A Biography*. New York: Crowell, 1968. 281 pages. (Ages 12 and up) *Biography*

In this biography for older children, Meltzer, a friend and colleague of Langston Hughes, has presented a warm and compelling portrayal of Hughes's life and work. Hughes and Meltzer collaborated on *A Pictorial History of the Negro in America* (Crown, 1968) and on *Black Magic: A Pictorial History of the Negro in American Entertainment* (Prentice-Hall, 1967). Meltzer's biography goes beyond an account of Hughes's family background, his travels, his involvement in causes, and his varied and prolific literary contributions. Meltzer has skillfully and impressively conveyed to the reader Hughes's intense feelings for black people as well as his belief in freedom, truth, and justice for people throughout the world.

Hughes is perhaps best known as a poet, but his writings took many forms of literary expression—short story, novel, play, song, musical comedy, opera, history, humor, and autobiography. Some of his most popular works are his books for children and young people. Always his writings were expressions of his own experiences and of his belief in individual achievement as a means of overcoming indifference and prejudice. His first book, *Weary Blues*, was inspired by the sound of a voice remembered from early childhood. The voice was singing the blues on Independence Avenue in Kansas City (p. ix). Years later in Harlem, after hearing a black man playing the piano and singing, he composed the folk portrait in the title poem of the book (p. 77). Hughes wrote about life as he saw it, and his life was a colorful one. From his birthplace in Joplin, Missouri, he moved with his mother to Topeka, Kansas, where he was the only black child in school. Spending his young manhood in Harlem and on his father's Mexican ranch, he began a series of travels that took him all around the world. Just as he drew material for his art from everyone he knew, his career, his character, and the spirit of his times have meaning for all people everywhere.

The book includes Meltzer's notes, acknowledgments, and a comprehensive bibliography of Hughes's published works. Readers will want to explore several of the books listed, especially the poetry in *The Dream Keeper*, the *Pictorial Histories*, and the eight books written particularly for young people.

182. Meyer, Duane. *The Heritage of Missouri: A History*. Illustrated with maps and photographs. St. Louis: State Publishing Company, 1973. 843 pages. (Ages 13 and up) *Nonfiction*

The Heritage of Missouri: A History, designed as a textbook for junior- and senior-high-school students, is an excellent reference source for any interested and able reader; it is one of the most comprehensive histories of Missouri presently available in a single volume. The material is organized into twenty chapters within six major units covering the broad scope of Missouri's social, economic, and political development from the prehistoric era to the space age. Unit 1, "Colonial Missouri," covers the prehistoric era, the arrival of the Europeans, the problems of settlement, and the French society in Missouri. Unit 2, "A Frontier Territory and State," explores territorial Missouri, statehood, Missouri and the West, and economic growth and social development from 1820 to 1860. Unit 3, "Conflict and Resolution," deals with the growing conflict over slavery, the Civil War, and its aftermath. Unit 4, "Growth and Reform," reviews the economic growth and social development from 1860 to 1910 and discusses progressive movements in Missouri. Unit 5, "Boom and Bust," contrasts the period of prosperity during World War I with the Great Depression in Missouri. Unit 6, "Contemporary Missouri," features Missouri in the 1940s, the space age, and the legacy of the state. Each chapter begins with a quotation identifying its theme and ends with a comprehensive bibliography for further reading. An appendix provides study aids for each chapter. An abundance of illustrative maps and photographs, a chronology, and an index add value to the book.

183. Meyer, Franklyn E. *Me and Caleb* (The Charles W. Follett Award). Illustrated by Lawrence Beall Smith. Chicago: Follett, 1962. 160 pages. (Ages 8–13) *Fiction*

The hilarious adventures of two young brothers are

told in the first person by Bud Wallings. He and his brother Caleb lived in Harleyville, Missouri, at the edge of the Ozark Mountains. Bud's description of life in the little town gives background for the activities that filled the boys' lives. While many of their exciting experiences were humorous, others were painful, as one might expect when two brothers, nine and twelve years old, are growing up. The boys cured Grandpa of fishing for eels, and they bravely accepted the death of their dog Weenie, injured during a hunting trip. But from all reports, the boys didn't exactly have the true Halloween spirit. There was also that fracas over the unusual Christmas gift (Carlyle, the goat) that Bud gave to Caleb. Then there was the time when Herbie Coggins was bombarded with snowballs when he arrived at the Wallings home to take Callie to the Christmas dance. Believable? Yes, if you've ever been a boy or grew up in a family with growing youngsters.

184. Meyer, Franklyn E. *Me and Caleb Again.* Illustrated by Charles Liese. Chicago: Follett, 1969. 185 pages. (Ages 8–14) *Fiction*

Caleb and Bud Wallings of Harleyville, Missouri, are back again. They are a year older, but most of their escapades continue to show only a growing skill at mischief-making. They delighted in annoying girls, especially their older sister Callie and the young visitor, Mildred Hungerford of Jefferson City. An infuriated Callie certainly did not appreciate the joke when she saw their dog, Petunia, racing around town dressed in her new bikini. But the boys met their match in the tree-house fracas when they collided with Mildred and her blackberry pie. Grouchy Mr. McLeod got his comeuppance when the boys turned Halloween tricks into treats by cleaning up his house and yard. In spite of all their carefree antics, the boys knew how to help when they were really needed. Readers of any age will find these realistic adventures delightfully funny, sometimes touched with sadness, but always unforgettable.

185. Miklowitz, Gloria. *Harry Truman* (A See and Read Biography). Illustrated by Janet Scabrini. New York: Putnam's, 1975. 62 pages. (Ages 6–9) *Biography*

The range of biographies dealing with the president from Missouri would not be complete without something for the very young. For those who are beginning to read, Miklowitz has provided a well-written story. While there is some fictionalized dialogue, the basic information is authentic except for incorrect information on page 42: Roosevelt died in 1945 (not 1944 as is printed in the book) when Truman had been vice-president for eighty-three days (instead of eighty-two days as printed in the book). The otherwise substantial content would also make the book appropriate for older children needing high-interest, low-vocabulary material.

Miklowitz characterizes Harry Truman as a happy, curious boy who took piano lessons and read a great deal, especially history. Making friends was not always easy for him as his family moved several times; poor eyesight also kept him from participating in many games that other children played. As a young man, Truman's service in World War I proved him to be a popular and respected leader. His political career, punctuated by his honesty, directness, and plain-speaking manner, began as a judge in Independence, Missouri, and reached its heights as the thirty-third president of the United States.

186. Miles, Miska (Patricia Miles Martin). *Uncle Fonzo's Ford*. Illustrated by Wendy Watson. Boston: Atlantic Monthly Press (distributed by Little, Brown), 1968. 56 pages. (Ages 7–10) *Fiction*

Uncle Fonzo always agreed with Grandma and Mama who said that the Riddle family could "make do" and get along happily with what they had. But things didn't always turn out right when Uncle Fonzo had a hand in the managing. A clock that struck fifteen after he had "fixed" it was one thing, but spilling green paint on Effie's new straw hat created another kind of disaster. Uncle Fonzo's impossible Ford was usually involved in some of his most provoking escapades. Worst of all was the time when he came to pick Effie up after school one rainy afternoon; the top of the Ford couldn't be raised, and everyone got drenched. Uncle Fonzo's Ford was even blamed for Norma Lou's being late for her own wedding.

There is no specific Missouri setting for this story, but Uncle Fonzo mentions that he had to go to the railroad station since the conductor was picking up some parts for his Ford in St. Louis, saying "He'll put them off the train at a quarter past six—leave them lying on the platform" (p. 39).

187. Monjo, F. N. *Willie Jasper's Golden Eagle: Being an Eyewitness Account of the Great Steamboat Race between the* Natchez *and the* Robert E. Lee. Illustrated by Douglas Gorsline. Garden City, N.Y.: Doubleday, 1976. 95 pages. (Ages 8–14) *Fiction*

Monjo has woven his story of Willie Jasper around an actual event and has made use of a number of real people, giving the reader a strong sense of history. The most famous of all steamboat races was the one between the *Natchez* and the *Robert E. Lee* in 1870, and Monjo's account of this great race is fascinating. In re-creating the heyday of the riverboats, he has provided a vivid picture of life and lore along the Mississippi as well as much information about boat captains and the luxurious steamboats. Endpaper maps and attractive drawings add interest. The story is narrated from the viewpoint of young Willie who, with his father (both imaginary characters), made a trip down the Mississippi from St. Louis to New Orleans. They were among the few fortunate travelers who booked return passage on the *Natchez*, piloted by the famous Capt. Tom Leathers, during its historic race with the rival steamer, *Robert E. Lee.* (Discerning readers will likely question a passage on page 37, first edition, where the text should read, "Osceola, Arkansas," instead of "Osceola, Missouri.")

An afterword: Thousands of spectators watched as the *Mississippi Queen* arrived at St. Louis four minutes ahead of the *Delta Queen* on the Fourth of July to win "The Great Steamboat Race of 1980." The race was a re-creation of the race 110 years ago between the *Natchez* and the *Robert E. Lee.* Perhaps some eyewitness will someday tell us more about this race, too.

188. Montgomery, Elizabeth Rider. *Lewis and Clark* (World Explorer Books). Illustrated by Edward Shenton. Champaign, Ill.: Garrard, 1966. 96 pages. (Ages 8–12) *Nonfiction*

This fictionalized account of the famous expedition to explore the West is presented in an easy-to-read format. A full-spread map with a clear legend provides helpful direction for the reader.

Inspired by the vision of a United States that would stretch from the Atlantic to the Pacific, Meriwether Lewis had longed to explore the West. So he was not only pleased but was also well prepared to accept Pres. Thomas Jefferson's assignment to organize such an expedition. Lewis chose his young friend and fellow army captain, William C. Clark, to lead the expedition with him. Besides being an excellent soldier and leader, Clark was also a fine mapmaker.

On 14 May 1804 the Lewis and Clark expedition left St. Louis, Missouri, to follow the Missouri River west. At Fort Mandan, the company hired Sacagawea, a Shoshone Indian, and her French trapper husband Charbonneau to guide them as they continued the journey through the dangerous Indian territories and over the rugged mountains. After much hardship and illness, the party finally reached the Pacific on 7 November 1805. They spent the winter on the Pacific Coast and on 23 March 1806 began the 4,135-mile trip home, arriving in St. Louis six months later. Lewis's detailed reports and Clark's carefully drawn maps strengthened the United States' claim on the land west of the Louisiana Territory.

189. Montgomery, Elizabeth Rider. *Walt Disney: Master of Make-Believe* (An Americans All Book). Illustrated by Vic Mays. Champaign, Ill.: Garrard, 1971. 96 pages. (Ages 8–12) *Biography*

Walt Disney's artistic talent supported by his determination and hard work brought him worldwide acclaim as a master of make-believe. He rose to fame for his cartoon characters Mickey Mouse and Donald Duck and continued to use his talent and lively imagination to pioneer new techniques in motion-picture animation. His vision, his confidence, and his willingness to take risks made Walt Disney Productions a famous and successful corporation. His entertaining movies and his magic kingdom of Disneyland continue to give pleasure to young and old. This book is one of the Americans All series featuring biographies of people who have contributed in a specific field to American life. Its high interest and low vocabulary make it suitable for reluctant readers in the upper grades as well as for average readers in the middle grades. An index is included.

190. Montgomery, Elizabeth Rider. *When Pioneers Pushed West to Oregon* (How They Lived Series). Illustrated by William L. Steinel. Champaign, Ill.: Garrard, 1971. 96 pages. (Ages 9–12) *Fiction*

Here is a book that clarifies the journey into our country's past. Using actual diaries, Montgomery has re-created the adventurous story of James and Jesse Applegate on the Oregon Trail in 1843. Leaving their Missouri home along with other members of the Oregon Emigration Company, they trekked two thousand miles across vast plains, trackless deserts, and perilous mountains to reach the Oregon Territory.

The first part of the book deals with the Missouri setting for the story, covering a period of several months from the early planning and preparation for the trip until the ox-drawn wagons pushed westward from Independence, Missouri. This easy-to-read story gives a clear picture of history and geography as the reader sees life in the past through the experiences of those Missouri pioneers who lived it. Beautiful full-color lithographed cover, endpapers, old prints, engravings, two-color drawings, and maps lend a lasting impression to the text. A table of contents, a glossary, and an index are included. Each of the ten chapters is headed by a theme with a date and place subheading.

191. Montgomery, Elizabeth Rider. *William C. Handy: Father of the Blues* (An Americans All Book). Illustrated by David Hodges. Champaign, Ill.: Garrard, 1968. 95 pages. (Ages 8–12) *Biography*

This easy-to-read fictionalized biography highlights the life of William Christopher Handy, acclaimed as "Father of the Blues." Montgomery has written an inspiring account of this remarkable man who, despite great odds, attained success and contributed something unique to the world of music. From early childhood, he had loved the spirituals sung in his father's church as well as the music that he was taught in school. By the time he was in high school, he was playing with a band and singing with a quartet. From then on, wherever he went he organized musical groups, taught others to read music, wrote his own arrangements, and published his own songs. "Saint Louis Blues," the song that made him famous, was inspired by his memories of the months he spent as a drifter in St. Louis, Missouri, at the age of nineteen. All these memories along with strains of long-ago songs of the black people, the "sorrow songs" and the "jubilation songs," blended in his mind to make up the tune that began "I hate to see de evenin' sun go down." For more than twenty-five years, the "Saint Louis Blues" was one of the most popular pieces of music in America, and Handy's memory still lives on in the hearts of music lovers throughout the world.

The book's format features high interest and low vocabulary and contains actual photographs; the picture on the cover shows this distinguished composer playing his famous trumpet against the background of the "Saint Louis Blues" sheet music.

192. Moody, Ralph. *Riders of the Pony Express* (North Star Books). Illustrated by Robert Riger; maps by Leonard Derwinski. Boston: Houghton Mifflin, 1958. 183 pages. (Ages 10–15) *Nonfiction*

Moody's well-written story of the Pony Express makes an excellent selection for reading aloud as well as for independent reading for all ages at the intermediate grade level and beyond. The emphasis of this book, as indicated by the title, is on the young riders who during 1860 and 1861 left an indelible mark on the history of the West. The Pony Express lasted only nineteen months, but no other mail service has so stirred the imagination of the American people. The stories of its brave riders, many of them only teenagers, are sagas of adventure into the Old West that are based on true experiences. Moody has vividly re-created events as eighty young riders rushed through an equal number of relay stations in a race against time across the treacherous country between St. Joseph, Missouri, and Sacramento, California. Johnny Frey, who carried the first pony mail westward from St. Joseph, was an expert horseman, but he was also well known up and down the Missouri valley as a race rider and a showman. He made a grand takeoff for the crowd at the train station that April evening, traveling three times faster than the California mail had ever before been carried. There was no wild celebration in Sacramento on 4 April as Sam Hamilton raced eastward to the next station where "Boston" Upson waited and hoped to make the rugged ride over the crest of the blizzard-ripped Sierras during daylight hours. Pony Bob Haslam has stood out above all the self-sacrificing riders as the greatest. In March 1861 he took part in the greatest and fastest ride ever made by the Pony Express. Seven days and seventeen hours from the time President Lincoln's inaugural address was telegraphed from Washington to St. Joseph, "a hard-spurring pony rider galloped it into Sacramento" (p. 179). The message saved California for the Union. Informative maps, diagrams, and an index make the book as useful as it is enjoyable.

193. Mosley, Jean Bell. *The Mockingbird Piano*. Philadelphia: Westminster Press, 1953. 192 pages. (Ages 13 and up) *Fiction*

Mosley has compiled fifteen short stories dealing with personal reflections on her early life with her family and neighbors in the St. Francois River valley of southeastern Missouri during the first quarter of this century. The stories are set clearly against the geographical background of the area, and her characterizations aptly reveal the philosophical attitudes of the sturdy, independent people who lived there. The reader will long remember Old Abraham Adams, the chronicler whose unique service to the community attracted visits from the old and young alike. Moving about the valley with Aunt Myra and Little Joe Rooks, one can share the inhabitants' happiness and contentment in everyday life. Nor would it be difficult to become a "hound-dog person" and to agree with Grandpa that there was never any music like hounddogs a-bayin' in the moonlight, "specially with Old Jethro leading them all the way!" (p. 53).

The stories hold appeal for children of all ages as well as for adults. In each story, the author tells how she and her sister Lou were involved with the people and events depicted. "The Stono Mountain Sweet Cream Shoes" tells how the family got her sister's graduation shoes. Although the "Mockingbird Piano" brought ridicule from Aunt Ange, it created a great deal of excitement for the girls along with a much-surprised church congregation. A table of contents identifies each story, and line drawings effectively introduce each theme. The volume provides many entertaining selections appropriate for reading aloud. *The Mockingbird Piano* won the Missouri Writers' Guild's top award for 1953.

194. Mosley, Jean Bell. "The Summer I Learned to See."
    Reader's Digest (August 1977): 88–90. (Ages 9–14)
    Fiction

A wise grandmother opens a small girl's eyes to the
treasures around her during the sticky end-of-the-summer
dog days in Missouri. "Take the bucket with you. . . . You'll
find something to fill it with," her grandmother had said
with anticipation.

Telling the story in the first person, Mosley recalls that
she hadn't wanted to take the bucket when she was going
after the mail, a mile's distance through fields and thickets
from the farmhouse where three generations of her family
lived. She was nine years old and didn't want to be both-
ered with the familiar half-gallon bucket that she'd carried
so often while doing various chores. Nevertheless she took
it repeatedly and filled it with such ordinary things as
pokeberries, peppermint, jewelweed, an oriole's nest, and
pennyroyal, all of which took on an interesting usefulness.
The day came when she brought home an empty bucket
but ecstatically described a clump of red sumac and a mon-
arch-butterfly migration, and her grandmother said,
"Honey, you don't need the bucket anymore."

195. Mosley, Jean Bell. *Wide Meadows*. Caldwell, Idaho:
    Caxton, 1960. 236 pages. (Ages 12 and up) *Fiction*

"Books are the treasured wealth of the world, and the
fit inheritance of generations and nations" (p. 127). This
quotation from Thoreau's *Walden* is a fitting theme for one
of the twenty short stories in *Wide Meadows*. Mosley has
drawn on her childhood experiences on a farm to supply
background for her humorous, homey, and inspirational
vignettes depicting country life in the Missouri Ozarks
soon after the turn of the century. A picturesque way of
life is stamped forever on the reader's mind as the events
of the farm year unfold at River Valley Farm in southeast
Missouri where three generations of the Bell family lived
in harmony as the seasons came and went.

The approach of fall was marked by the gathering of corn and by other winter preparations amid the smell of wood smoke and frosty air. An unusual Thanksgiving gathering as a result of Dad's "great retreat" (p. 37), a Christmas program that settled a longtime community quarrel, Mama's purchase of the set of encyclopedias, and the political fox were just a few of the episodes that marked the passing year. The family anxiously awaited the days when spring freed them from the grip of winter and life would be filled with growing crops, gardenmaking, and country auctions. Summer crowned the year with highlights of harvesting and visiting relatives.

196. Moyer, John W. *Famous Frontiersmen*. Illustrated by James L. Vlasaty. Chicago: Rand McNally, 1972. 112 pages. (Ages 10 and up) *Nonfiction*

The illustrations are the most impressive aspect of this extralarge volume that includes the profiles of eleven men famed in the opening of the West. A full-color painting of each frontiersman precedes the accompanying narrative, and more than thirty black-and-white drawings illuminate the entire text. Of the eleven frontiersmen included in the book, the lives of seven are a part of the history of Missouri: Daniel Boone, William C. Clark, Meriwether Lewis, James Bridger, Christopher "Kit" Carson, James Butler "Wild Bill" Hickok, and William Frederick "Buffalo Bill" Cody. While much of the same information about each of these men can be found in other full-length books, the simplified text as well as the attractive format will appeal to a wide audience. The style of writing is mediocre with careless attention to facts in the story of Wild Bill Hickok and with the reference to the frontier town of Springfield, Missouri, in 1865. The author is affiliated with the Field Museum of Natural History in Chicago.

197. Murphy, Lila B., writer-editor. *Our City, St. Louis*. Illustrated with photographs. St. Louis: St. Louis Board

of Education, 1976 (paperback). 87 pages. (Ages 8–12) *Nonfiction*

An appreciation of St. Louis is provided early in the elementary grades through *Our City, St. Louis*, prepared by the division of curriculum services of the St. Louis public schools. Important facts about the city are presented in a brief and simplified text and in an attractive format suitable for young readers. Informative photographs and clearly drawn maps accompany each topic to assist the child's interpretation and increased understanding of the subject. The content is organized into five major topics: "The History of St. Louis," "The Neighborhood Community," "The City Community," "Industry in St. Louis," and "Leisure and Learning." Subtopics in bold type feature outstanding people, places, and events related to each of the major headings. A glossary is included.

198. Musick, John R. *Stories of Missouri*. Illustrated. New York: American Book, 1897. 228 pages. (Ages 12 and up) OP. *Fiction*

According to the introduction of this book, care was taken to select unquestionably true stories that were typical of the time and characteristic of the people. The stories were also selected for the light that they shed on the history of Missouri. There is no index, but the stories are arranged in chronological order; chapter headings indicate the nature of the content. The story "Western Boatman" is an account of the origin of the legendary character Mike Fink. In "The First Schoolmasters," Musick relates the less familiar story about the followers of Aaron Burr in his unsuccessful attempt to seize the western territories and annex them to Mexico. These followers were men of education and refinement who, unable to return home, became itinerant pedagogues and spread throughout Missouri.

While the book rightfully belongs in a historical collection, it is a good reference source, especially for anecdotal materials. Many later authors have credited this book as their source of information; the works of others who have used the material freely frequently reflect this early source.

199. Myers, Hortense, and Ruth Burnett. *Joseph Pulitzer: Boy Journalist* (Childhood of Famous Americans). Illustrated by Robert Doremus. Indianapolis: Bobbs-Merrill, 1975. 200 pages. (Ages 8–12)   *Biography*

Joseph Pulitzer was born in Mako, Hungary, in 1847 and lived there and in Buda until he was seventeen years old. The story is told that as a child he was fascinated by the gypsies and once slipped away from home to visit their camp near the edge of the village. Pride in his ancestors was heightened by the legend of the white stag that led the Magyars to Hungary, the promised land. Always an eager listener and a quick learner, interested in people and in the world, Pulitzer came to America in 1864 to join the Union army. After the war, he went to St. Louis where he eventually became a newspaper reporter. His experience as a political reporter led to a seat in the state legislature, but deciding that he could be more effective as a publisher, he purchased the *St. Louis Post-Dispatch*, which became increasingly prosperous. Later, as owner of the *New York World*, he campaigned for many issues among which was the completion of the Statue of Liberty in New York harbor. Pulitzer promoted journalism as a profession, and in 1908 the University of Missouri established the first school of journalism. He founded the Pulitzer Prize to reward creative efforts in journalism, literature, drama, and music.

The closing pages of the book include facts about the period when Pulitzer lived, review questions, ideas for discussion, things to do, books to read, and a glossary. The readability level of the book is about fourth grade, but the content appeal extends well into the upper grades as much interesting information is given about this impressive man.

200. Nagel, Paul C. *Missouri: A Bicentennial History* (States and the Nation Series). Illustrated with a photographer's essay by A. Y. Owen; original maps by Harold Faye. New York: Norton, 1977. 205 pages. (Ages 12 and up) *Nonfiction*

"Whether by the pen of Samuel Clemens, the brush of George Caleb Bingham, or the flight of Charles A. Lindbergh's *Spirit of St. Louis*, America has come to Missouri for glimpses of a life and outlook which once seemed so promising when the nation and Missouri were young" (p. 9). *Missouri: A Bicentennial History*, one of the volumes of the States and the Nation series, is designed to give a perspective of the ideals espoused and the experiences undergone in the history of the nation. The significant aspects of each state's past add to an understanding of the history of the nation as a whole. Nagel's portrait of Missouri is written in essay form; each of the nine chapters discusses significant themes in the development of the state. His unifying thread amid the state's great diversity is the upholding of Jeffersonian precepts. The first chapter is concerned with reflections about Missouri by authors, artists, journalists, and other imaginative citizens. A discussion of Missouri's early years and of her brief time of national leadership follows. The influence of Thomas Hart Benton and Harry S. Truman is explored in two chapters. Between these eras, Missouri suffered years of internal division and violence. The book concludes with an interpretation of how Missouri has responded to the major forces at work in America since 1875. The volume includes an index and annotated suggestions for further reading.

201. Neville, Emily Cheney. *Garden of Broken Glass*. New York: Delacorte, 1975. 228 pages. (Ages 10–14) *Fiction*

"Broken glass seemed to grow in St. Louis like part of the earth. . . . The crop flourished" (pp. 4–5). Thirteen-year-old Brian Moody tried hard to survive the squalor and poverty of his life in the slums of St. Louis. Abandoned houses, broken windows, and scattered trash were only part of the reason why he wanted to shut out his hopeless surroundings. He found that making his mind a blank made it easier to forget that his father had deserted the family and easier to ignore his alcoholic mother and the way that she favored his younger brother Andy. He could even pretend not to hear his older sister Eve, who was always telling him what to do. School was his refuge, because it was the only safe place. There he could come and go without being noticed much, even though he was one of the few white children in the seventh grade. Then Fat Martha, Dwayne Yale, and Dwayne's girl friend Melvita befriended Brian. These black children helped him to find other ways to make his life bearable. Finally, he was able to show his sister and brother how the three of them could be a family.

202. Noble, Iris. *Joseph Pulitzer: Front Page Pioneer*. New York: Messner, 1957. 191 pages. (Ages 13 and up) *Biography*

This biography written for advanced readers tells the dramatic story of how Joseph Pulitzer shaped the course of American journalism and left a legacy to future journalists as well as to the entire literary world. In 1864, at the age of seventeen, Pulitzer, a penniless Hungarian immigrant, came to America to join the Union army. He loved America because of its promise of freedom and equality, and in St. Louis he began his rise to fame as a reporter, editor, and publisher. He was a reformer, a crusader against corruption, and a champion of unbiased reporting; he was devoted to the public and stood for what he believed was right, even when it meant standing alone. He began his journalism career as a reporter for the St. Louis *Westliche Post*, owned by the famous Carl Schurz, U.S. senator from Missouri, and his partner, Dr. Emil Preetorius, who recognized Pulitzer's ability and gave him his first experience as a political reporter. In 1878 Pulitzer bought and merged the *St. Louis Post-Dispatch* and created one of the strongest independent papers in the country. Then in 1883, still a young man of thirty-six, he reached further heights of success when he purchased the *New York World*. Always he continued his determination to produce a newspaper dedicated to the public welfare and to progress.

In addition to an excellent characterization of Pulitzer, Noble has provided information about Pulitzer's family life, about St. Louis society, and about the political and economic situation in the state and nation during the last part of the century. The book has a bibliography and is indexed.

203. Nolan, Jeannette Covert. *The Gay Poet: The Story of Eugene Field*. Illustrated by Robert S. Robertson. New York: Messner, 1940. 254 pages. (Ages 12 and up) *Biography*

The theme of Nolan's biography as indicated in the title is overshadowed by Eugene Field's many steadfast and endearing qualities as well as by his literary legacy to the world; yet his characteristic sense of humor was a well-known aspect of his life. His fun-loving disposition, which made him prone to rowdy practical jokes, is reflected in many episodes that provide unity to the story. Nolan skillfully blends the circumstances and time of Field's life and introduces many important people with whom he associated. His early life is seen against the background of a devoted family with considerable culture and education; his father, Roswell Martin Field, was a highly respected lawyer, widely known for his role in the historic Dred Scott decision. While young Field showed potential talents, his academic pursuits were less worthy than expected. The story provides a good picture of his life while attending the University of Missouri, of his subsequent courtship and marriage to Julia Comstock of St. Joseph, and of his professional achievements. In 1873 he began his career as a reporter for the *St. Louis Journal* and within two years moved to the editorship of the *St. Joseph Gazette*. Advancing rapidly in the newspaper world, he returned to St. Louis for an editorial position on the *Journal and Times-Journal*.

By the time he was thirty, he was managing editor of the *Kansas City Times*, and a year later (1881) he made the big step to become a highly successful managing editor of the *Denver Tribune*. His last move, two years later, was to Chicago where he worked for the *Chicago Daily News* and concentrated on his own creative writing of poetry and short stories. Throughout his demanding career, his devotion to his family was unswerving as was his enjoyment of people and his sense of good humor. His verses won for him the hearts of readers everywhere and a place in American literature.

204. Norman, James. *Kearny Rode West* (American Battles and Campaigns). Cover illustration by Ted Xaras. New York: Putnam's, 1971. 190 pages. (Ages 10 and up) *Nonfiction*

When the Mexican War broke out in 1846, Brig. Gen. Stephen Watts Kearny was placed in command of the U.S. Army of the West; he was ordered to organize this army and to lead it on an extraordinary expedition that was to expand the nation to the Pacific. In this narrative, Norman has presented a dramatic account of Kearny's army of Missouri Volunteers as they moved westward to seize Santa Fe and to take over the Mexican territory now included in the state of New Mexico. After establishing a civil government there, Kearny led a small force on to California where he joined forces with Commodore Robert F. Stockton. By January 1847 their combined forces had occupied Los Angeles and had set up a territorial government. There also began the controversy that was to make dire enemies of the four good friends—Kearny, John Charles Frémont, Thomas Hart Benton, and Christopher "Kit" Carson—whose conquests had fulfilled America's continental destiny. The story provides an interesting picture of St. Louis in the 1840s, of Jefferson Barracks, and of the First Dragoon Regiment, the army's elite corps of horsemen, which had been under Kearny's command since 1833. Included is one of the few available accounts of the Missouri Volunteers who made up the Army of the West. Mostly farm boys, they were rugged frontiersmen but were unskilled and undisciplined in army tactics. Yet the two infantry companies proved their endurance by marching through unexplored country, always going ahead of the mounted volunteers. Several Missourians participating in this campaign later became famous in American history: Ulysses S. Grant, Meriwether Lewis Clark, Tom Fitzpatrick, William T. Sherman, and Sterling Price; Alexander William Doniphan and his First Regiment of Missouri Volunteers became a national legend.

The book is indexed. Erroneous information that appears on page 13 states, "The United States at that time [1843] was still small. There were eighteen states, the most westward being Missouri." In order to counter bias, the reader should also read biographies of John Charles Frémont and Jessie Benton Frémont, as well as Julia Davis's *Ride with the Eagle: The Expedition of The First Missouri in the War with Mexico, 1846*; Betty Baker's *The Dunderhead War* provides interesting fiction set against the background of this same period.

205. North, Sterling. *Mark Twain and the River* (North Star Books). Illustrated by Victor Mays. Boston: Houghton Mifflin, 1961. 184 pages. (Ages 10 and up) *Biography*

This nonfictional biography of Mark Twain, one of America's greatest literary figures, can be enjoyed by young people and adult scholars alike. North's skillfully written material is historically accurate and retains the mood of Twain's own books. This book covers Twain's entire life from his birth at Florida, Missouri, in 1835, to his death near Redding, Connecticut, in 1910. The story is built around eight major episodes that each mark a chronological period of time. The setting for the life of this famous man is described as "A Frontier Paradise" with the river an ever-appealing scene for the young growing boy. Four sections of the book portray Samuel Clemens as a wandering typesetter, a proud steamboat pilot, a luckless miner, a successful newspaper reporter, and an entertaining teller of tales. The final chapters recount his romantic courtship and marriage to Olivia Langdon of Elmira, New York; his devoted family life; his distinguished literary accomplishments; and his worldwide travels. The book is indexed.

206. Nothdurft, Lillian. *Folklore and Early Customs of Southeast Missouri*. New York: Exposition Press, 1972. 77 pages. (Ages 12 and up) *Nonfiction*

This collection of folklore and early customs attributed to the southeast Missouri area is organized under nine major topics containing information on a wide range of subjects including home life, rural schools, and churches. Discussions of community gatherings and entertainment reveal the cooperative spirit that existed among the people and explain some of the popular games. Among the descriptions of typical folk characters are those of the Circuit Rider, Country Doctor, Schoolteacher, Storekeeper, Blacksmith, Water Witch, and Mail Carrier. Examples of picturesque expressions, tall tales, folk dances, "singin' games," and superstitions make up more than half of the book. Most of this folklore could be found in any part of the state or, for that matter, throughout the nation, but it is reminiscent of life as people knew it during the early part of this century. (Note: the preface incorrectly labels these stories as being about the nineteenth century.) Children today could enjoy learning some of the folk dances, comparing life then and now, and particularly contrasting the characterizations such as those of the Doctor, Teacher, or Storekeeper. Also, young readers might be surprised to find out how many of the same superstitions exist today.

207. Orrmont, Arthur. *James Buchanan Eads: The Man Who Mastered the Mississippi* (A Hall of Fame Book). Englewood Cliffs, N.J.: Prentice-Hall, 1970. 143 pages. (Ages 12–16) *Biography*

In this fascinating biography, Orrmont has re-created the inspiring life of James Buchanan Eads, whose engineering achievements have been monumental. The story begins with Eads's arrival in St. Louis in 1833 when he was thirteen years old. As a youngster, Eads sold apples on the streets and worked as an errand boy to help meet family expenses. He was unable to obtain a formal education, yet he became the greatest self-taught engineer that the world has ever known. He survived grave personal tragedies and huge financial losses. He overcame natural obstacles, strong public opinion, and powerful government opposition in his efforts to improve the Mississippi River and its tributaries. Among his greatest achievements were the salvage of sunken steamboats, the construction of the iron-clads that hastened the Union victory in the Civil War, the spanning of the Mississippi by Eads Bridge completed in 1874, and the building of jetties (false banks) that opened the south pass of the Mississippi for a clear channel of commerce to the Gulf. Eads was the first American to be awarded the Albert Medal by the British Society for the Encouragement of Art, Manufactures and Commerce (1884). The thread of Eads's personal life is woven into this account of his distinguished career, and the man is characterized by his kindly manner as well as by his devotion to his family. A chronology and a list of books for further reading are included.

208. Painter, Allyson, and Irving Dillard. *"I'm from Missouri!" Where Man and Mule Shaped the Heart of a Nation.* Illustrated with photographs. New York: Hastings House, 1951. 104 pages. (Ages 10 and up) *Nonfiction*

Within these pages of striking photographs and pictorial maps complemented by informative text, the photographer and the author have presented a distinguished portrait of Missouri. Painter has captured the many-sided beauty of Missouri in seventy-five pages of black-and-white captioned photographs of historic and scenic places across the state. Dillard, the author, portrays Missouri as "All America in one place" as he reveals in expressive language the complex nature of the state, its people, its culture, its industry, and its commerce. But he also proves that "Missouri is itself as well" as he describes the natural beauty of its ancient mountains, surging springs, and unspoiled streams. The material in this book is arranged in six parts, each preceded by an attractive pictorial map of the area depicted: "Introduction: Missouri Is All America"; "Area I, Down by Old Man River"; "Area II, Hills, Hollows, and Hermits"; "Area III, Crossroads of the Country"; "Area IV, Up Where the West Begins"; and "Area V, Land of Tom and Huck and Dan'l Boone." The material is compact but impressively inclusive.

209. Phegley, Mallie. *The Father of Texas: Stephen F. Austin.* Illustrated with maps and drawings. San Antonio: Naylor, 1960. 123 pages. (Ages 12 and up)   *Biography*

Missouri's influence on the growth of the American nation was far-reaching and was particularly evident in the state's role as the mother of the West. One of those famous Missourians who have made an impact on history was Stephen F. Austin, founder of the state of Texas; the capital of Texas bears his name.

Texas in 1820 was a province of Mexico. It was a sparsely settled territory, and Moses Austin planned to colonize it with Missourians. Austin, an enterprising and successful lead-mine operator who had lost his fortune in a St. Louis bank failure, had received a charter from Mexico permitting him to bring settlers into Texas. He died before he could realize his ambitions, but his son, Stephen, took up his father's grant of thousands of Texas acres. He had no difficulty attracting colonists as many people in the Missouri Territory had suffered from the economic failures of the times and were eager to seek new homes. They had confidence in this man who had served in the territorial legislature and whose father had contributed so much to the growth and wealth of the territory.

Within the pages of this fictionalized biography, Stephen Austin and his band of adventuring colonists live again to inspire the reader with their brave and courageous deeds. The demands of colonization were great as Mexican laws, Mexican bandits, hostile Indians, and rebellious colonists constantly hampered the settlers. Austin made many hazardous trips to Mexico to confer with high government officials and even suffered unjust imprisonment in Mexico City. This dedicated man left a memorial that stretches the length and breadth of the land called Texas. The book is indexed.

210. Phelan, Mary Kay. *The Story of the Louisiana Purchase.* Illustrated by Frank Aloise. New York: Crowell, 1979. 149 pages. (Ages 10–14) *Nonfiction*

Phelan begins her informal but dramatic story of the Louisiana Purchase by telling of a journey downriver to New Orleans in 1800; she then gives the reader a brief review of the previous 118-year history of New Orleans and of the province of Louisiana as well as a description of everyday life in New Orleans and on the American frontier during the early 1800s. The fast-moving story proceeds from President Jefferson's inauguration to the events leading to the United States' purchase of the Louisiana Territory from France for $15 million in 1803. Louisiana had changed hands several times since La Salle had claimed the region for France in 1682, but Spain's agreement in 1800 to accept the secret Treaty of San Ildefonso and to return Louisiana to France created a threat for the new republic and stirred widespread speculations. The intrigue and excitement of the secret negotiations are strikingly revealed through the author's vivid portrayal of the fascinating participants, including Jefferson, Madison, Livingston, Bonaparte, and Talleyrand. The story closes with a summary of events from 1803, through the war of 1812 and General Jackson's victory over the British, to the final negotiations with Spain for the purchase of Florida in 1819. The Louisiana Purchase, the largest single territorial gain in U.S. history, almost doubled the size of the young country, greatly increased its economic resources, and provided a powerful impetus to westward expansion. In addition to Louisiana, the states of North and South Dakota, Missouri, Nebraska, Iowa, Arkansas, Oklahoma, and much of Minnesota, Kansas, Colorado, Montana, and Wyoming were eventually carved out of this territory. The importance of the transaction has been ranked next to the Declaration of Independence and the adoption of the Constitution. Chapter headings and chronologies, as well as a bibliography and an index, provide additional value to the book.

211. Pinkerton, Robert E. *The First Overland Mail* (Landmark Books). Illustrated by Paul Lantz. New York: Random House, 1953. 185 pages. (Ages 10–14) *Nonfiction*

This book is one of the few that deals with the first successful overland mail service from Missouri to California. The Southern Overland Mail, a stagecoach line commonly known as the Butterfield Line, crossed the country from St. Louis to San Francisco. The book also tells the story of John Butterfield, who established the line in 1858; it continued until the beginning of the Civil War in 1861. The story furnishes background on the political arguments involved in awarding the government contract and tells how Butterfield overcame tremendous difficulties in planning the route, in providing supplies and equipment, and in protecting the passengers and employees. Descriptions of the relay system and the schedules; the way stations and their agents; the roads, stagecoaches, and drivers; as well as Indian encounters, both friendly and hostile, are realistically presented. The main stagecoach line left Tipton, Missouri, the end of the 160 miles of the Missouri Pacific Railroad west from St. Louis, and traveled south 318 miles to Fort Smith where it joined the branch line from Memphis to continue westward. Of particular interest is the first trip, which is recounted in chapter 8. As soon as the mail arrived after a ten-hour train trip from St. Louis, the stagecoach left Tipton on the Butterfield Trail, reaching Springfield two days later. On the morning of the third day, after traveling over rough and dangerous roads through the Ozark Mountains, the stage arrived at Fort Smith. The entire route covering a distance of 2800 miles in twenty-five successive days made almost a half-circle across the western part of the continent. Butterfield's Southern Overland Mail preceded the central route of the Overland Mail, the Pony Express, the telegraph, and the railroad. The book is especially useful for social-studies units on the postal service, transportation, and the westward movement. There are excellent illustrations and an index.

212. Place, Marian T. *Mountain Man: The Life of Jim Beckwourth*. Illustrated by Paul Williams. New York: Macmillan, 1970. 120 pages. (Ages 11 and up) *Biography*

Jim Beckwourth was the son of a white Virginia planter and a black slave. In 1805, when he was about seven years old, his father moved the family to St. Louis, Missouri. He later settled on a section of land between the forks of the Mississippi and Missouri rivers twelve miles below St. Charles; the area was known for many years as "Beckwourth's settlement." The region at that time, according to Jim, was "a howling wilderness inhabited only by wild beasts and merciless savages" (p. 4). When Jim was fourteen, his father apprenticed him to a blacksmith in St. Louis. Evidently his father was fond enough of him to want him to be more than a field hand; a blacksmith was an important and respected craftsman. By the time Jim had completed his apprenticeship, he had decided to see "the great western wilderness." He signed on as company blacksmith for a trapping expedition bound for the Rocky Mountains, thus beginning his lifelong association with the Rocky Mountain Fur Company, headquartered in St. Louis and owned by Andrew Henry, an educated gentleman, and Gen. William H. Ashley, lieutenant governor of the newly formed state of Missouri. Although on his first trip Jim reached no farther than where the Missouri turned north, he was a confirmed mountain man from that time on. He enjoyed the challenge of pitting his wits and endurance against the hazards of the wilderness, the wild animals, and the Indians. He lived with the Indians and even became a Crow chief. He became a successful trapper and trader who was famous from coast to coast. He knew all the great mountain men—Jed Smith, Jim Bridger, Kit Carson, Tom Fitzpatrick, and others; he traveled in their company as an equal. When these frontiersmen lounged around their campfire, they entertained each other by telling tall tales. While Jim became known as an accomplished storyteller, his yarns were always based on actual happenings. In his late fifties, he told his life story to T. D. Bonner, a newspaperman, who published it in 1856 under the title, *The Life and Adventures of James P. Beckwourth, Mountaineer, Scout and Pioneer, and Chief of the Crow Nation of Indians.* This biography is based on Bonner's book. It has twelve titled chapter divisions and contains a selected bibliography and an index.

213. Pond, Alonzo W. *Caverns of the World.* Illustrated with photographs. New York: Norton, 1960. 178 pages. (Ages 12 and up) *Nonfiction*

Pond's fascination with underground passages led him into caverns in many parts of the world; this book tells about some of his favorite "worlds-within-a-world," the surprising, mysterious, and sometimes hazardous caverns beneath the earth. Pond discusses various types of caves and how they were formed. The flowers and the creatures that live within the caves are as interesting as the pools and rock formations. Throughout the book, the author discusses several Missouri caves and underground water streams including Boiling Springs, Crystal Cave, Cathedral Cave, Fairy Cave, Jacobs Cave, Lone Hill Onyx Cave, Roaring Spring, Tavern Cave or Zell Cave, and Tunnel Cave. Several of these are identified in the chapter entitled "Caverns Are Born below the Water Table." Boiling Springs on the Gasconade River is described as one of the largest natural springs in the world, flowing forty-two million gallons of water daily. Mark Twain Cave and Cameron Cave were once a connected system that is now cut in two by the living stream that drained these caverns. More than twenty openings from the Mark Twain Cave on the side to the river valley have been discovered. In the chapter "Caverns in Music, Legend, and History," the author points to the intricate network of passages as convincing evidence that Tom Sawyer should have tied a string to the wall of the cave when he led Becky Thatcher on the cave expedition; he also directs the reader to Mark Twain's *Adventures of Tom Sawyer* saying, "No one before or since has better described the terrible fear of cave darkness when the last candle burns down. No one has made more clear the basic rules of cave exploration" (p. 128). Other information about Missouri caves is included in the chapters dealing with cave formations, stories about how some of the caves were discovered, and the varied uses that caves have served. The index is essential to this book.

214. Potter, Marian. *Milepost 67*. Cover by George Mocniak. Chicago: Follett, 1965. 224 pages. (Ages 9–12) *Fiction*

Ten-year-old Evaline Stevens lived with her family in a yellow section house along the railroad right-of-way in the small community of Middling, Missouri, during the early 1920s. Between their house and the depot was a sign on a white flat post, "Milepost 67," which meant that it was sixty-seven miles from there to Union Station in St. Louis. Evaline's father was foreman of the railroad section gang whose job it was to keep the tracks and the right-of-way in order. Life was filled with simple everyday pleasures for a girl whose family loved each other and who knew how to make the most out of their meager earnings. The danger and the excitement of a flood on the river and of a trip on the train to St. Louis are among the highlights of this appealing story. This book gives a good picture of the life led by the children of railroad section workers during that period in history. It is also one of the few books that give children a link with the railroading past. Since each chapter is a separate episode, any chapter would serve as a good read-aloud story. A brief introduction to characters and setting would create the background.

215. Powers, William K. *Indians of the Southern Plains* (American Indians Then and Now). Illustrated with photographs. New York: Putnam's, 1971. 223 pages. (Ages 12 and up) *Nonfiction*

Factual information about the Indians of the southern plains, both in the past and in the present, is presented in explicit language and in logical patterns. This entertaining account of these Indian tribes is told within the setting of American history. The Indians of the Great Plains were the first known inhabitants of the vast territory extending westward from the Mississippi to the Rocky Mountains and south and north from the Gulf of Mexico to the Canadian prairies. Among the twenty principal tribes identified by the author were the Missouri, Oto, and Osage, the three tribes living within the present area of the state of Missouri. Information about each of these tribes includes a discussion of distinctive chracteristics of the people; an explanation of their language, tribal organization, and ceremonies; a description of their dwellings and their way of life as well as their means of obtaining food, clothing, shelter, and transportation; short biographical sketches of famous people; and commentaries on their costumes, crafts, music, dance, rituals, and the powwow. An excellent bibliography and an index add to the value of the book.

216. Rabe, Berniece. *Naomi*. New York: Nelson, 1975. 192 pages. (Ages 14 and up) *Fiction*

During the depression years of the 1930s in the farming area of southeastern Missouri, Naomi Bradley struggled to find her own way in the harsh environment. Mom had said, "Y'll soon turn fourteen. Y'll be graduatin' from the eighth grade in May. Y're old enough to be considerin'. But we ain't lettin' you marry no Catholic. . . . And y'ain't gonna date nobody. They can come to the house like Lenny did" (p. 164). When marriage was the only hope for a girl's future, it was Mom's responsibility to teach her daughters early the requirements for getting and holding a husband. But Naomi decided that she wanted to do her own thinking and to listen to her own voice instead of doing what others expected of her. In the end, it was the visiting nurse, Sarah Mitchell Haller, who helped Naomi to learn that there were important services for women to perform in life as well as to recognize her own real goals. While the grim elements of the story are lightened by the author's use of humor, the main content of the novel is starkly realistic.

217. Rabe, Berniece. *Rass*. New York: Nelson, 1973. 176 pages. (Ages 12 and up) *Fiction*

Rass is mostly about a teenaged boy named Rass; it is also about his sharecropper family on a southeast Missouri farm during the Great Depression. This is one of the few children's books written clearly about this period in American history. Self-willed Rass clashed so frequently with his dad's narrow-minded and harsh manner that Rass once vowed, "I'll hate him until I die" (p. 15). Yet there was no one that he longed to please more than his dad. As Rass saw his father over the years, as well as through the eyes of others and in contrast to his Uncle Jake, he came to accept the fact that his father was an unhappy coward and that he could love his father without liking his faults. *Rass* is more than a story resolving father-and-son conflicts; it is a chronicle of the hardships, the sorrows, and the good times of a large sharecropper family. Readers will sympathize with Rass as readily as they will be amused at his trials. This is an exceptionally well-written story that goes beyond its theme and locale. The book should have wide appeal and lasting value. *Rass* was one of the twenty-one books on the 1974–1975 Missouri Mark Twain Award list.

218. Rabe, Berniece. *The Girl Who Had No Name*. Jacket illustration by Muriel Wood. New York: Dutton, 1977. 149 pages. (Ages 12 and up) *Fiction*

Set against a background of rural southeast Missouri during the depression days of 1936, this story is marked by abundant details of domestic economy and by effectively sketched characters. Twelve-year-old Girlie, the youngest of a poor, motherless family, was passed from one to another of her nine sisters, who were either unable or unwilling to cope with her upbringing. But with fearless courage, she finally managed to piece together the reason why she was never given a real name and why her father declined to take care of her after her mother's death. Besides resolving these major issues and coping with the everyday problems encountered during this period of hard times, Girlie was able to face the seemingly endless changes in her life. By the time she graduated from the eighth grade under a successful work-study program, she not only had a name but also had a solid home life with a hopeful future. Biological questions related to Girlie's parentage are discussed naturally and forthrightly as are other details related to the background of the story.

219. Rabe, Berniece. *The Orphans.* Jacket illustration by Donna Diamond. New York: Dutton, 1978. 184 pages. (Ages 10–14) *Fiction*

Southeastern Missouri during the depression of the 1930s is the background for *The Orphans*, a story depicting the hard times but characterized by the will and spirit of the people. As young men struggled with the responsibilities of making a living for their families, they often repressed their fears with laughter and jokes and sometimes with reckless actions. The women and children more readily expressed their actual feelings as they dealt with the harsh realities of life. So it was with the orphans, especially Little Adam Braggs.

Ten-year-old twins Little Adam and Eva were orphans who were left homeless a second time when their uncles were killed trying to beat a train to the crossing. The twins' determination to belong to a family took them on an unusual but surprisingly successful quest. After being rejected by their unknown Aunt Aggie on their arrival in St. Louis, they were taken to an orphanage. But they soon convinced the authorities to send them back to the promising security of G-Mama, their stepgrandmother. It was there at the backwoods cabin that Sheriff Erica Wheeler discovered the twins trying to manage for themselves while taking care of G-Mama who had broken her hip. Erica took the three of them into town to stay with her until G-Mama had recovered. In the meantime, Little Adam's matchmaking plot failed to get a husband for Erica or to persuade G-Mama to marry her longtime suitor, the owner of the general store. However, a favorable decision by Judge Nagle finally made the twins a part of a real family, and "Little" no longer a part of Adam's name.

220. Randall, Ruth Painter. *I Jessie: A Biography of the Girl Who Married John Charles Frémont, Famous Explorer of the West*. Illustrated with photographs; jacket design by Robert J. Lowe. Boston: Little, Brown, 1963. 223 pages. (Ages 12 and up) *Biography*

Randall has provided an excellent portrait of a most unusual life and has shown how Jessie Benton Frémont, with her husband, shared a career that contributed vitally to the history of this country's expansion. Jessie Ann Benton, a favorite daughter of Missouri's famous senator, Thomas Hart Benton, grew up in the comfortable society of St. Louis and Washington, D.C. But her strong will and independent nature had destined her for a remarkable life far beyond the ordinary. Despite opposition from her family, she married John Charles Frémont, who rose to fame and popularity as a soldier and an explorer who was known as "the Pathfinder." Their adventures, marked by the hazards and hardships of the wilderness as well as by long and desolate separations from each other, took them to the peaks and valleys of spectacular fame and fortune. Jessie's steadfast belief in her husband and in his work in opening California helped him to overcome many adversities. She fought against political intrigue in Washington and against his court-martial. Land investments in California had made them wealthy forty-niners, but when Frémont lost the fortune trying to establish a southern railroad to the Pacific, Jessie courageously supported the family through the sale of her stories and books. It is on these volumes and on Allan Nevins's biography of Frémont that Randall has based her story. The index adds to the book's value. Mature readers will also be interested in Irving Stone's novel, *Immortal Wife* (Doubleday, 1948).

221. Randolph, Vance, editor. *An Ozark Anthology*. Jacket design by Thomas Hart Benton. Caldwell, Idaho: Caxton, 1940. 374 pages. (YA) OP. *Fiction*

Vance Randolph, a recognized authority on Ozark dialects and folklore, searched the literature published about the Ozark hill people and selected fifteen stories for *An Ozark Anthology*. Among the selections are "Paid in Full" by Rose Wilder Lane, "America's Yesterday" by Thomas Hart Benton, "The Hired Man" by Rose O'Neill, and "The Witch Doctor of Rosy Ridge" by MacKinlay Kantor. Each selection is preceded with bibliographic notes, and each author has lived in the Ozark country. As Randolph points out in his introduction, the background for the stories was drawn from an isolated region characterized by a way of life that progress has rapidly eliminated. The picturesque Ozark Mountain countryside known by these authors was peopled by an old American stock with customs and traditions held for many centuries. The log cabins were there as were the cord beds and muzzle-loading rifles, the spinning wheels, and handlooms, along with the men and women whose dialect was as quaint as their superstitions and as colorful as their old English ballads. Although the volume is intended for adults, some of these stories, judiciously chosen and used, would be appropriate for the young adolescent reader or for reading aloud to children in the upper elementary grades.

222. Reeder, Col. "Red" (Russell P., Jr.). *Omar Nelson Bradley: The Soldiers' General* (Defenders of Freedom Series). Illustrated by Herman B. Vestal; map by Henri A. Fulchere. Champaign, Ill.: Garrard, 1969. 112 pages. (Ages 9–12) *Biography*

This simplified, easy-to-read biography highlights for children in the middle grades the major events in the life of a famous Missourian and a great American. It is a highly dramatic story emphasizing Omar Bradley's sturdy character and his personal determination. Each phase of his illustrious career is set against a background sufficiently detailed to allow the reader a full understanding of the time and place of events as well as of Bradley's achievements and successes. The fictionalized conversation readily involves the reader. Almost the entire first half of the book deals with Bradley's boyhood and his West Point years. One chapter touches briefly on his next twenty-five years as an infantry officer. Then the remainder of the book discusses Bradley's action during World War II, which revealed his exceptional ability as a commanding leader on the battlefronts, and his subsequent years as a five-star general and as chairman of the Joint Chiefs of Staff.

Omar Nelson Bradley was born at Clark, Missouri, on 12 February 1893. Following his father's death, he and his mother moved to Moberly, Missouri, where he was captain of his high-school baseball team. This athletic skill won him a place in both baseball and football at West Point. In December 1916, at Columbia, Missouri, he was married to his high-school friend and classmate, Mary Quayles, who had just graduated from the University of Missouri School of Journalism.

Bradley's decisiveness in command of his army resulted in spectacular victories. His genuine concern for his men in battle won their respect and earned him the title "the Soldiers' General." He has received distinguished awards from twelve foreign countries as well as many from his own country. In 1967, when Gen. Emmett O'Donnell of the air force presented him with the United Service Organization's distinguished award, he said, "He [Omar Nelson Bradley] truly belongs to the Nation" (p. 110).

The book is indexed and contains a preface letter written by Bradley about the author, Colonel Reeder, who was a West Point classmate and commander of the Twelfth Infantry on D-Day.

223. Reeder, Col. "Red" (Russell P., Jr.). *Ulysses S. Grant,
Horseman and Fighter* (A Discovery Book). Illustrated
by Ken Wagner. Champaign, Ill.: Garrard, 1964. 80
pages. (Ages 7–10) *Biography*

In the easy-to-read text common to all the books in
this series, this fictional biography presents brief highlights
of the life of Ulysses S. Grant. Mention is made of some of
his boyish pranks, but for the most part themes of courage
and bravery underlie serious episodes depicting his military career. The story begins with eleven-year-old Ulysses
displaying his horsemanship at a circus in Georgetown,
Ohio, and moves quickly into his period of training at West
Point. During his first assignment at Jefferson Barracks
near St. Louis, he met Julia Dent, whom he later married.
While little attention is given to her role in his life, she and
their children are mentioned as living at various places
where he was stationed. The final chapter deals briefly and
superficially with his presidency and final years, omitting
the tragic realities of those years. Chapter headings and
maps of the major battlefields add interest and clarity for
the reader. The value of the book, as with others in the
series, lies in its usefulness as an introduction to biography
and to research in new areas.

224. Rees, Ennis. *Windwagon Smith.* Illustrated by Peter P.
Plasencia. Englewood Cliffs, N.J.: Prentice-Hall, 1966.
Unpaged. (Ages 8–12) *Fiction*

In unrhymed verse, Rees tells the tale of Windwagon
Smith as his prairie schooner rolls over the great plains
toward the fabled land of American tall tales. Practically
everyone in Westport, Missouri, laughed at Mr. Smith and
his strange wagon until a man from St. Joseph offered him
money to build others like it for "hauling trade to Santa Fe
and all points west." Then the windwagon became Westport's pride and joy, at least for a while. Some of the leading citizens went for a ride in the "Prairie Clipper" which
"was ten times as large as a regular wagon and built with a
platform, or bridge, on top where Windwagon Smith

could stand and steer. The sail was as big as the side of a barn." At the end of the story, Rees gives credit to the source of the legend, which grew from an incident said to have happened in 1853. While the book is unpaged, the text is longer and more difficult to read than other recent versions including Mary Calhoun's *High Wind for Kansas*, Edna Shapiro's *Windwagon Smith*, and Ramona Maher's *When Windwagon Smith Came to Westport*.

225. Reid, Loren. *Hurry Home Wednesday: Growing Up in a Small Missouri Town, 1905–1921*. Illustrated with photographs and maps. Columbia: University of Missouri Press, 1978. 320 pages. (YA) *Nonfiction*

Hurry Home Wednesday provides a vicarious experience into Missouri's past that will interest a wide audience from adult readers to able readers in the upper grades and even younger listeners who can appreciate selected portions of the book. Like many small towns across the nation, Gilman City makes no claim to fame, but Reid has re-created a memorable picture of everyday small-town life as it was during the early part of this century. The story recalls Reid's own boyhood as he grew up there and helped to publish the town's weekly newspaper. The biographical sketches of Reid and his family, the characterizations of the individual townspeople, and the detailed descriptions of the varied aspects of life in the once-thriving town convey the author's full understanding of the time and the place. His sense of humor casts a genial glow over the book that becomes more focused in the telling of specific amusing incidents. Since the Reid family's livelihood centered around the publication of the town's only newspaper, the detailed account of their activities is exceptionally realistic as well as entertaining. Schoolchildren today who visit modern newspaper offices would enjoy this look into the contrasting newsroom of the past; likewise, older students learning about the production of today's newspapers could come away from this account with grateful appreciation of their forebears who set type by hand or operated a Linotype. The information about the local school's activities points out the importance of education to the small community. While today's young people are not likely to be enthusiastic about routine that includes *The One Hundred and One Best Songs* or the problems from Milne's *Standard Arithmetic*, they will find drama in many activities of yesteryear, and many would be willing to hurry home on Wednesday to chores as challenging as those that Reid reports. The photographs make interesting browsing.

226. Reinfeld, Fred. *Pony Express*. Illustrated with photographs. New York: Macmillan, 1966. 126 pages. (Ages 12 and up) *Nonfiction*

Reinfeld's excellent historical narrative provides the mature reader with a detailed account of the establishment of the first rapid communication between the East and the West. The record of the Pony Express is woven into the comprehensive history and the political background of the struggles to provide cross-country transportation. Despite all the problems encountered by the Russell, Majors, and Waddell transportation company, these enterprising Missourians wrote a glorious chapter in American history. The personal character of each of these men is as fascinating as the story of their venture is. While they were eager for financial success, they were equally concerned with certain values as was evident in the pledge, composed by Majors, required of each employee. Frequent quotations from newspapers and other sources, including Mark Twain, disclose interesting bits of information and support the author's interpretations. For example, one account from the *New York Sun* reported that the mail car used on the run from Hannibal to St. Joseph was the first car constructed for mail purposes in the United States. Furthermore, "The engine, named 'The Missouri,' was a woodburner. From an artistic standpoint it was a much handsomer machine than" the locomotives of today (p. 57). The immortal words of Twain's famous description of the Pony Express, "a whiz and a hail, and the swift phantom of the desert was gone" (pp. 52–54), are sure to stir the imagination and to keep the reader turning the pages. Indians on the warpath kept the newspapers active with pleas for help from the government as the *St. Louis Globe-Democrat*'s reaction shows: "It is a matter, therefore, of highest importance that the bold and daring spirits who risk their necks in carrying a sack of letters through the defiles of the mountains, over unbroken prairies and through the rapid rivers which divide us from the Pacific, should be protected" (p. 80). As the Pony Express came to an end, glowing tributes appeared in newspapers across the nation. Even though the telegraph lines replaced the Pony Express, the epic of the pony riders will live as long as the spirit of adventure exists in the hearts and minds of readers. Several old photographs help to capture the genuine spirit of the Old West.

227. Rhodes, Richard, and the editors of Time-Life Books. *The Ozarks* (The American Wilderness). New York: Time, Inc., 1974. 184 pages. (Ages 12 and up) *Non-fiction*

Magnificent, precisely captioned photographs match the beautifully written text of this volume about the Ozarks. The material is organized into six major sections: "Another Kind of Wilderness: A Water-Sculptured Land"; "A Collection of Caverns"; "Miracles from Rock"; "Floating with the Current"; "A Natural Refuge for Migrants: A Botanical Home away from Home"; and "The Rituals of a Long Spring." As these expressive titles indicate, information comes to the reader not in the usual manner of discussions on geography, topography, fauna, and flora, but with unforgettable descriptions and explanations depicting this land of beauty and wonder. Long after the book is closed, the sensitive impressions shared by the author-photographers will linger satisfyingly to challenge the mind of the reader. Into his discussion, Rhodes has woven human-interest stories about early inhabitants with impressions from the chronicles of the early explorers of the Ozark wilderness. He points out that this region is as yet "a wilderness intact in the middle of a continent" (p. 20) and can still be seen much as it was when man first saw it. Some two-and-a-half million acres of the Ozarks are preserved in national forests. Likewise, its rivers are deemed as national treasures by the Ozark National Scenic Riverway Act of 1964. The information about Ozark caverns, three thousand caves in the Missouri Ozarks alone, is especially interesting, and the description and accompanying photographs of Tumbling Creek Cave near Forsythe, Missouri, as a "fantastical show in an underground gallery" (p. 68), is a masterpiece of literary imagery. The volume contains a bibliography and index.

228. Robertson, Keith. *Ticktock and Jim* (Famous Horse Stories: Grosset and Dunlap). Illustrated by Wesley Dennis. Philadelphia: John C. Winston, 1948. 240 pages. (Ages 10–14) *Fiction*

When it is spring in southern Missouri, a twelve-year-old boy's spirits can be rapidly aroused, particularly if he lives on a farm and has a horse named Ticktock. One day, while his parents were shopping in town, Jim Meadows traded his heirloom watch to an itinerant horse trader for a scrawny horse that few people would have claimed. But to Jim, this little western mustang was something special from the first time he saw him tied to the end of a string of other horses trailing a trader's wagon. Many times during the following months the little pony proved to be the fine animal that Jim had believed it to be. Even Jim's father, who had been angered over the trade, relented as family and friends became convinced of Ticktock's worth. The first victory came when the pony successfully chased a dangerous bull out of the yard. Ticktock came to the rescue of Jim's younger sister Jean when she was hurt during a secret rendezvous. Then finally, it was Ticktock who, in the deep of the night, alerted the family that their barn was on fire. While these events that depict the horse's trustworthiness mark exciting and sober elements, the story also contains many humorous episodes.

229. Robertson, Keith. *Ticktock and Jim, Deputy Sheriffs*. Illustrated by Everett Stahl. Philadelphia: John C. Winston, 1949. 215 pages. (Ages 10–14) *Fiction*

Readers who have already encountered *Ticktock and Jim* will be interested in the further adventures of the little mouse-colored mustang and its owner Jim Meadows. The scene is the farm country of southern Missouri and the Ozark Mountains, probably during the 1930s. Many of the realistic episodes are drawn from the author's boyhood experiences, since he did in fact once trade his watch for a horse.

Ticktock and Jim were going about their Pony Express business one Saturday morning when they discovered a mysterious package in the road. But before Jim could examine it, two rough men overtook him, pushed him into a ditch, and rushed away with the box. The situation became even more puzzling when Jim found a diamond nearby, presumably lost by the men during the scuffle. Jim's younger sister Jean and her Welsh pony played their own important role in the story. Jim's new neighbor Larry Grant not only joined him in helping to solve the mystery but also became a full partner in an expanded Pony Express business. Both boys and Ticktock were made honorary deputy sheriffs.

The book is divided into chapters with title headings and contains numerous black-and-white illustrations.

230. Robinson, Ray. *Baseball's Most Colorful Managers* (Sports Shelf Books). Illustrated with photographs. New York: Putnam's, 1969. 191 pages. (Ages 12 and up) *Biography*

In the introduction, Robinson states that, while winning records, popularity, and knowledgeability were important considerations, the selection of biographical subjects, for the most part, included those managers who had "become legends through force of personality, character, temperament, publicity skills, articulateness, instinct, and ability to project that inscrutable quality called color" (p. 10). One of the six biographical sketches appearing in this book describes the unforgettable Casey Stengel. The sketch of Stengel deals almost entirely with his managerial positions except for brief accounts of his early life as a ball player and of his marriage to Edna Lawson of Glendale, California. Charles Dillon Stengel was born on 10 July 1890 in Kansas City, Missouri, where he grew up participating in sports. Early in his career he acquired the nickname K. C., which was transformed into Casey. Stengel's spectacular success with the New York Yankees was a complete contrast to his reputation as a loser in the National League. From 1912 to 1925, Casey was a celebrated performer in the National League and was known for his batting championship as well as for his comical antics. But as a manager, only one of his National League clubs, the 1938 Boston Braves, was able to win more games than it lost. During his twelve years with the Yankees, he won ten pennants and seven world titles. On his return to the National League in 1961 as the manager of the New York Mets, he again fell heir to a losing team; the club held the distinction of having the worst players in baseball history. (Five years later, Yogi Berra, another Missourian, was to bring them out of their slump.) Soon after his departure from the Mets in 1965, Stengel was unananimously elected to baseball's Hall of Fame. An index adds to the book's usefulness.

231. Robinson, Ray. *Stan Musial: Baseball's Durable "Man."* Illustrated with photographs. New York: Putnam's, 1963. 192 pages. (Ages 10 and up) *Biography*

Robinson effectively characterizes Stan Musial as a durable baseball player and as a human being, a hero to millions of fans including his devoted family and a host of loyal friends. This biography includes the statistical record of Musial's achievements as well as numerous examples of his attractiveness as a personable individual. Musial signed with the St. Louis Cardinals when he was seventeen years old and played his first game in a Cardinal uniform, wearing number six, in 1941; he played his last game in 1963. He was one of the few players who spent his whole career in the uniform of a single ball club, and so his story is also the story of the St. Louis Cardinals. During his outstanding career, both Musial and the St. Louis club earned numerous baseball records. By 1962, when this book was written, his final batting average was .330, the third highest in the National League. But it was during some of his most unforgettable games against the Brooklyn Dodgers in 1948 that he acquired the simple but respectful nickname, "The Man." His successful performance in the game was equally matched by his many favorable personal qualities and wholesome life-style. The book contains an index and a table of statistics listing Musial's record with the Cardinals along with his World Series and All-Star Game records.

232. Robinson, Ray. "Yogi Berra: Living Legend," in *The Greatest Yankees of Them All* (Sports Shelf Books). Illustrated with photographs. New York: Putnam's, 1969, pp. 135–50. (Ages 12 and up)   *Biography*

This book features fifteen biographical sketches of the all-time great players from the New York Yankees. Among these spectacular and durable players was the colorful catcher Yogi Berra. Lawrence Peter Berra was born in a section of St. Louis named the Hill on 12 May 1925. As a youngster his main interest was sports, including baseball, soccer, softball, hockey, and boxing. He got his nickname from his pals who thought that he walked "like Yogi." One of his closest friends both on and off the baseball field was Joe Garagiola who lived in the same neighborhood, the Little Italy of St. Louis. (Garagiola became a catcher for the St. Louis Cardinals, played on the New York Yankee team, and ultimately became a highly paid announcer for the National Broadcasting Company.) In 1964, after twenty years with the Yankees, Berra terminated his active career as a player and became the team's manager. But he lost his position that same year when the Yankees lost the World Series to the St. Louis Cardinals. (Another Missouri player,

Ken Boyer, led his team to victory in that year.) Berra's zeal and durability made him a living legend; he appeared in a record fourteen World Series, played a record seventy-five games, and made another record of seventy-one hits. He won three Most Valuable Player Awards (1951, 1954, and 1955). Toward the end of his career, he played under the management of Casey Stengel, another Missourian, and was succeeded as a catcher by Elston Howard, also of St. Louis. At the time of the writing of this biographical sketch, Berra, in his early forties, was a coach with the New York Mets. He, his wife, the former Carmen Short of St. Louis, and their three sons were living in Montclair, New Jersey. The book is indexed.

233. Rossi, Paul A., and David C. Hunt. *The Art of the Old West, from the Collection of the Gilcrease Institute.* New York: Knopf, 1971. 335 pages. (Ages 12 and up) *Nonfiction*

A large, heavy, and lavish volume, this book is designed for viewing and reading at a reference table. It is a collection of representative paintings, drawings, watercolors, sculptures, and lithographs from the Thomas Gilcrease Institute of American History and Art in Tulsa, Oklahoma. Among the book's 300 plates, 134 are in full color. Twenty scenes of cowboy and Indian life are by Charles M. Russell (1864–1926), born in St. Louis. There are twenty-four paintings, studies, and sketches of George Catlin's observations on his journey from St. Louis to Fort Union, New Mexico. The narrative accompanying the collection closely relates the art to the life and history of the frontier.

234. Rounds, Glen. *Mr. Yowder and the Lion Roar Capsules.* Illustrated by the author. New York: Holiday House, 1976. Unpaged. (Ages 8–12) *Fiction*

Xenon Zebulon Yowder was a sign painter who lived near Lee's Summit, Missouri, during the time of the Great Depression. People had very little money to spend, but Mr.

From *Mr. Yowder and the Lion Roar Capsules* (Rounds)

Yowder was a clever man, and when his customers didn't have money to pay him, he would accept things that he could use, sell, or trade. One day he did some work for a circus and ended up with an old lion. Even though he found himself with a problem that almost stumped him, he was determined to prove that he had made a good bargain. How that lion's roar could be heard as far away as Lone Jack and Knob Noster makes a real tall tale indeed.

235. Rounds, Glen. *Sweet Betsy from Pike*. Verses selected and illustrated by Glen Rounds. Chicago: Childrens Press (A Golden Gate Junior Book), 1973. Unpaged. (All Ages) *Fiction*

Rounds presents a picture-book version of the popular American folk song about Sweet Betsy from Pike County, Missouri, and her faithful lover Ike. The artist's black-and-white line drawings are boisterous and imaginative. Betsy is pictured as a rough, tough pioneer woman

From *Sweet Betsy from Pike* (Rounds)

who could fight Indians or dance the light fantastic. Big, awkward, lovable Ike is devoted to Besty throughout their hardships to California and back home again.

A simple piano arrangement is included along with seventeen verses and two refrains. While Rounds's version is laughter-provoking, it is best suited to older children. The Abisch and Kaplan adaptation, *Sweet Betsy from Pike*, is a much more colorful and appropriate version for young children and would also be appealing to all ages.

236. Rounds, Glen. *The Prairie Schooners*. Illustrated by the author. New York: Holiday House, 1968. 95 pages. (Ages 8–12) *Nonfiction*

In entertaining text, Rounds has presented an authentic account of the prairie schooners and has brought dramatically to life the people who made the trip westward during the years of the great Oregon migration. This author-illustrator has provided a well-marked, two-page map showing the route of the prairie schooners on the Oregon Trail during the years 1843–1868. Then, following a concise but clear introduction describing the prairie schooners and their place in American history, he has re-created an excellent picture of Independence, Missouri, "the Prairie Port" of the frontier days. The reader has been given not only a fascinating account of a journey across the country on a wagon train but also an extra bonus of colorful details. For example, an amazing amount of consideration went into choosing equipment and supplies. Unscrupulous and conniving traders often took advantage of ignorant and inexperienced travelers. A little ginger, lampblack, or paint might conceal many a weakness until the unsuspecting emigrant was delayed or turned back on the trail. Getting a wagon train underway demanded a great deal of effort and skill in organization and preparation. Discarding household possessions was often complicated as was finding space for absolutely essential items. There were endless discussions among the travelers about the best types of wagons, the safest trails to follow, the advantage of oxen as compared to horses or mules, and dozens of other problems. Each page of text is illuminated with detailed and realistic drawings.

237. Rubin, Robert. *Satchel Paige: All-Time Baseball Great* (Sports Shelf Books). Jacket illustration by George Loh. New York: Putnam's, 1974. 157 pages. (Ages 10 and up) *Biography*

Whether or not they are sports fans, readers will find the Satchel Paige story exceptionally interesting as the author tells how a penniless black boy won a place in baseball's Hall of Fame. Rubin makes use of his special ability to combine baseball facts and personal details to portray a durable athlete and a personable human being. With the use of a great deal of dialogue and the subject's own quotations, Rubin discusses Paige's long career in baseball and his phenomenal success as a pitcher. Born in Mobile, Alabama, in 1906, Leroy "Satchel" Paige struggled against poverty and racial discrimination. But, fortunately, early in life he realized that his skill in throwing, his speed and control, were natural gifts; once he picked up a baseball, neither Satch nor the game were ever the same. After years of independent professional baseball played with various teams throughout the world, he settled permanently in Kansas City where he pitched for the Kansas City Monarchs of the Negro League for the next ten years. He was forty-two years old before his great desire to pitch in the major leagues was realized. By 1948 blacks had been admitted to the major leagues, and Paige made his debut with the Cleveland Indians; he joined the St. Louis Browns in 1951. Ten years later, at the age of fifty-five, he had his final fling at pitching for organized baseball, although he pitched three innings for the Kansas City Athletics in 1965. At last, in 1971, Paige finally took his rightful place in baseball's Hall of Fame in Cooperstown, New York.

238. Russ, Lavinia. *Over the Hills and Far Away*. Jacket design by Eveline Ness. New York: Harcourt, 1968. 160 pages. (Ages 10–14) *Fiction*

Growing up at Marlborough near Kansas City, Missouri, in 1917 was somewhat different for Peakie Maston than it was for most children. The reason perhaps was that Peakie's family, especially her mother, was somewhat different from the families that Peakie knew. If mother wasn't quoting something, she was laughing at something or doing something to make other people laugh. When Peakie said that she didn't think mothers should laugh at their children, her mother gave her a notebook and said, "don't tell me about what mothers ought to do. Write it down in a book. . . . Then, when you've grown up and have children of your own, you'll remember" (p. 11). Needless to say, Peakie filled quite a few pages with things that mothers shouldn't do.

The book is written in the first person as Peakie tells her own story about how she feels growing up in her world. She reveals a parade of characters as she recounts episodes reflecting the activities and behavior of the various members of her family including Father, sister Beatrice, Aunt Hattie, Aunt Cornelia, and Uncle Ned. But it was Mother Jane at the French Convent School who encouraged her spirit of adventure to go "over the hills and far away." Young readers will quickly identify with Peakie as they surely have experienced similar feelings and reactions in their own lives. The story is told with humor, understanding, and affection. The author has also captured the flavor of the period, giving the reader a glimpse into the way of life in 1917.

239. Ryle, Walter H., and Charles Garner. *The Story of Missouri.* Illustrated with photographs and maps. New York: American Book, 1938. 326 pages. (Ages 10–14 and up) OP. *Nonfiction*

Using a textbook format, Ryle and Garner have presented a composite picture of Missouri life up to the copyright date. Chapter and topic headings aid the reader as do the previews, review questions, and references for each chapter. An index and a table of contents are also provided. The first nine chapters and chapter 15 remain appropriate reference material since they deal with Missouri's early history and with Missouri folklore. Several legends and historical tales include "How Arrow Rock Got Its Name," "Legend of Mina-Sauk," "Origin of the Osage Indians," "An Old Lead Mine," "The Lost Copper Mine," "Price's Kavalry," and "Ghost Towns." Further reference to Missouri's colorful folklore cites Vance Randolph's *The Ozarks and American Survival of Primitive Society* (Vanguard, 1931) and *Ozark Mountain Folks* (Vanguard, 1932).

240. Sanderlin, George. *Mark Twain: As Others Saw Him.* Illustrated with photographs. New York: Coward-McCann, 1978. 173 pages. (Ages 12 and up) *Nonfiction*

Scholarly works of literary criticism usually belong to the mature reader, but Sanderlin has compiled a volume of material that should challenge the young critic who is familiar with Mark Twain and with the immortal characters that he created. The book is divided into three major sections. In the first section, the author reviews the life of

Samuel L. Clemens, using many quotations from Twain's own material. In the second section, Sanderlin presents Twain's opinions on a wide variety of topics such as war, religion, politics, and sex. The third section is a compilation of comments about Twain by famous people as well as by ordinary folks from Twain's own period of time to the present. Readers are given a revealing and interesting portrait of a highly complex literary figure and will certainly agree with the critic who pointed out that the better one knew Mark Twain, the better one liked him. The volume contains a list of Twain's books, a selected bibliography, and an index.

241. Schmidt, Thusnelda, and Laura E. Cathon, compilers. *For Patriot Dream*. Illustrated by Sarah Kurek. New York: Abingdon, 1970. 206 pages. (Ages 8–12) *Anthology*

For Patriot Dream is an anthology of fact and fiction in story and verse about people who have helped to make America a great nation. The theme of these selections bears out the idea that a nation is more than land, rivers, and trees; it is the thoughts and dreams, the courage and fervent support of its people. The selections are organized into six groups under themes taken from the lines of Katherine Lee Bates's "America the Beautiful." The compilers have included four selections by Missouri authors Dorothy Heiderstadt and Laura Ingalls Wilder. Two selections are about two famed Missourians—Langston Hughes and George Washington Carver.

242. Schwartz, Charles W., and Elizabeth R. Schwartz. *The Wild Mammals of Missouri*. Illustrated by Charles W. Schwartz. Columbia: University of Missouri Press, 1959, 1980. 341 pages. (All Ages) *Nonfiction*

This large volume is an excellent guide to the identification of the wild mammals of Missouri as well as a comprehensive reference to information about their lives. More than sixty species of wild mammals are identified.

The clearly written text, which is complemented by over four hundred distinguished illustrations, presents important facts about each mammal including its description, habitat, home, food, reproduction, management, and control. An introductory chapter acquaints the reader with the characteristics and life-styles of mammals in general and has a list of the wild mammals of Missouri and an explanation of how to identify the mammals and their tracks. The final chapter covers material about wild mammals that have lived in Missouri within historic times as well as about several mammals that may possibly be found in Missouri today. All other chapters present detailed information about the wild mammals of Missouri grouped into seven orders: Pouched Mammals, Insect-eating Mammals, Flying Mammals, Hare-shaped Mammals, Gnawing Mammals, Flesh-eating Mammals, and Even-toed Hoofed Mammals. Selected references following the discussion of each mammal and an index add to the usefulness of this valuable book. While the text is designed for both the layman and the professional biologist, teachers and pupils will find that the book holds essential information for an increased understanding and appreciation of wild animals and their environment.

243. Seifert, Shirley. *The Key to St. Louis* (Keys to the City Series). Illustrated with photographs. New York: Lippincott, 1963. 128 pages. (Ages 9–14) OP. *Nonfiction*

While the content is only as up-to-date as the copyright date (1963), the book does contain interesting, easy-to-read material on the history of St. Louis.

Beginning in 1763 when Pierre Laclede selected the site for a fur-trading post, the author traces the city's progress through two centuries. Laclede had prophesied that St. Louis would become one of the finest cities in America. Only the Old St. Louis Cathedral, built in 1830, remains as a symbol of the original townsite, but in a prophesy of her own, Seifert foretold the completion of another symbol that honors a later name for St. Louis—the Gateway City. The final page of the book provides a photograph of the

Saarinen model of the Jefferson National Expansion Memorial with the Gateway Arch. Looking westward through the arch, a person could view the "mass of the modern city." But "a few steps beyond Fourth Street would take him into what was once the common fields outside the Spanish wall. A little further along he would come to what was the Grand Prairie, where the townspeople used to gather wild strawberries in May, or to the forest where in Autumn they gathered nuts and persimmons and wild grapes and firewood" (p. 19).

St. Louis prospered as a French, a Spanish, and finally an American town, enriched by the fur trade, by river traffic, by the railroad boom, by flourishing industries, and by its position as the gateway to the West. Parks, museums, schools, music, and baseball are some of the contributions making St. Louis the fine city it is today. In addition to photographic reproductions, the book is fully indexed and contains a map of metropolitan St. Louis.

244. Serl, Emma. *The Story of Kansas City*. Illustrated with photographs. Kansas City: Board of Education, 1924. 150 pages. (Ages 8–12) OP. *Nonfiction*

This three-book publication, bound together in one volume for reference purposes, provides information in simplified text for children in the public schools of Kansas City. The book is worthwhile for its historical value and for its collection of old photographs. Book 1 deals with the early history of Kansas City, and book 2 continues with an account of its industries and how the city provided for its citizens. Book 3 tells about the services of private utility companies and how citizens have contributed to the maintenance and growth of the city. Discussion suggestions follow each short chapter. Other similar volumes published at later dates are reviewed within this bibliography.

245. Seymour, Flora Warren. *Sacagawea: Bird Girl* (Childhood of Famous Americans). Illustrated by Robert

Doremus. Indianapolis: Bobbs-Merrill, 1959. 200 pages.
(Ages 8–12) *Biography*

While three other books reviewed within this bibliography have stressed Sacagawea's role as a guide and interpreter for the Lewis and Clark expedition, this book deals for the most part with her childhood. The fictionalized story begins in 1794 at the valley homeland of the Shoshone, high in the Rocky Mountains in what is now the state of Wyoming. The account of her childhood, which takes up three-fourths of the book, provides interesting details based on known Indian customs and traditions of the time. Seymour notes that, although the name "Sacagawea" has been pronounced a number of different ways, she prefers Sah-kah´-gah-way´-a as being nearest to the way the Indians say it. She was called "Bird Girl" because her mother had seen a great, beautiful bird fly to the sky, singing, when Sacagawea was a baby. Every incident in the young girl's life seemed to bear out that prophetic name; this thoughtful and courageous girl was to go far beyond the high hills of her homeland. Her name became a symbol for bravery, endurance, and wholehearted loyalty. The last two chapters of the book briefly summarize the seventeen-year-old Sacagawea's reunion with the Shoshone tribe and her journey with Lewis and Clark. The story closes in 1806, leaving Sacagawea at the Mandan Indian village with the promise of sending her son to St. Louis to be educated. Facts about landmarks and statues honoring Sacagawea are accompanied by a map of the United States that outlines the Louisiana Purchase and marks the route of the Lewis and Clark expedition from St. Louis to the Pacific Ocean.

246. Shapiro, Edna. *Windwagon Smith* (A Reading Shelf Book). Illustrated by Frank Aloise. Champaign, Ill.: Garrard, 1969. 35 pages. (Ages 7–12) *Fiction*

A red-haired sailor drove into Westport, Missouri, in a windwagon to show people a way to travel west faster

From *Windwagon Smith* (Shapiro)

than going by covered wagon. The hilarious adventure took passengers right over an Indian camp, straight through a stampeding buffalo herd, and into a rain storm. Blown by roaring winds, the wagon rolled across the prairie so fast that no one could see where they were going until the windwagon fell apart. Although the text is easy to read, this tall tale is interesting enough for all ages. Delightful illustrations including endpapers enhance the story. Other versions include Mary Calhoun's *High Wind for Kansas*, Ennis Rees's *Windwagon Smith*, and Ramona Maher's *When Windwagon Smith Came to Westport*.

247. Sheaff, Virginia, Alice Lanterman Hammond, Emma Serl, and Louise Gex. *The Story of Kansas City*, 4 vols. Illustrated by students of Kansas City high schools. Kansas City: Board of Education, 1958, 1967. (Ages 8–14) *Nonfiction*

The Story of Kansas City has undergone several revisions as well as expansion into four volumes since the publication of the original volume in 1924. Four volumes written by Hammond and Sheaff were published from 1944 to 1947. The first two volumes were revised by Sheaff in 1954 and 1957. Then in 1958 Sheaff and Gex revised the third volume. The 1967 editions were revised by Sheaff under the direction of the Elementary Curriculum Department. An unusual feature of these books is the original artwork done by students of the Kansas City high schools. Both the illustrations and the text convey the importance of this story, which is also a significant part of the story of our nation. The four-volume series of *The Story of Kansas City* includes *Early Kansas City* (grade three), *The City Beautiful* (grade four), *The City at Work* (grade five), and *Your City and You* (grade nine). The 1967 edition of *The Story of Kansas City: Early Kansas City* comprises stories of long-ago life in the area including the Indians, the trail to Santa Fe, early settlers, and the early towns of Independence, Westport, and Kansas (Kansas City, Missouri). Each section is followed with study questions and with directions for activities to reinforce the reader's understanding and appreciation of the subject. While the 1958 and 1967 editions of *The Story of Kansas City: The City at Work* cover similar content, both volumes are useful in meeting individual differences among readers. The 1967 edition is written at a more complex level of difficulty than the earlier edition and includes more extensive subject matter. The material is divided into four sections entitled "Crossroads of the Nation," "Spreading the News," "The World at Work," and "The City and You." At the end of each section is a list of more things to know about Kansas City including a list of firsts in Kansas City. A recent paperback publication, *My Kansas City*, compiled and written by The Learning Exchange of Kansas City is described in the selected bibliography at the back of this book. Both *The Story of Kansas* and *My Kansas City* are excellent examples of school and community projects that promote interest in local history.

248. Shoemaker, Floyd Calvin. *Missouri's Hall of Fame: Lives of Eminent Missourians.* Illustrated with photo-

graphs. Columbia: Missouri Book Company, 1921. 269 pages. (Ages 12 and up) OP. *Biography*

This 1921 edition presents profiles of thirty-one Missourians who, at that time, had won fame not only in the state but as a part of the history of the nation. These profiles include renowned authors, artists, explorers, inventors, scientists, journalists, reformers, soldiers, and statesmen. While many familiar names appear, a number of these famous Missourians may be unknown to today's schoolchildren. The book has use today not only as a reference to the lives of highly regarded Missourians and to their contributions but also as a reference to the points of view of the period. Photographs accompany most of the profiles. Shoemaker, longtime secretary to the State Historical Society of Missouri, himself became an eminent Missourian.

249. Shura, Mary Francis. *The Gray Ghosts of Taylor Ridge*. Illustrated by Michael Hampshire. New York: Dodd, Mead, 1978. 128 pages. (Ages 10–14) *Fiction*

Taylor Ridge, located somewhere near Lexington, Missouri, was thought about only as a good site for the local fourth grade's annual field trip until one cold January day. Nan Miller had lost her father's prized compass while on her class outing and in desperation had persuaded her reluctant thirteen-year-old brother Nat to help her find it. Nat hated winter, and he wasn't too crazy about his ten-year-old sister. But the course of events on Taylor Ridge during the next few days gave Nat a new perspective on himself as well as on Nan. During their search of the old Civil War homestead, they met an old blind man who warned them about gray ghosts that came "chinking" around there after dark. Old Boomer, who lived with his dog Bubba in a cabin at the foot of the ridge, believed that there were century-old treasures hidden on the windswept ridge and that the ghosts of the family that hid them haunted the area. The strange happenings on the hill turned out to be more than just an old man's imaginations. As Nat and Nan encountered mystery and danger in their final search for Bubba and the compass, they rescued a young man from an old abandoned well and located the long-lost Civil War treasure. Told in the first person by Nat, the story is fast-paced and entertaining.

250. Silverberg, Robert. *Bridges.* Illustrated with photographs. Philadelphia: Macrae Smith, 1966. 189 pages. (Ages 12 and up) *Nonfiction*

The development of the world's great bridges is traced from the dawn of humanity to the present time and concludes with tomorrow's proposed bridges. When man first placed a log across a stream, a chain of progress began that led to the stone and creeping-vine structures that were transformed into the majestic beam, arch, and suspension bridges of today. The first four chapters deal with a general discussion of the early history of bridges covering primitive times, the Middle Ages, and the iron age; the remaining content identifies spectacular bridges of the world and provides excellent information about their construction including the engineers and builders whose imagination and courage have marked these amazing achievements. One of these magnificent structures is the Eads Bridge, completed in 1874. An essay on bridging the Mississippi in St. Louis is contained in chapter 5, "Captain Eads Builds a Bridge." In addition to the twelve consecutive pages covering this subject, numerous other references are made throughout the text to James Buchanan Eads and to the dramatic influence of this bridge on the building of other bridges; contrasts and comparisons are made in connection with the John Roebling theory of the suspension bridge, the Brooklyn Bridge, bridges for a new century, the Forth Bridge, the Quebec Bridge, steel-arch bridges, and the George Washington Bridge. Many attractive photographs, a bibliography, and an index add to the value of the book's very readable text.

251. Stanley, Caroline Abbot. *Order No. 11, a Tale of the Border*. Illustrated by Harry C. Edwards. New York: Century, 1904, reprinted by Democrat Publishing Company, Clinton, Missouri, 1969. 420 pages. (YA) OP. *Fiction*

Stanley lends credence to her story with the following dedication: "To Mrs. Jessamine Wallace, of Jackson County, Missouri, a participant in these scenes, and the faithful friend of three generations, this book is inscribed."

Set against the background of the border conflict between Missouri and Kansas before and during the Civil War (1859–1865), this melodramatic novel gives a detailed account of the involvement of two families who lived in Jackson County. While the story is fiction, the devastation resulting from General Order No. 11 is historically documented as are the characterizations of a number of historical figures. The underlying theme depicting the romance of Virginia Trevilian and Gordon Lay captures the reader's attention throughout the story even though the author uses a great deal of detailed description and lengthy narration. The accounts of the personal behavior of the people involved are reflections of the pleasures as well as the struggles of the times.

Although not a *Gone with the Wind*, this book could have appeal to the adolescent who is reaching for more mature reading and for more lengthy novels. Loula Grace Erdman in *Life Was Simpler Then*, her reminiscences of her own childhood, remarked that of course every child growing up in western Missouri read *Order No. 11*.

252. Steinberg, Alfred. *Harry S. Truman* (Lives to Remember). Jacket by Frank Aloise. New York: Putnam's, 1963. 223 pages. (Ages 12 and up) *Biography*

Steinberg's adult biography, *The Man from Missouri: The Life and Times of Harry S. Truman* (Putnam's, 1962), was followed by this version for teenaged readers. In highly readable text, he surveys Truman's boyhood and youth, his army service in World War I, his early political experiences, and his years in Washington, D.C., as senator from Missouri and as president of the United States. Steinberg deals objectively with the account of Truman's rise from obscurity to the presidency, skillfully showing how the man was modeled by his times. His presidency was one of the great personal triumphs of modern times. He held the office during a period in which there was great international tension due to the conflict between communism and democracy, and the Western world looked to his leadership with hope and respect. He took vigorous part in the political strife that marked his administration. His efforts to meet the demanding problems that faced the nation and the world shaped policies that still affect the lives of people today—the formation of the United Nations, the decision to use the atomic bomb against Japan, the cold war against Communist aggression, the Marshall Plan, and the Korean War. Steinberg's portrait of Truman expresses the depth of the man's character through his earthy humor, his interest in people, his spirit of determination, his honesty, and his dedication to duty. The book contains a bibliography and an index.

253. Stevens, Eden Vale. *Buffalo Bill* (A See and Read Biography). Drawings by Joseph Ciardiello. New York: Putnam's, 1976. 63 pages. (Ages 6–9) *Biography*

This simplified story for beginning readers traces the life of William Frederick Cody, known as Buffalo Bill, from his childhood in Iowa, through his great adventures in the West, to his worldwide success with his Wild West Show. When he was eight years old, his family moved to Weston, Missouri, on the Kansas border. At Fort Leavenworth, the young lad saw much that interested him, especially the soldiers on horses; he was fascinated by the men in buckskin shirts and wide-brimmed hats who were scouts for the cavalry. He watched as his father traded beads and blankets to the Indians for horses and he made friends with a boy of the Kickapoo tribe. After his father died, he went to work for Alexander Majors whose wagon trains carried supplies to Salt Lake City. At the age of fourteen, he became a rider for the Pony Express in Missouri and gained a reputation for his courage and endurance. He became lifelong friends with Kit Carson, Jim Bridger, and Wild Bill Hickok, all famous scouts of the American frontier. He served as a scout and sometimes as a spy for the Union army during the Civil War; while he was stationed in St. Louis, he met and married Louisa Frederici. He earned the nickname "Buffalo Bill" while working for the Kansas Pacific Railroad; he risked his life hunting thousands of wild buffalo to supply food for the workmen who were laying the railroad tracks across the prairie. By the age of twenty-five, he was a legend of his own time. Even though the Wild West was gone, he made it live again through his Wild West Show, which brought him fame and fortune throughout the world.

254. Stevenson, Augusta. *Buffalo Bill: Boy of the Plains* (Childhood of Famous Americans). Illustrated by E. Joseph Dreany. Indianapolis: Bobbs-Merrill, 1959. 189 pages. (Ages 8–12) *Biography*

Stevenson's biography is a step beyond the beginning-to-read level and provides middle-grade readers with substantial information about the life of William Frederick Cody with an emphasis on his childhood. The book is especially worthwhile for its description of Weston, Missouri, and the surrounding frontier life, including St. Joseph, Missouri, and the Pony Express. Bill Cody, like many other frontier youths, grew up rapidly, and, at an early age, took his place beside the men in hunting, scouting, and fighting Indians. At the age of fourteen, he watched with fascination as the first Pony Express rider set out from St. Joseph on 3 April 1860 to carry the mail across the western part of the continent. He was so impressed with the work of the pony riders that he persuaded Mr. Russell of the Pony Express Company to hire him. While riding on his 116-mile stretch of the route, he had many thrilling and narrow escapes from Indians, robbers, buffalo, and other dangers. On one of his rides, he arrived at his destination to find that the relief rider had been killed by Indians, so he continued riding for a record-making 322 miles. The book contains a chronology, study questions, suggested activities, a bibliography, and a glossary.

Buffalo Bill, a picture-story biography suitable for ages seven to ten, by Ingri and Edgar d'Aulaire (Doubleday, 1952) is more outstanding than either this book or Eden Vale Stevens's version, although only brief mention is made of Missouri and of Cody's riding for the Pony Express.

255. Stevenson, Augusta. *George Washington Carver: Boy Scientist* (Childhood of Famous Americans). Illustrated by Wallace Wood. Indianapolis: Bobbs-Merrill, 1959. 200 pages. (Ages 8–12) *Biography*

Several other biographies of George Washington Carver, which have already been reviewed in this bibliography, cover much of the same content included in Stevenson's book. However, Stevenson introduced the Childhood of Famous Americans series, and her books have been popular with children of a wide age-range and at varying levels of reading achievement. Her formula, which has been followed by other authors of the series, provides an easy-to-read vocabulary with much dialogue and a fast-moving plot. In Stevenson's story, Carver becomes a very real person to the reader as he reveals the thoughts, feelings, and concerns about plants and growing things that led to his remarkable achievements in life. The story is told with skill and understanding; some humorous incidents are included such as the time that the ripe milkweed pods opened in Mrs. Carver's kitchen. These and other events in Carver's life are portrayed with interest that enables the reader to share his adventures, to appreciate his struggles, and to admire the famous scientist.

256. Stevenson, Augusta. *Kit Carson: Boy Trapper* (Childhood of Famous Americans). Illustrated by Robert Doremus. Indianapolis: Bobbs-Merrill, 1962. 200 pages. (Ages 8–12) *Biography*

Kit Carson becomes very real to children as they read

the story of his growing up on the Missouri frontier. While he had no formal education, the disciplined lessons that he learned in that rugged wilderness prepared him for his dangerous and adventurous life as a western trapper, scout, and guide. The book provides a vivid picture of life in a settler's home near Franklin, Missouri, as well as of life at Fort Hempstead; this was a neighborhood fort in the Boone's Lick region of central Missouri where the settlers fled when Indians attacked. The story portrays events in young Carson's life that reflected his increasing skills, his daring and honest nature, and his determination to become a western scout. The reader is given a brief glimpse of Franklin, Missouri, the last town on the western frontier during the early 1820s. It was also one of the busiest towns in the country as colorful travelers and their equally fascinating caravans gathered there in preparation for their long trips southwest to the old Spanish settlement of Santa Fe. Into the saddlemaker's shop where the fifteen-year-old Kit was apprenticed came demanding customers who opened the way for him to begin his western adventures. The last chapter of the story presents a brief account of Carson's life as an invaluable scout and guide for the expeditions of John Charles Frémont during the years 1842–1848. Appendix material contains supplementary facts about Carson's life and times.

257. Stocking, Hobart E. *The Road to Santa Fe*. Illustrations and maps by the author. New York: Hastings House, 1971. 372 pages. (Ages 14 and up) *Nonfiction*

"Across western Missouri, southwest across Kansas, the Oklahoma Panhandle and eastern New Mexico, is a line engraved in sod. . . . The engraving, less distinct each year, begins at Franklin, Missouri. Incised by toil beset with trouble the shallow trough, an antiphonary of history, is the mark of tens of thousands of rolling wheels. It is the Road to Santa Fe" (p. 1). It began in 1821 as a route of commerce through Indian country, across arid land and the Cimarron Desert, and was, until rails were laid west from Kansas City, the only link between the Mississippi and the Southwest. In 1846 it was the route of an army of invasion and the wagons that supplied it, and by 1848 many travelers were following the road to Santa Fe to the California gold fields. Stocking researched journals, histories, and official records and made personal inquiries along the road to Santa Fe in order to present this detailed epic of southwestern history. To trace the road to Santa Fe, he compiled precisely detailed hand-drawn maps, which have now been placed in the National Archives. The book, organized around sixteen chapter headings, contains a chronology, a bibliography of sources, an index, and a table of contents in addition to the maps and illustrations. The mature reader will find a wealth of information in this fascinating account.

258. Stover, Marjorie Filley. *Trail Boss in Pigtails*. Illustrated by Lydia Dabcovich. New York: Atheneum, 1972. 220 pages. (Ages 10–14) *Fiction*

In the epilogue, Stover states that Emma Jane Burke really lived back in the 1800s and that this story is based on an actual incident when the thirteen-year-old girl as trail boss drove eighty-one longhorn cattle from Waco, Texas, to Chicago in 1859. The Burke family had lived in Texas only three years but, because of Pa's illness, decided to return to Illinois where they had relatives. With the money from the sale of their home, they bought eighty-two longhorn steers that they planned to drive to Chicago. The price that the cattle would bring there would pay for a farm on which the family could live comfortably. The long journey took them "over the plains of Texas. Through the territory of the civilized Indian tribes; swerving up through the state of Missouri; crossing the great Mississippi into Illinois; and finally getting back to the little village of Avoca almost across the state" (p. 7). Pa and the whole family counted on Emma Jane to take them through. Even Pa, who didn't live through the journey, hadn't counted on all the problems that they would encounter, but Emma Jane's resourcefulness enabled the family to handle many difficulties and dangers such as storms and floods, unfriendly Indians, and protesting Missourians. In order to protect their herds from diseased Texas cattle, Missouri farmers had set up roadblocks along the border and refused to let Texas cattle through. (This incident, told on page 101, was based on authentic procedures of that time.) How Emma Jane outwitted the guards at the Grand River Bridge near Clinton, Missouri, makes fascinating reading as does the legend of the Piasa bird told in the account of the family's crossing of the Piasa country as they neared the Mississippi. (Another book reviewed in this bibliography, *Indian Legends of the Piasa Country* by George McAdams Clifford, contains an elaboration of this same legend.)

259. Sullivan, Peggy. *The O'Donnells.* Illustrated by Mary Stevens. Chicago: Follett, 1956. 160 pages. (Ages 10–14) *Fiction*

Set in Kansas City, Missouri, during the early 1900s, the story of the O'Donnells provides the reader with exciting adventures that reflect their warm family life. Papa was a great one for doing things that kept Mama and their five lively daughters (Grace, Ella, Margaret, Rose, and Cecilia) involved in many appealing experiences. The girls especially enjoyed their parents' stories about life in the old country, the Emerald Isle. Mama once said, "If we're not looking to the past, then we're off dreaming of the future" (p. 45). But Papa was confident that if their girls were dreamers, he would not worry as long as they had the stuff to work for their dreams. They proved their ability by helping him to lay the bricks for the sidewalk, by driving the "summer" horse Papa bought each year, and by their many other activities. Visits from Aunt Ella, graduations, parties, and holidays were glad times for the O'Donnells. There were also sad times such as when Papa's friend and partner McLaughlin was killed in the line of duty. An exciting time occurred when Papa bought a house and had it moved across town. The entire O'Donnell family got up at midnight to watch when the power lines were taken down so that the house could be moved across the trolley tracks.

260. Teasdale, Sara. *Stars To-Night.* Illustrated by Dorothy P. Lathrop. New York: Macmillan, 1958. 49 pages. (Ages 6–12) *Poetry*

Among the twenty-five poems contained in *Stars To-Night* are several commonly found in anthologies. These favorites include "Night," "Stars," "The Falling Star," "The Coin," and "April." Teasdale, winner of a Pulitzer Prize for poetry, was one of America's greatest lyric poets. While many of her lyrics are descriptive and complex in form, the poems selected for this volume show a simplicity of phrase and a musical rhythm that appeal to children. The themes reflecting her characteristic observations of the beauty of nature are expressed imaginatively. Once children grasp the mood of her verse, their appreciation is bound to grow. Lathrop's pen-and-ink drawings add immeasurably to the quality of the book as well as to a child's understanding of these sensitive poems. *Stars To-Night* is a book of rare beauty that every child should have the opportunity to know.

261. Terzian, James P. *Defender of Human Rights: Carl Schurz.* Jacket design by Dave Dippel. New York: Messner, 1965. 192 pages. (Ages 12 and up) *Biography*

On the campus of Columbia University in New York City is an impressive memorial of a man's courage and devotion to principle. The inscription on the base of this nine-foot-high bronze statue reads: "Carl Schurz, Defender of Liberty and a Friend of *Human Right*." German-born Carl Schurz, who came to the United States in 1852, became a distinguished citizen who had far-reaching influence on many aspects of American life. He was a leading figure in the founding of the Republican party. He served briefly as U.S. ambassador to Spain and resigned to join the Union forces as a brigadier general under Maj. Gen. John Charles Frémont. After the war, Schurz became the editor and part-owner of the *Westliche Post* in St. Louis. From 1869 to 1875, he served as an esteemed U.S. senator from Missouri and was an able secretary of the interior from 1877 to 1881. He became an editor for the *New York Evening Post* and later was associated with *Harper's Weekly*. His achievements in the areas of civil service and Indian affairs marked his great leadership as a defender of human rights. Schurz's life as a Missourian was particularly interesting since, as a crusading editor and a determined state politician, he forcefully expressed his ideas for reform during an era of graft and corruption. Terzian points out how President Johnson's impeachment trial had an important bearing on Schurz's career. He also includes interesting discussions of Missouri's method of electing U.S. senators in those days, the controversies and struggles over Schurz's candidacy, and Schurz's strong denunciation of the corruption of the Grant administration. The book contains a bibliography and an index.

262. Thomas, Henry. *Ulysses S. Grant* (Lives to Remember). Jacket portrait and design by Joseph Cellini. New York: Putnam's, 1961. 192 pages. (Ages 11 and up) *Biography*

Thomas has provided young people with an interesting and easy-to-read biography of Ulysses S. Grant. While this story of Grant's life emphasizes his involvement in the Civil War and his presidency of the United States, other aspects of his life are brought into appropriate focus. On his graduation from West Point, he was stationed at Jefferson Barracks near St. Louis where he met Julia Dent, a prominent socialite; they were married four years later. Discouraged with army life, he resigned and spent several bleak years with his family in the St. Louis area where he engaged in unsuccessful business ventures. With the outbreak of the war, Grant considered it his duty to join the Union forces; his first assignment as colonel of the Twenty-first Illinois Volunteers was in Missouri. He soon became known for his capacity for discipline, organization, and decisionmaking. In August 1861 he was promoted to brigadier general and was assigned to a command in Jefferson City. His military potential continued to be recognized when he overcame southern resistance and, as major general, led the Union forces to victory at Appomattox on 9 April 1865. Grant served two successive presidential terms despite fraud and corruption within his administration. Thomas deals fully and objectively with these infamous scandals in which Grant's personal integrity emerged intact. An appreciation of his postwar accomplishments as well as of his military genius overshadowed his weaknesses and mistakes. Grant was known for his quiet and kind manner and was characterized as honorable, courageous, and loyal. He received many honors in America as well as in Europe and Asia. A bibliography and an index are included.

263. Thum, Marcella. *Exploring Black America: A History and Guide*. Illustrated with photographs. New York: Atheneum, 1975. 402 pages. (Ages 11 and up) *Nonfiction*

Exploring Black America is a guidebook to museums, monuments, and historic sites commemorating the achievements of black Americans. The first part of each chapter discusses a specific aspect of black history and culture, and the second part lists appropriate sites that may be visited. Missouri figures clearly in many aspects of black history. For example, the oldest college in America established specifically to provide higher education for black students is Lincoln University at Jefferson City, Missouri (pp. 328–31); a new era in black music was begun when Scott Joplin's "Maple Leaf Rag" was published in 1899 while he was working in Sedalia, Missouri (pp. 282–95, 305); Missouri-born Langston Hughes constantly experimented with all forms of poetry and also wrote songs, novels, plays, history, and biography (pp. 216, 254–56); and the St. Louis Sports Hall of Fame (pp. 372–73) holds many pictures of famous black Cardinal baseball players. The table of contents and the index furnish help in browsing for other subjects covered in this comprehensive volume.

264. Thum, Marcella. *Exploring Literary America*. Illustrated with photographs. New York: Atheneum, 1979. 236 pages. (Ages 12 and up) *Nonfiction*

While only a few of Missouri's literary landmarks, sites, and settings are included in this American travel and reference guide, the material given provides worthwhile background information on selected authors and on the location of places of interest. The section on Missouri cites Becky Thatcher's Home, Hannibal; Eugene Field Home, St. Louis; Laura Ingalls Wilder Home and Museum, Mansfield; Mark Twain Boyhood Home, Hannibal; Mark Twain State Park and Museum, Florida; Shepherd of the Hills Farm, Branson; and Tom Sawyer Dioramas, Hannibal. The book contains geographical, author, title, and subject indexes, as well as a table of contents and an introduction. *Show Me the Arts: A Guide to Missouri's Cultural Resources* contains a comprehensive coverage of Missouri's literary landmarks (see the selected bibliography at the back of this book).

265. Thum, Marcella. *Mystery at Crane's Landing* (Winner of the Mystery Writers of America Edgar Award). New York: Dodd, Mead, 1964. 141 pages. (Ages 12 and up) *Fiction*

Paula Jordan's spring vacation brought her straight into a baffling web of mysterious events. Soon after she arrived at New Madrid, Missouri, during the town's Civil War centennial, Paula discovered that her roommate, Lucy Crane, was in deep trouble—she was a prisoner in her own home. Paula's bewilderment about her hosts at Crane's Landing changed to fear when Lucy fell from a horse under strange circumstances. Then as Paula tried to grasp the meaning of Lucy's desperate message about a hidden photograph, she realized that her own safety was equally threatened. Finally, her handsome friend Dave Rawlings, who had thought that Paula was imagining things, reluctantly came to her assistance and helped to solve the mystery. A reenactment of a decisive Civil War battle provides

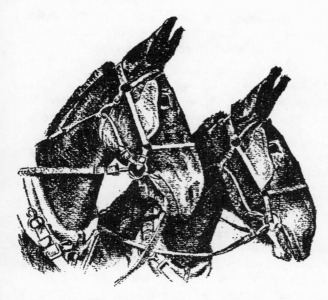

From *Treasure of Crazy Quilt Farm* (Thum)

authentic background history of the area as do the "Open House" at the elaborately furnished antebellum home and the period fashions worn at the centennial festivities.

266. Thum, Marcella. *Treasure of Crazy Quilt Farm.* Illustrated by Elinor Jaeger. New York: Franklin Watts, 1965. 209 pages. (Ages 9–12) *Fiction*

When twelve-year-old Denise Louise Schultz and her family moved from St. Louis to the countryside, she had a difficult time adjusting to her new home. More than anything else, Dee wanted to go back to St. Louis to visit her friend Sue Benson and to attend the 1904 world's fair. Dee's efforts to earn the money for the trip produced some surprising answers to a mystery that surrounded Crazy Quilt Farm. At the same time she learned some important lessons about friendship as her schoolmates helped to make her dream come true. Details involving the domestic and social activities of the family and the neighborhood are skillfully interwoven into the story to present a realistic picture of life in Missouri during the early 1900s.

267. Tippett, James S. *Crickety Cricket! The Best-Loved Poems of James S. Tippett*. Pictures by Mary Chalmers. New York: Harper, 1973. 76 pages. (Ages 5–10) *Poetry*

Tippett, a native-born Missourian, has written about important things remembered from his childhood—trains and trucks, animals and birds, summer and autumn, icicles, snow, and Christmastime. These poems represent children's everyday experiences, and Tippett's simple rhymes and clear images appeal to young readers or listeners. Some of the poems such as "Trains" and "Tracks in the Snow" are favorites for choral reading and for creative dramatization. Each page of *Crickety Cricket!* is decorated with expressive pictures, and the book is just the right size for youngsters to handle comfortably. *I Live in the City* (1927), *I Go A-Traveling* (1929), *I Know Some Little Animals* (1941), *A World to Know* (1938), and *Counting the Days* (1940) are other Tippett collections published by Harper. Almost all anthologies of literature for children and youth include his poems.

268. Towne, Peter. *George Washington Carver* (Biographies for Young Readers). Illustrations in color by Elzia Moon. New York: Crowell, 1975. 33 pages. (Ages 7–10) *Biography*

This famous scientist was born on the Moses Carver farm outside of Diamond Grove, Missouri, around 1860. He was a quiet, shy, little boy with a special gift for learning things on his own. By the time he was ten years old, he was known in the community as "the Plant Doctor" because of his interest and skill in growing plants. Since George was eager to learn and there were no schools nearby for black children, he left the security and kindness of the Carver home to begin his long struggle for an education. As an orphan in the post–Civil War period, he grew up mostly on his own, living with various people and going to several different schools. He was not only the first black man to graduate from the Iowa State College of Agriculture at Ames but was also the school's first black teacher. He realized a lifetime opportunity when Booker T. Washington invited him to teach at his school in Tuskegee, Alabama. There he was able to help his own people to learn skills to help themselves; he could also continue his own experimentation in his study of plants.

Attractive, colored-picture cover, large print, and effective illustrations along with well-written content give this book special appeal for seven- to ten-year-olds. This age-group will also find this book with its additional information a step beyond Aliki's beautiful picture-story of Carver's life, *A Weed Is a Flower*.

269. Truman, Margaret. *Harry S. Truman*. Illustrated with photographs. New York: Morrow, 1973. 602 pages. (Adult) *Biography*

Because of its unusual portrait of a president by his daughter, this biography is a valuable contribution to a collection of materials dealing with the life and times of the president from Missouri. Fully indexed and clearly written, the volume serves as a practical reference that can be read by a wide age-range. The scope of the biography covers Truman's life from his early days and political career in Missouri through the momentous years in Washington where he served as U.S. senator, vice-president, and president. It concludes with his retirement and his enjoyment of being a grandfather of four boys. The author describes the dramatic events of the 1948 presidential campaign when Truman won the presidency against all odds. She also portrays her father as a family man in the very highest sense of the word. The most important people in his life were his wife, his daughter, his mother, and his sister. Truman's letters to his family, written in his unique style, contain fascinating descriptions of great events and of world leaders as he saw them. The book includes personal recollections from many people who knew the president as well as Margaret Truman's own reminiscences of the man who was both her father and the president.

270. Tunis, Edwin. *Frontier Living*. Illustrated by the author. New York: Crowell, 1961. 161 pages. (Ages 10 and up) *Nonfiction*

Tunis has re-created the American frontier in lively text and in attractive illustrations. More than two hundred intricate drawings faithfully interpret the text and greatly enhance the information. Authentic details of everyday life on the frontier are presented in relation to appropriate historical and geographical perspectives. The story, which covers a period of almost two centuries, moves westward across the continent from the seaboard colonies, through the wilderness, beyond the Mississippi, and over the mountain trails to the Far West. Descriptions of homes, household articles, clothing, food, and transportation reflect the character and the way of life of men, women, and children as do the explanations about farming, hunting, religion, government, education, entertainment, and other significant activities. Inserted historical essays and maps help the reader to link time and place with each account. Particular references to Missouri are included in the sections entitled "The 'Permanent' Indian Frontier," "Beyond the Mississippi," "Caravans to Santa Fe," "The Fur Trade and the Mountain Men," "The Bitter Road to Oregon," "The Overland Mail," "The Pony Express," "The Civil War in the West," and "'Bleeding Kansas.'" Among the prominent Missourians mentioned are William Becknell, Jessie Benton, Jim Bridger, John Butterfield, Kit Carson, William C. Clark, John Charles Frémont, Stephen Watts Kearny, Pierre Laclede, and Meriwether Lewis. The material is indexed. The author's companion volume, *The Young United States, 1793–1830* (World, 1969), also includes information about Missouri. Both of these distinguished books could contribute immeasurably to units in social studies.

From *Frontier Living* (Tunis)

271. Tutt, Clara. *Carl Schurz, Patriot.* Illustrated by Susan
B. Duetsch. Madison: State Historical Society of Wisconsin, 1960. 107 pages. (Ages 10–14) *Biography*

More than half of Tutt's biography is devoted to
Schurz's life in Germany under the Prussian rule of King
Wilhelm. The story covers Schurz's early childhood, his
schooling, his brief role as a patriot and soldier of the revolutionary army in the Rhineland in 1848, and an account
of his escape from the siege of Rastatt and the rescue of
Herr Kinkle, the leader of the revolutionary army. Tutt
touches briefly on Schurz's life as a refugee in England and
on his marriage to Margarethe Meyer of Hamburg, Germany. The last part of the book deals with Carl and Margarethe's arrival in the United States and with their establishment of a home near Watertown, Wisconsin, where he
opened a law office and she opened a kindergarten. As the
story continues, Schurz's dream of becoming a patriot
drew nearer to realization when he helped to organize
the Republican party, campaigned for Abraham Lincoln
throughout the northern states, and served briefly as minister to Spain and later as an officer in the Union army.
One short chapter is devoted to his life in Missouri as the

editor of a newspaper and to his political career in Washington, D.C., as U.S. senator from Missouri. The last few pages summarize his later years including a final visit to Wisconsin in 1905; Shurz died in 1906 at the age of seventy-seven. Although his life of service was given to his adopted country, the German people, as well as others throughout the world, have been inspired by his ideals. Tutt's book makes a good introduction, for all readers, to Terzian's more comprehensive treatment of the subject in *Defender of Human Rights* and provides an easy-to-read version for younger or less able readers.

272. Twain, Mark (Samuel L. Clemens). *Life on the Mississippi*. Illustrated by Walter Stewart and Frank Schoonover. New York: Harper, 1874, 1883. 227 pages. (Ages 13 and up) *Fiction*

Life on the Mississippi is more than an interesting collection of reminiscences about the early steamboat days; it is a romantic history of the river and a storehouse of realistic character sketches of people associated with the river and with the growth of America. Twain's narrative is skillfully interwoven with detailed accounts of vivid events and humorous incidents. The first part of the book is concerned with Twain's experiences as a steamboat pilot; the second part is an account of his travels as a passenger when he returned to the river twenty years later. Twain re-creates the glory and grandeur of the old Mississippi days of steamboating as seen from the pilothouse. He explains in glowing details the hazards of the deceptive but fascinating river and the difficulties experienced by a young apprentice learning how to navigate under the guidance of Horace Bixby, the most famous pilot on the Mississippi. He also conveys the eagerness felt by the cub pilot earning his license as well as the excitement and enjoyment of life on the river. The river seemed very different when Twain returned many years later. This time, he traveled as a passenger and looked on the changes with considerable regret. *Life on the Mississippi*, *The Adventures of Tom Sawyer*, and *The Adventures of Huckleberry Finn* represent the best of

American literature from the viewpoint of a keen observer of the American frontier in the mid-nineteenth century. These original stories have been a source of inspiration to each succeeding generation of authors as well as a source of pleasure for readers.

273. Twain, Mark (Samuel L. Clemens). *The Adventures of Huckleberry Finn*. Illustrated by Baldwin Hawes. New York: World, 1885. 405 pages. (Ages 12 and up) *Fiction*

In a sequel to *The Adventures of Tom Sawyer*, Twain continues the saga of boyhood in the town of Hannibal and on the Mississippi. The theme of friendship and social justice distinguishes the story that highlights the travels of Huck Finn and the slave Jim as they go down the Mississippi on a raft. Tom Sawyer also participated in some of Huck's escapades; in fact, it was Tom's planning that led to the attempt to free Jim from the jail.

A more difficult and mature story, *The Adventures of Huckleberry Finn* was written for an adult audience and is often called one of America's great novels. The book gave rise to controversy when it was first published, and many passages in the book are considered derogatory today, particularly those that portray the black character, Nigger Jim. However, the author's blend of satire and social criticism with humor enabled him to present complex characters that overshadow the elements of black stereotyping. Both black and white characters speak in dialect and both perform warm, humane, and tolerant acts.

274. Twain, Mark (Samuel L. Clemens). *The Adventures of Tom Sawyer*. Illustrated by Louis Slobodkin. New York: World, 1876. 292 pages. (Ages 10 and up) *Fiction*

Any list of classics in literature for children and youth is sure to include *The Adventures of Tom Sawyer*; the book won universal acclaim soon after its appearance in 1876 and has continued to maintain a wide popularity. The background for the adventures of Tom and his friends in

their midwestern town along the Mississippi River provides a true picture of the American scene a hundred years
ago. But their adventures never grow old, and beyond the
excitement and humor emerges the author's unforgettable
portrayal of human nature. Twain, one of the first authors
to bring realism and humor into literature for young
people, based his story on his recollections of his own boyhood in Hannibal, Missouri. Once readers have encountered Twain's characters, they will know what it means to
be forever young in America. Favorite episodes include
"The Glorious Whitewasher," "The Cat and the Painkiller,"
"The Pirate Crew Set Sail," "Pirates at Their Own Funeral," "Tom and Becky in the Cave," and "Found and Lost
Again."

275. Veglahn, Nancy. *Getting to Know the Missouri River*
     (Getting to Know Series). Illustrated by William Plum-
     mer. New York: Coward-McCann, 1972. 71 pages.
     (Ages 9–14) *Nonfiction*

In an interesting and informative account of people
and events that marked the history of "Big Muddy," Veglahn gives the reader a concise and clear picture of the
river's role in the development of the nation as a whole.
Since the state of Missouri is linked closely to the Missouri
River, many familiar personalities and places figure impor-
tantly in this story. While Father Jacques Marquette in
1673 was the first to see the Missouri River, it was Etienne
de Bourgmont who traveled up the lower Missouri in 1714
and identified it with the Missouri Indians living in that
area. By the early 1800s, the little village of St. Louis had
become the base of exploring expeditions, trade, and
travel along the Missouri and its tributaries. Besides Meriwether Lewis, William C. Clark, and Sacagawea, other colorful personages who became part of the Missouri scene
included Manuel Lisa, Pierre Chouteau, Joseph la Barge,
Grant Marsh, and John Neihardt. The first expedition by
steamboat up the Missouri River in 1819 took thirteen
days to get two hundred miles from St. Louis to Franklin,

Missouri, but by 1845 the steamboat was the primary mode of travel. Three events in the 1840s—the annexation of Texas, the gold rush to California, and the Mormon migration—made the lower Missouri River a vital waterway. The Santa Fe Trail began at the steamboat landing at Franklin. St. Louis, Independence, Westport Landing (Kansas City), and St. Joseph were also important jumping-off places along the river during the westward movement. The concluding chapter highlights the projects resulting from the 1944 Flood Control Act. A table of contents with chapter headings, an index, and a list of some important dates in Missouri history add to the usefulness of this well-written book.

276. Walton, Bryce. *Cave of Danger*. New York: Crowell, 1967. 263 pages. (Ages 12 and up) *Fiction*

Suspense and adventure abound as teenager Matt Wilde becomes so intent on discovering a cave that he disregards the spelunker's rules of safety. For months he had been exploring the rugged Ozark hills near his home in south Missouri. He was confident that there was an unexplored cave somewhere in the rocky wilderness known as the Karst. More than anything, Matt wanted to find a cave that no human being had ever seen before, and he spent all his spare time looking for it. When he wasn't in the hills, he and his best friend Spotty (Merton) Jessup were either planning their search or attending the Cave Club Grotto under the leadership of their science teacher, Mr. Ernst Fuller. Everything could have been under control, even with the threat of Kurt Moseby, but things didn't turn out quite as expected. The discovery of the long, winding corridors, underground rivers, and echoing chambers with glittering stalactites and quiet lakes was overshadowed by the loneliness and fear of being trapped underground. All the thrills and excitement of caving, as well as the dangers and techniques of underground exploration, are pictured with skill and authenticity.

277. Weber, Lenora Mattingly. *My True Love Waits*. New York: Crowell, 1953. 262 pages. (Ages 14 and up) *Fiction*

People in the small town of Topley, Missouri, in the 1860s held fast to time-honored conventions. When Mary Conroy jilted Zach Topley, the son of the town's leading citizen, and married a newcomer, Armen Neff, most of the townspeople reacted to such conduct by ostracizing the couple. Regarded as a "nobody," Armen was unable to find work to support his wife. Finally in desperation he went to the Colorado gold fields to seek his fortune, leaving Mary in Topley until after their baby was born. Mary again disregarded convention by starting out to join Armen without waiting for him to return for her. Accompanying her and the baby on the journey were her twelve-year-old brother, her nineteen-year-old sister, and their Uncle Thad and his wife. Mary was eventually reunited with her husband, but not before having to overcome innumerable hardships along the way. Weber skillfully weaves a realistic picture of the period's mores and traditions as well as of the hazardous trip across the prairies and over the mountains in the covered wagons.

278. Weeks, Raymond. *The Hound-Tuner of Callaway*. New York: Columbia University Press, 1927. 277 pages. (Ages 12 and up) OP. *Fiction*

"The Hound-Tuner of Callaway" introduces a collection of twenty-eight short stories, some of which may be of interest to students engaged in a study of Missouri folklore. Some of the stories contain familiar names of actual people and places within the Missouri valley and in Jackson, Boone, and Callaway counties in particular. As Weeks states in his preface, "These unpretentious stories lay no claim to please the popular taste. They are merely remembered happenings and imaginings of the time of later pioneers in the Missouri Valley" (p. vii). Most likely, the reader or listener would be impressed with their simplicity and quaintness, although the writing contains superfluous expressions, and the dialect in some of the stories is labored. Despite these drawbacks, the book should be conserved as a historically valuable object.

279. Weiss. Harvey. *The Sooner Hound*. Illustrated by the author. New York: Putnam's, 1959. 46 pages. (Ages 5–9) OP. *Fiction*

Author-artist Weiss makes his own adaptation of a famous railroad yarn about a shaggy mutt with a "hangdog look." But this pooch had a secret gift; in fact, the crazy hound didn't like to do anything but run! He also had a proud master who was a railroad fireman known as a "boomer." The master's claim that the dog always went with him wherever he went makes for a rollicking tale from the railroad roundhouses. Appropriate illustrations furnish added humor to this tall tale written in easy-to-read text. Jack Conroy and Arna Bontemps first published this same story under the title, *The Fast Sooner Hound*.

280. Wellman, Manly Wade. *Rebel Mail Runner*. Illustrated by Stuyvesant Van Veen. New York: Holiday House, 1954. 221 pages. (Ages 12 and up) OP. *Fiction*

This story begins and ends at Bowling Green in Pike County, Missouri, but in the meantime, the scenes shift between there and St. Louis to strategic points throughout the Deep South. The theme is an almost forgotten aspect of the war between the states—the Confederate Underground Mail Service from Missouri. The story is imaginary as is the character of the hero, Barry Mills, but Absalom Grimes, the leader of the mail runners, was a real person, and the memoirs of his exploits formed the basis of this junior novel.

Once seventeen-year-old Barry Mills had become involved in helping Captain Grimes to escape the Union soldiers, he knew that he couldn't return home; he would be called a rebel spy. So his decision to join the Confederate mail runners was easy. His father had already enlisted with the South, and home life with his cousin Buckalew Mills was becoming unbearable. As Grimes's assistant, Barry was in constant danger as he slipped through Union lines carrying letters back and forth between the rebel soldiers and their families. His adventures took him up and down the Mississippi from St. Louis to Memphis, Vicksburg, and beyond. He traveled by steamboat and train, horse and mule, and on foot. He risked his life in blockades, battlefields, and even prisons to deliver his underground communications. An interesting thread of the story was the role played by the young women and matrons who served as couriers taking the mail between St. Louis, the distributing point, and the Missouri towns.

281. West, Tom. *Heroes on Horseback: The Story of the Pony Express*. Illustrated with photographs. New York: Four Winds Press, 1969. 160 pages. (Ages 8–12) *Nonfiction*

Hero stories have strong appeal to eight- to twelve-year-olds, and West offers them exciting heroes in his account of the Pony Express. Every exacting trip was filled with fascinating adventure as the daredevil rider raced along a trail over blizzard-swept mountains, across blazing deserts, or through hostile Indian country. Many of the young men who joined the Pony Express were brought up on farms in the Missouri area and were expert riders; among them were J. W. "Bill" Richardson, Johnny Frey, and Bill Gates. These colorful riders were issued bright red shirts and blue pants, but many preferred to wear range garb. Mark Twain immortalized them, saying, "Both rider and horse went 'flying light.' The rider's dress was thin and fitted close; he wore a 'roundabout' and a skull cap, and tucked his pantaloons into his boot tops like a race rider. . . . his horse . . . wore a little wafer of a saddle, and no visible blanket" (p. 101). Covering the saddle was the treasured mochila, ingeniously designed to get the mail through with or without the rider. The entire nation shared the excitement on 3 April 1860, as the first rider left St. Joseph, Missouri, the jumping-off place for the Pony Express. (St. Joseph was already a stagecoach terminal and was linked by railway with Hannibal.) For one month the hardy riders made good the company's slogan, "Ten Days from Coast to Coast." Then tragedy struck when the Paiute Indians went on the warpath. The long chain of stations across Nevada and western Utah were wide open to attack as were the lone pony riders. But the determined Missourians would not accept defeat and soon the Russell, Majors, and Waddell Company restored the mail service to California. Many old photographs and an index add to the appeal and usefulness of the book.

282. White, Dale. *Steamboat up the Missouri*. Illustrated by Charles Geer. New York: Viking, 1958. 185 pages. (Ages 12 and up) *Fiction*

This story, set against the background of the Civil War, presents an interesting account of some of the complex problems encountered in our expanding country during that period. By March 1863 Dave MacLaren was as angry, impatient, and disappointed as a fifteen-year-old boy could be who hadn't been able to sign up for military service. Neither the Union army nor the navy would take him because he was a cub pilot. It would be three or four years before he completed his apprenticeship aboard the *Osage Queen*, a luxurious passenger packet making weekly trips between St. Louis and Kansas City. But Dave was soon drawn unexpectedly into an important mission that enabled him to help his country in a very special way. According to couriers from upriver, Indian tribes, encouraged by Confederate sympathizers and by British spies, were threatening to join the Sioux in an uprising that would take Union forces away from their field of action. The South thought only of winning the war, and the British were taking advantage of the situation since they could more easily regain control of the vast plains and mountain country if the upper Missouri River posts were undefended. Dave's father, who was highly regarded by the Indians, was determined to placate the tribes, and he needed dependable and skillful men to help him. Their service involved an exciting and dangerous journey by steamboat up the Missouri. As the plot unfolds, Dave met the difficult challenges with honor, copiloting the *Eagle*, a privately rigged boat, in a tense and desperate race against a rival company.

283. Whitehouse, Arch. *John J. Pershing* (Lives to Remember). Jacket illustration by Frank Aloise. New York: Putnam's, 1964. 191 pages. (Ages 11–15) *Biography*

While the style is mediocre with some poorly chosen words and biased as well as inept expressions, Whitehouse's book is a good source of facts about Pershing's life and about his influence on the character of the time in which he lived. It also provides worthwhile information not included in the Pershing biographies by Castor, *America's First World War*, and by Foster, *John J. Pershing: World War I Hero*. In this full-length biography, a brief chapter deals with Pershing's family background and his early childhood; attention is called to his German-French ancestors who came to America in 1749 and to the fact that he, their great-grandson, was sent to liberate their homeland as commander in chief of the American Expeditionary Forces during World War I. The main part of the story features the varied military activities of his adult life with more than half of the book devoted to an account of World War I and America's involvement under Pershing's distinguished command. A bibliography and an index add to the usefulness of the book. Whitehouse was a veteran of World War I, serving in England's Royal Flying Corps.

284. Whitman, Virginia. *Ozark Obie*. Illustrated by William Hutchinson. Nashville: Broadman Press, 1961. 160 pages. (Ages 10–14) *Fiction*

Fourteen-year-old Kent O'Brien, known as Obie, lived with his family near Missouri's scenic Lake of the Ozarks. His father operated a district fire tower, and Obie himself worked during the summer as a guide at the Niangua Cave and Boat Docks. His ambition was to earn enough money to buy a rifle by the time the deer season arrived, because more than anything else he wanted to kill a deer. He also wanted to prove that he was grown up enough for his family to stop referring to him as their baby boy or their baby brother. Obie and his friend Tom explored a secret entrance to the Niangua Cave and discovered an Indian burial mound. On returning to the cave alone to find a shovel that he had left behind, Obie encountered a stranger and led to the capture of an escaped convict. As a fishing guide, he assisted with the catch of a prize fish that earned him an extra bonus. But one boat trip with a couple of honeymooners ended in their having to be rescued from an isolated island. Obie's experiences during that summer brought him to the realization of his goal. Readers are also provided with some exciting and realistic adventures, which are given additional interpretation through the endpaper maps. *Secret of the Hidden Ranch* (Zondervan, 1964) is a sequel to this story.

285. Whitney, Alex. *Sports and Games the Indians Gave Us*. Drawings and diagrams by Marie and Nils Ostberg. New York: McKay, 1977. 82 pages. (Ages 10 and up) *Nonfiction*

A ball game played by the Osage Indians of Missouri as well as by almost every other North American tribe was shinney, the ancestor of both field and ice hockey. The game was played for pleasure, as well as for prizes, but was mainly considered a war-training exercise for Indian braves; women, girls, and young boys played a modified version of the sport. Long before the white man's historic arrival, the Indian tribes of the North American continent were playing their versions of many other sports enjoyed here today, such as baseball, football, soccer, lacrosse, wrestling, shuffleboard, bowling, and skydiving. These and many other sports and games that the Indians gave us are identified and explained in this fascinating book. (Some of these games are also mentioned in Barrett's *Shinkah, the Osage Indian*. Whitney's survey includes step-by-step instructions and clear diagrams for making some of the equipment. A map of North America shows eleven different areas originally occupied by major Indian tribes. A three-page listing identifies each of the major tribes of the North American continent according to their geographical area. Among the eighteen different tribes occupying the Prairie area, which includes the present state of Missouri, are the Osage and Missouri Indians. A selected bibliography and an index are provided.

286. Wilder, Laura Ingalls. *On the Way Home: The Diary of a Trip from South Dakota to Mansfield, Missouri, in 1894.* Setting by Rose Wilder Lane. Illustrated with photographs. New York: Harper, 1962. 101 pages. (Ages 10 and up) *Biography*

Laura Ingalls Wilder made daily notes of her family's 650-mile journey from De Smet, South Dakota, to Mansfield, Missouri, in 1894. Her descriptions of what they saw and did along the way provide the reader with an accurate glimpse of the prairie frontier. The journey ended when the long line of ten wagons arrived at Mansfield, but Laura's story continues to live on. In Mansfield, arrangements were made to buy the land that has become known as Rocky Ridge Farm and the one-hundred-dollar bill was discovered missing, creating a mystery that was eventually solved. The house that Laura and Almanzo Wilder built of materials from the farm is now preserved as a memorial museum by the Laura Ingalls Wilder Home Association of Mansfield. It was there that Laura wrote her "Little House" books, which have become classics. Two explanatory sections written by Rose Wilder Lane accompany her mother's diary along with actual photographs of the family and of their farm home.

287. Wilkie, Katherine E. *Daniel Boone: Taming the Wild* (A Discovery Book). Illustrated by Don Sibley. Champaign, Ill.: Garrard, 1960. 80 pages. (Ages 7–10) *Biography*

Wilkie's brief, fictionalized biography of Daniel Boone introduces the young reader to the famous explorer. The story begins with his early childhood on the edge of the

Pennsylvania woods and continues with a series of action-filled adventures in the life of the man who opened the way westward for thousands of settlers. Each episode is based on factual events and developed in a simplified style appropriate for the young reader. Selected incidents include scenes with young Daniel's Indian friends, the family's move to the Yadkin valley, a home of his own, on to Kentucky, the Wilderness Road, a rescue, saving the fort, and Boone's reward. The closing chapter highlights his final settlement in Missouri. The ease of reading, coupled with the brief text and high-interest content, makes this book appealing to older children who lack the skills to read more difficult material.

288. Winders, Gertrude Hecker. *Jim Bridger: Mountain Boy* (Childhood of Famous Americans). Illustrated by Harry H. Lees. Indianapolis: Bobbs-Merrill, 1955. 188 pages. (Ages 9–13) *Biography*

In this fictionalized biography that follows a format similar to those of other books in the series, Winders has presented interesting and substantial content at an easy-to-read level of difficulty that has wide age-range appeal. Jim Bridger, American fur trader and scout, began and ended his pioneering career in Missouri. His fascination with the mountains began in his early childhood in Virginia. In 1812, when his family journeyed west by covered wagon and riverboat and settled in an area near St. Louis (Six-Mile Prairie in Illinois), the growing boy came nearer to seeing the big mountains of the West. For a time, Jim operated a ferry across the Mississippi to St. Louis and later worked in a St. Louis blacksmith shop. There he learned much about the mountain country as well as something about river life and about the languages of the Spanish, French, and Indians; among those who came to this shop were well-known traders, trappers, and boatmen such as Manuel Lisa, Auguste and Pierre Chouteau, and Mike Fink. When Jim was eighteen, he joined Gen. William H. Ashley in a fur-trading expedition to the upper Missouri River. During the next forty years, he became the most famous scout of the West. He discovered the Great Salt Lake, built Fort Bridger on the Oregon Trail, explored the Yellowstone region, and served as a guide for the Union Pacific Railroad surveys. Among his friends were other famous mountain men from the Missouri area including Tom Fitzpatrick, Hugh Glass, Jedediah Smith, Milton and William Sublette, and Kit Carson. Many of the stories that Jim and his friends told about their exploits seemed unbelievable until later accounts proved them to be true. In 1871 Jim Bridger retired to his farm in Jackson County, Missouri, where he died ten years later. A list of his achievements is inscribed on the monument to his memory, located in Mount Washington Cemetery at Independence.

289. Wise, William. *Charles A. Lindbergh: Aviation Pioneer* (An American Hero Biography). Illustrated by Paul Sagsoorian. New York: Putnam's, 1970. 95 pages. (Ages 9–12) *Biography*

The historic flight of Charles A. Lindbergh's *Spirit of St. Louis* in 1927 focused national attention on Missouri and gave evidence once again of Missouri's prominence in the course of American history. Lindbergh was able to convey his vision and imagination to several concerned Missourians; their financial support and encouragement enabled him to achieve worldwide fame as an aviation pioneer. His flight was one of the most daring endeavors of the twentieth century; in a frail little airplane, he accomplished the first solo transatlantic flight from New York to Paris.

This biography surveys Lindbergh's early interests and his career in flying, his year as a cadet in the Army Air Force Flying School, and his plan to win the Orteig Prize. It also provides an account of the construction of the *Spirit of St. Louis* as well as a description of the hazardous flight. The last chapter deals briefly with the tragedies and contributions of his later life. The text is straightforward with no dialogue and, for the most part, is appropriately simplified for the nine- to twelve-year-old age-group. The content is a step beyond David R. Collins's *Charles Lindbergh: Hero Pilot*. There are chapter headings and an index.

290. Withers, Carl, compiler. *A Rocket in My Pocket: The Rhymes and Chants of Young Americans*. Illustrated by Suzanne Suba. New York: Holt, Rinehart and Winston, 1948. Unpaged. (Ages 5–10) *Poetry*

This collection of more than four hundred chants, sayings, riddles, jokes, tongue twisters, and nonsense rhymes makes fun reading for all ages and is especially entertaining for listeners in early childhood. Amusing illustrations match the text to perfection. Withers's informative essay about this kind of folklore and its significance is also a valuable feature of the book. The collection illustrates how nonsense and humor travel from country to country and how people the world over, regardless of language differences, have a common folklore. Withers, a distinguished folklorist, was born and reared on a Missouri farm; he spent years collecting from children and teenagers their own folklore—their rhymes and chants, jokes and riddles, ditties, superstitions, stories, songs, and games. His other collections include *A World of Nonsense: Strange and Humorous Tales from Many Lands* (Holt, Rinehart and Winston, 1968), *I Saw a Rocket Walk a Mile* (Holt, Rinehart and Winston, 1965), and *Rainbow in the Morning* (Abelard-Schuman, 1956).

291. Witherspoon, Margaret Johanson. *Remembering the St. Louis World's Fair*. Illustrated with pen-and-ink drawings by Frances Johanson Krebs and photographs by Elinor Martineau Coyle. St. Louis: Folkestone Press, 1973 (paperback). 96 pages. (Ages 10 and up) *Nonfiction*

Inspired by the stories told by parents and grandparents as well as by memories of her own childhood spent in the fairgrounds area of Forest Park, the author and the designers of this book have brought back visions of the splendor of the 1904 St. Louis World's Fair. This fair, claimed to be unsurpassed in beauty, embellishment, and variety, was geographically the largest of all time. Many buildings and monuments, thousands of pictures and documents, and countless souvenirs cherished by their owners remain today as reminders of those golden days. Each chapter of the book provides a delightful experience for the reader to explore an age of never-to-be-forgotten St. Louis history. From the beginnings of plans to celebrate the one-hundredth anniversary of the Louisiana Purchase to the fair's demolition, an unfolding drama reveals matchless men, states at home, ways of travel, the pike, the Olympics, and other fascinating exhibition sites along with interesting trivia and memorabilia. One of the finest legacies of the fair to the city of St. Louis is the Jefferson Memorial standing symbolically at the main entrance to the former fairgrounds.

292. Wolfe, Louis. *Let's Go to the Louisiana Purchase* (Let's Go Series). Illustrated by Charles Dougherty. New York: Putnam's, 1963. 47 pages. (Ages 8 and up) *Nonfiction*

This easy-to-read story gives a brief account of the purchase of the Louisiana Territory from France in 1803. The reader, assumed to be a participant in the story, is taken from Washington, D.C., to Paris where the difficult secret negotiations were concluded. Important historical facts are included as well as clear portrayals of the prominent statesmen involved in the purchase. The book is especially suitable for older children needing high-interest, low-vocabulary material in the social studies. Appropriate illustrations accompany the text, and a glossary defines difficult words and terms.

The able young reader would likely find Phelan's *The Story of the Louisiana Purchase* more challenging, while Chidsey's *Louisiana Purchase* would appeal to able readers in the upper elementary grades or in high school.

293. Wooldridge, Rhoda. *And Oh! How Proudly*. Illustrated by John Livesay. Independence, Mo.: Independence Press, 1972. 171 pages. (Ages 10–14) *Fiction*

An adventure from New Orleans to the St. Louis settlement in 1769 during French and Spanish rivalry over the Louisiana Territory provides suspense and fascination for students in the upper elementary grades and in junior high school. The reader is immediately drawn into the lives of the principal characters, the members of the Dubois family and their friend, nineteen-year-old Chris Mueller, with enough detail and character delineation to keep interest high. Chris helps a French merchant, Jacques Dubois, to escape from Spanish soldiers and as a result finds himself responsible for the Dubois children, Demetre and Mimi, and their Acadian companion, Toinette. The strength of character and resourcefulness of Chris and others are dramatically painted as the story unfolds. Toinette is seen as strong and courageous, a match for both Chris and Demetre's display of mature judgment. Encounters with the Houmas and Tunica Indians give insight into both friendly and hostile tribes along the Mississippi River. The historical significance of this novel with its focus on the early settlement of America makes it an ideal piece of literature to use during history and social-studies units.

294. Wooldridge, Rhoda. *Chouteau and the Founding of Saint Louis*. Independence, Mo.: Independence Press, 1975. 215 pages. (Ages 12 and up) *Fiction*

The role played by Auguste Chouteau in the founding of the St. Louis trading post is accounted against authentic historical background of the period. In 1763 fourteen-year-old Auguste left his home in New Orleans to begin a dangerous journey that was to take him to the confluence of the Mississippi and Missouri rivers. As a clerk on the cargo boat of the trader Pierre Laclede, the young boy's knowledge and skills were invaluable in dealing with the different Indian tribes as well as with many other hazardous situations. In building the new settlement, Auguste proved to be an equal to Laclede's determination and perseverance. By 1764 their dream of a trading post that was destined to be the gateway to the vast new western America was realized. Eighteen months after he began his journey from New Orleans, Auguste was made a participating partner and was put in charge of the St. Louis post while Laclede further explored the Missouri countryside.

Wooldridge's book provides by far one of the best stories available about Chouteau and the founding of St. Louis. Her realistic characterizations and her use of historical figures along with accurate historical background are so effective that the novel approaches the genre of biography. The story makes an excellent enrichment for social-studies units dealing with this period in American history.

295. Wooldridge, Rhoda. *Hannah's Brave Year*. Jacket illustration by Robert Quackenbush. New York: Bobbs-Merrill, 1964. 151 pages. (Ages 10 and up) *Fiction*

In spite of the neighbors' deciding to separate the children, twelve-year-old Hannah Harelson was determined to keep the family together when her parents died of cholera. With the help of her younger sister Marty, she managed the household chores while sixteen-year-old Nat worked in the fields and their eighteen-year-old brother Joel went fur trapping to earn enough money to pay the mortgage on the farm. Life on the Missouri frontier was not easy for the children as thieves, blizzards, and illness added to their hardships and misfortunes. However, Osage Indian Sagameeshee, storeowner Cambright, Grandma Peabody, and Pierre Roubeau were among those loyal and helpful friends who gave the orphaned but courageous family renewed hope. Set in the area of Fort Osage at Old Sibley near Independence, Missouri, this is more than just another pioneer story. The many domestic details of cooking, planting, and harvesting are vividly described as are the children living in the two-room cabin on their mortgaged land.

Both *Hannah's Brave Year* and *Hannah's House* are among

the few available stories for children and youth that depict the details of frontier living in Missouri. These books are increasingly popular with children today, and they should be conserved for children of future generations.

296. Wooldridge, Rhoda. *Hannah's House*. Illustrated by Alta Adkins. Independence, Mo.: Independence Press, 1972. 182 pages. (Ages 10 and up) *Fiction*

In this sequel to *Hannah's Brave Year*, the six orphaned Harelson children continue the struggle to survive in the wilderness of Jackson County, Missouri, in the early 1840s. Fighting drought, grasshoppers, and fire, the children work hard to pay off the mortgage and to keep the farm that their parents had homesteaded. When the old sorghum mill and a corner of clay land provided a profitable means of exchange between the Cambrights and the Harelsons, Hannah's dream of a new house became a reality. The action-filled plot is supported by a strong theme depicting the spirit of love that binds the close family and their neighbors together. Authentic details of pioneer living combined with realistic characterizations and free-flowing sytle create a vicarious experience with our country's past that is certain to leave a vivid impression on young readers.

Both *Hannah's House* and *Hannah's Brave Year* are among some of the finest historical fiction published today. These books have lasting value for future generations of children and youth; they tell a story that will always be a part of America's background.

297. Wooldridge, Rhoda. *That's the Way, Joshuway*. Illustrated by Alta Adkins. Independence, Mo.: Independence Press, 1965. 152 pages. (Ages 10–14) *Fiction*

That's the Way, Joshuway is a fast-moving story set around Arrow Rock, old Blue Mills landing, and Independence, Missouri, during the exciting frontier days when riverboats plied the Missouri River and wagon trains moved westward along the Santa Fe Trail near Lexington and Independence. While Josh Carver's dream of going

From *That's the Way, Joshuway* (Wooldridge)

west is never realized, he does learn the satisfaction of belonging to a family and to a homeland carved in the wilderness of Missouri. He is helped along the way by George Caleb Bingham, the artist whom he had encountered while working in his uncle's harness shop in Arrow Rock. This historical novel reflects familiar scenes across mid-Missouri and describes the life, customs, and people of the 1840s, but its main theme features a young boy's taking pride in his work and learning to become independent while sharing the joys of family life.

That's the Way, Joshuway is especially worthwhile for its realistic setting. Many of the towns and roads in the area have retained the same names, and several buildings, including the entire old town of Arrow Rock, have been restored to their original appearance. The reader who has traveled in this area can readily identify with Joshuway, and all who become acquainted with him can take pride in the historic landmarks that were once so important to this storybook character.

298. Wright, Louis B. *Everyday Life on the American Frontier* (Life in America Series). Illustrated with photographs. New York: Putnam's, 1968. 256 pages. (Ages 12 and up) *Nonfiction*

Details of everyday life on the American frontier are described in an easily read narrative matched equally by numerous well-chosen illustrations that include copies of famous paintings, lithographs, woodcuts, and engravings representing the times. Throughout this volume, Wright stresses the influences that lured people westward toward new frontiers. He points out that for some the fur trade, the mines, the farms, and the ranches provided motivation in the search of fortunes; for others, it was the excitement and adventure of living a different way of life in a new land. Mountain men, explorers, missionaries, and adventurers led the way. While the general discussions of frontier living—the homes, food, work, religion, education, transportation, and entertainment—are worthwhile, the specific accounts of individuals connected with the American frontier maintain variety and interest in the material. A large portion of the book contains numerous references to Missouri and to related topics since this area figured greatly in the movement of the frontier beyond the Mississippi. In chapter 4, attention is given to the Louisiana Purchase, to the Lewis and Clark expedition, and to the St. Louis frontier of 1846. An account of "a tour of curiosity and amusement" quoted from *The Oregon Trail* by Francis Parkman provides a vivid and entertaining account of a steamboat trip up the Missouri to Kansas landing and to the towns of Westport and Independence. The frontier town of St. Louis is a focal point of chapter 5, which deals with an account of the mountain men who organized fur companies and established fortified trading posts. The impact on Missouri of the gold rush and the westward expansion beyond the Rocky Mountains is cited in chapter 6. The book is an excellent reference and provides interesting browsing. A list of suggested references and an index are included.

299. Yeager, Rosemary. *James Buchanan Eads: Master of the Great River*. Illustrated by John Hackmaster. Princeton: Van Nostrand, 1968. 126 pages. (Ages 9–12) *Biography*

The genius and courage of James Buchanan Eads, as well as his abiding interest in St. Louis and in the Mississippi, won him a place of worldwide distinction. Eads, a self-taught engineer and inventor, was born in Lawrenceburg, Indiana, in 1820 and came to St. Louis when he was thirteen years old. By the age of twenty-one, he had invented the diving bell, which made him a fortune in the boat-salvaging business. A fleet of seven ironclad gunboats that he designed and built for use in the Civil War enabled the Union navy to gain control of the Mississippi and hastened the final victory. His most amazing achievement was the construction of the famous Eads Bridge spanning the Mississippi at St. Louis. This bridge with its structural-steel arches was a bridge of many firsts, including the excessive use of a cantilever design; it was even the subject of a commemorative U.S. postage stamp. Yeager tells about the bridge being such a favorite place for Sunday afternoon walks and drives that signs had to be posted warning "high rollers" (speeders on horses) and "scorchers" (speeders on bicycles) against traveling too fast. Eads's continuing interest in the difficulties associated with the Mississippi led him to even more remarkable achievements. His construction of jetties at the mouth of the Mississippi kept the channel deep enough to permit ocean vessels to reach New Orleans. The Eads Plaza, a square at the foot of Canal Street in New Orleans, still honors him. Yeager includes an interesting epilogue about "Operation *Cairo*," the salvaging of one of Eads's ironclads near Vicksburg, Mississippi. The book contains a bibliography and an index and is dedicated "in memory of Barrett Williams, who so generously offered his private library to James Buchanan Eads.'"

300. Yeo, Wilma, and Helen K. Cook. *Maverick with a Paintbrush: Thomas Hart Benton.* Illustrated with reproductions and "A Portfolio of Paintings by Thomas Hart Benton." Garden City, N.Y.: Doubleday, 1977. 125 pages. (Ages 12 and up) *Biography*

"America's muralist never stopped searching for new frontiers among the lights and shadows of his boundless American scene" (p. 124). Born in Neosho, Missouri, in 1889 into a family of lawyers and politicians, Tom Benton was expected to follow his father's footsteps. He was named after his great-uncle, Thomas Hart Benton, who was one of Missouri's first two U.S. senators. While Benton felt strongly about his country, he was to interpret it in his paintings instead of in political oratory. During his early years, while his father was serving four terms in the House of Representatives (1897–1905), Benton became increasingly interested in drawing and decided to study art. At the age of seventeen, he was hired as a cartoonist for a local newspaper in Joplin, Missouri. But he soon left for Chicago, Paris, and New York to study and work as a serious artist. In 1935 Benton returned to Missouri to begin work on the now-famous mural, *A Social History of the State of Missouri*, in the Missouri state capitol. While Benton's paintings have stirred considerable controversy, his unmistakable style and his keen gift for portraying America as he saw it leave no question about his success in capturing both the spirit and the imagination of the American people.

301. Zemach, Harve. *Mommy, Buy Me a China Doll* (adapted from an Ozark children's folk song). Illustrated by

Margot Zemach. New York: Farrar, Straus & Giroux, 1975. Unpaged. (Ages 5–8) *Fiction*

Young children should delight in the humor and repetition in this adaptation of an old Ozark folk song. Effective illustrations accompany the ballad in which little Eliza Lou solves the problem of money to buy a china doll from a mountain trader. "We could trade our Daddy's featherbed. Do, Mommy, do!" But each solution poses a new problem as does each alternative suggestion of sleeping arrangements for the entire family and their horses, kittens, chickens, and pigs.

Literary Map of Missouri

Stories as Varied as the Locales That Dot the Landscape

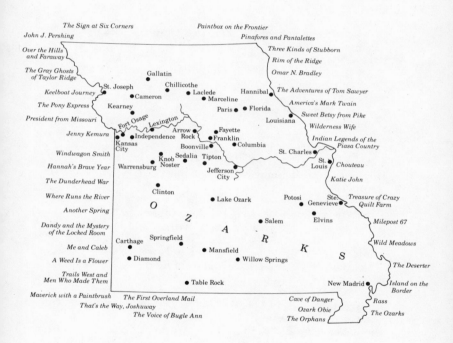

The Sign at Six Corners

John J. Pershing

Over the Hills and Faraway

The Gray Ghosts of Taylor Ridge

Keelboat Journey

The Pony Express

President from Missouri

Jenny Kemura

Windwagon Smith

Hannah's Brave Year

The Dunderhead War

Where Runs the River

Another Spring

Dandy and the Mystery of the Locked Room

Me and Caleb

A Weed Is a Flower

Trails West and Men Who Made Them

Maverick with a Paintbrush

That's the Way, Joshuway

The Voice of Bugle Ann

The First Overland Mail

Paintbox on the Frontier

Pinafores and Pantalettes

Three Kinds of Stubborn

Rim of the Ridge

Omar N. Bradley

The Adventures of Tom Sawyer

America's Mark Twain

Sweet Betsy from Pike

Wilderness Wife

Indian Legends of the Piasa Country

Chouteau

Katie John

Treasure of Crazy Quilt Farm

Milepost 67

Wild Meadows

The Deserter

Island on the Border

Rass

The Ozarks

Cave of Danger

Ozark Obie

The Orphans

Gallatin

Chillicothe

St. Joseph

Cameron

Laclede

Marceline

Hannibal

Kearney

Paris

Florida

Louisiana

Fort Osage

Lexington

Arrow Rock

Fayette

Kansas City

Independence

Franklin

Columbia

St. Charles

Boonville

Knob Noster

Sedalia

Tipton

St. Louis

Warrensburg

Jefferson City

Clinton

Lake Ozark

Potosi

Ste. Genevieve

Elvins

O Z A R K S

Salem

Carthage

Springfield

Mansfield

Diamond

Willow Springs

Table Rock

New Madrid

Selected Bibliography

Profiles of Missouri Authors

These profiles appeared in *Language Arts* (formerly *Elementary English*). Champaign, Ill.: National Council of Teachers of English.

Crosson, Whilhelmina M. "Florence Crannell Means." 17 (December 1940): 321–24, 326.

Darby, Ada Claire. "The Negro in Children's Books." 21 (January 1944): 31–32 (describes the author's defense of black dialect in her stories, particularly *"Jump Lively, Jeff"*).

Fitzgerald, A. Irene. "Rhoda Wooldridge: Author of Historical Fiction." 55 (February 1978): 218–21.

Flanagan, Frances. "A Tribute to Laura Ingalls Wilder." 34 (April 1957): 203–13.

Griese, Arnold A. "Clyde Robert Bulla: Master Story Weaver." 48 (November 1971): 766–78.

Hopkins, Lee Bennett. "Aileen Fisher." 55 (October 1978): 868–72.

———. "Negro Poets: Through the Music of Their Words." 45 (February 1968): 306–8 (Langston Hughes, p. 307).

Noyce, Ruth. "Art History for Children: Shirley Glubok." 55 (May 1978): 626–29.

Painter, Helen W. *"Rifles for Watie*: A Novel of the Civil War." 38 (May 1961): 287–91, 297 (Harold Keith).

Parker, Pat. "Glen Rounds: Artist and Storyteller." 55 (September 1978): 744–48.

Ramsey, Irvin L., and Lola B. Ramsey. "Aileen Fisher: Like Nothing at All." 44 (October 1967): 593–601.

Toothaker, Roy E. "A Conversation with Alberta Wilson Constant." 53 (January 1976): 23–26.

———. "Mary Francis Shura: Why She Writes." 57 (February 1980): 193–99.

Ward, Nancy. "Laura Ingalls Wilder: An Appreciation." 50 (October 1973): 1025–28.

Handbooks, Books, Booklets, and Films

American Association of University Women, Missouri State Division. *Pause in Missouri, People, Places, Events*. Edited by Margaret

A. Witt and volunteer staff; illustrated by Linda L. Wilson. Columbia, Mo.: Computer Color-Graphics, 1979. 140 pages. (*Pause in Missouri* Editorial and Business Office, Box 2144, Stephens College, Columbia 65201).

This book, a collection of short essays written by local residents and AAUW branch members of various parts of the state, is divided into seven sections; regional maps help readers to locate places and areas mentioned in the stories.

American Association of University Women, Ferguson–Florissant Branch. *Show Me the Arts: A Guide to Missouri's Cultural Resources.* Florissant, Mo.: Show Me the Arts, 1979.

This guide to the museums and other points of interest across the state includes information on facilities and prices (available at Auto Club of Missouri Bookstore, 3917 Lindell Blvd., St. Louis, or address inquiries to Show Me the Arts, 550 Rue St. Francois, Florissant, Mo. 63031).

Anderson, Paul. *The Reptiles of Missouri.* Illustrated with maps, drawings, and photographs. Columbia: University of Missouri Press, 1965. 354 pages.

This volume provides a systematic account of twenty turtles, eleven lizards, and fifty snakes. Their distribution areas are identified along with their natural history, habits, and descriptions.

Anderson, William. *Laura Wilder of Mansfield.* Mansfield, Mo.: Laura Ingalls Wilder–Rose Wilder Lane Home and Museum, 1974 (paperback). 36 pages.

Illustrated with photographs, this brief biography, as well as magazine article reprints and a map of Laura's travels, is available at the museum.

Caldwell, Dorothy. *Missouri Women in Public Life.* Edited by Bev Jensen Katirayi. In commemoration of the United Nation's International Women's Year, 1975, and the nation's bicentennial anniversary. Pamphlet sponsored by MFA, 1975. Unpaged.

Chapman, Carl H., and Eleanor Chapman. *Indians and Archaeology of Missouri.* Missouri Handbook No. 5. Columbia: University of Missouri Press, 1978. 161 pages.

Dark, Harry, and Phyl Dark. *The Greatest Ozark Guidebook.* Illustrations by Richard Lewis. Springfield, Mo.: Greatest Graphics, 1979 (paperback). 240 pages.

This travel guide provides information about caves, wineries, festivals, state parks, scenic drives, national rivers, and other attractions.

Hall, Leonard. *Stars Upstream: Life along an Ozark River.* Illustrated with photographs. Columbia: University of Missouri Press, 1969 (paperback). 264 pages.

In an informal narrative, the author vividly describes the sights and sounds along America's first national scenic riverway located within Missouri's Ozark highlands.

Harr, Helen K. *Bushwhacker's Annual.* A Missouri History Calendar. Calligraphy and drawings by Margaret Stookesberry. St. Joseph, Mo.: Helen Harr, 1979, 1980.

Keller, W. D. *The Common Rocks and Minerals of Missouri.* Missouri Handbook No. 1. Columbia: University of Missouri Press, 1961. 78 pages.

My Kansas City. Illustrated with drawings. Kansas City: The Learning Exchange, 1980 (paperback). 105 pages.

This resource booklet, written for students in the elementary grades, traces Kansas City's rich historical heritage from 1800 to the present and provides realistic activities that reinforce learning. *My Kansas City*, compiled and written by the Learning Exchange in cooperation with the Junior League, is appropriate for home as well as for school. Currently available exclusively from the Learning Exchange at 2720 Walnut Street, Kansas City, Missouri 64108. The project is an excellent example of what communities can do to promote an appreciation of local history.

Official Manual of Missouri. Feature articles from the manual are indexed by the School of the Ozarks, compiled by Karen McClaskey; microfiche available through Southwest Missouri Library Network, Box 737 MPO, Springfield, Missouri 65102.

Ramsey, Robert L. *Our Storehouse of Missouri Place Names.* Missouri Handbook No. 2. Columbia: University of Missouri Press, 1973. 160 pages.

Rickett, Theresa C. *Wild Flowers of Missouri.* Missouri Handbook No. 3. Columbia: University of Missouri Press, 1954. 148 pages.

Settergren, Carl, and R. E. McDermott. *Trees of Missouri.* Columbia: University of Missouri Agricultural Experiment Station, 1969.

Trimble, Barbara, Barbara Abernathy, and Mary H. Trimble, compilers. *Rose O'Neill*, 1968 (no other publication information given). Information about the booklet and other Rose O'Neill memorabilia may be obtained from the School of the Ozarks, Order Department, Point Lookout, Missouri 65726.

A list of books and magazine articles about Rose O'Neill was published in *The Ozark Visitor*, December 1971, pp. 6–7, RP 3/ 79, a news sheet distributed by the School of the Ozarks. Missouri Ozark Materials, compiled by Karen McClaskey, is indexed by the School of the Ozarks and is available through interlibrary loan.

Terry, Dickson. *There's a Town in Missouri* . . . (Hermann • Hannibal • Springfield • St. Joseph • Joplin • Cape Girardeau • Independence • St. Louis, 1902). St. Louis: New Sunrise Publishing, 1979. 136 pages.

An anthology of articles previously published in *The Midwest Motorist.*

Tetrick, James. *Independence Missouri in Historic Jackson County.* Independence, Mo.: Herald Publishing House. A Technicolor product. Unpaged booklet.

Unklesbay, A. G. *The Common Fossils of Missouri.* Missouri Handbook No. 4. Columbia: University of Missouri Press, 1973. 98 pages.

Filmstrips and Records (available from Missouri State Teachers Association, Columbia): *The Story of Missouri*:
  Missouri: A Government of the People
  Missouri: Her Geography and Natural Beauty
  Missouri: Playground of America
  Missouri: Her Heritage from the Past
  Missouri: Education for Life
  Missouri: Land of Plenty

Magazines and Brochures

Bittersweet. Lebanon, Mo.: Bittersweet, Inc. Four issues annually ($8.00). This student publication, which focuses on the Ozark culture, is a project of the language-arts department of the Lebanon High School.

Missouri Conservationist. Jefferson City, Mo.: Missouri Department of Conservation, P.O. Box 180. Published monthly (subscriptions free to adult Missouri residents). The department also has a number of available books, bulletins, circulars, and leaflets related to Missouri's natural resources; limited requests are filled without charge.

Missouri Highways. Published by the Missouri Highway Commission, 1968–1973. Contains photographs and information about the state's towns and people as well as descriptions of Missouri's highways and roads. An index has been compiled by Darla Parkes, reference and interlibrary loan librarian at the Missouri State Library, Jefferson City.

Missouri Historical Review. Columbia, Mo.: The State Historical Society of Missouri. Published quarterly ($2.00).

Missouri Life. Jefferson City, Mo.: Missouri Life, Inc. Published bimonthly ($12.00).

Missouri: Travel Guide. Jefferson City: 1980, Missouri Division of Tourism, Department NR-O, P.O. Box 1055. Free booklet.

Missouri: Vacation Guide. Jefferson City: Missouri Division of Tourism, Department MO75, P.O. Box 1055. Free booklet.

Show-Me Libraries. Jefferson City: Missouri State Library. Published monthly. Contains useful information about library programs, resources, and other aspects of librarianship throughout Missouri.

The Midwest Motorist. Maryland Heights, Mo.: Auto Club of Missouri. Published bimonthly ($3.00).

About the Author–Compiler

Alice Irene Fitzgerald has a B.S. in Education, M.Ed., Ed.D., from the University of Missouri. A professor emeritus of education at the University of Missouri–Columbia, she taught graduate and undergraduate courses in literature for children and youth. She has taught in the public schools of Missouri, has supervised student-teachers in the University Laboratory School, and has taught graduate courses at Northeast Missouri State University. Her publications include magazine articles covering various aspects of literature for children and youth. A member of the Missouri State Teachers Association, she has served on the Reading Circle Committee, which compiles the association's *Selected List of Children's Books*. An active member of American Association of University Women, she has held offices at the local, state, and national level and is presently serving as UMC corporate representative to AAUW.

Index of Missouri Authors and Their Books about Missouri

Appropriate age-groups are given in parentheses; references are to entry numbers, not to pages.

Chapman, Carl H., and Eleanor F. Chapman. *Indians and Archae-ology of Missouri* (12 and up), 58

Chittum, Ida. *Tales of Terror* (10 and up), 60

Churchill, Winston. *The Crisis* (YA), 61

Clayton, LaReine Warden. *Now Be a Little Lady* (YA), 62

Clifford, Georgia McAdams. *Indian Legends of the Piasa Country* (10 and up), 65

Collins, Arthur Loyd, and Georgia I. Collins. *Hero Stories from Missouri History* (All Ages), 66

Collins, Earl A. *Folk Tales of Missouri* (10 and up), 67

Collins, Earl A. *Legends and Lore of Missouri* (10 and up), 68

Collins, Earl A., and Felix Eugene Snider. *Missouri Midland State* (14 and up), 69

Conroy, John C. (Jack), and Arna Bontemps. *The Fast Sooner Hound* (7–12), 73

Constant, Alberta Wilson. *Paintbox on the Frontier: The Life and Times of George Caleb Bingham* (11 and up), 74

Cook, Olive Rambo. *Coon Holler* (8–14), 75

Cook, Olive Rambo. *Locket* (10 and up), 76

Cook, Olive Rambo. *Serilda's Star* (8–12), 77

Cook, Olive Rambo. *The Sign at Six Corners* (12 and up), 78

Darby, Ada Claire. *Gay Soeurette* (9–12), 82

Darby, Ada Claire. *Hickory-Goody* (10–14), 83

Darby, Ada Claire. *"Jump Lively, Jeff"* (9–12), 84

Darby, Ada Claire. *Peace-Pipes at Portage, a Story of Old Saint Louis* (10 and up), 85

Darby, Ada Claire. *Pinafores and Pantalettes; or, The Big Brick House* (8–12), 86

Darby, Ada Claire. *Pull Away, Boatman* (12 and up), 87

Darby, Ada Claire. *"Scally" Alden* (9–12), 88

Darby, Ada Claire. *"Show Me" Missouri* (10 and up), 89

Darby, Ada Claire. *Skip-Come-a-Lou* (9–12), 90

Darby, Ada Claire. *Sometimes Jenny Wren* (9–12), 91

Dooley, Thomas A., M.D. *Doctor Tom Dooley, My Story* (12–16), 98

Draper, Cena Christopher. *Dandy and the Mystery of the Locked Room* (10–14), 100

Draper, Cena Christopher. *Ridge Willoughby* (8–12), 101

Draper, Cena Christopher. *Rim of the Ridge* (10–14), 102

Draper, Cena Christopher. *The Worst Hound Around* (9–14), 103

Erdman, Loula Grace. *Another Spring* (13 and up), 107

Erdman, Loula Grace. *Life Was Simpler Then* (12 and up), 108

Erdman, Loula Grace. *Lonely Passage* (YA), 109

Erdman, Loula Grace. *Save Weeping for the Night* (13 and up), 110

Erdman, Loula Grace. *Separate Star* (13 and up), 111

Erdman, Loula Grace. *The Far Journey* (YA), 112

Erdman, Loula Grace. *The Years of the Locust* (YA), 113

Evans, Mark. *Scott Joplin and the Ragtime Years* (10 and up), 115

Missouri Poets and Their Books of Poetry for Children and Youth

Title Index

Appropriate age-groups are given in parentheses; references are to entry numbers, not to pages.

Credit Lines (continued from page iv)

This simplified, easy-to-read biography highlights for children in the middle grades the major events in the life of a famous Missourian and a great American. It is a highly dramatic story emphasizing Omar Bradley's sturdy character and his personal determination. Each phase of his illustrious career is set against a background sufficiently detailed to allow the reader a full understanding of the time and place of events as well as of Bradley's achievements and successes. The fictionalized conversation readily involves the reader. Almost the entire first half of the book deals with Bradley's boyhood and his West Point years. One chapter touches briefly on his next twenty-five years as an infantry officer. Then the remainder of the book discusses Bradley's action during World War II, which revealed his exceptional ability as a commanding leader on the battlefronts, and his subsequent years as a five-star general and as chairman of the Joint Chiefs of Staff.

Omar Nelson Bradley was born at Clark, Missouri, on 12 February 1893. Following his father's death, he and his mother moved to Moberly, Missouri, where he was captain of his high-school baseball team. This athletic skill won him a place in both baseball and football at West Point. In December 1916, at Columbia, Missouri, he was married to his high-school friend and classmate, Mary Quayles, who had just graduated from the University of Missouri School of Journalism.

Bradley's decisiveness in command of his army resulted in spectacular victories. His genuine concern for his men in battle won their respect and earned him the title "the Soldiers' General." He has received distinguished awards from twelve foreign countries as well as many from his own country. In 1967, when Gen. Emmett O'Donnell of the air force presented him with the United Service Organization's distinguished award, he said, "He [Omar Nelson Bradley] truly belongs to the Nation" (p. 110).

The book is indexed and contains a preface letter written by Bradley about the author, Colonel Reeder, who was a West Point classmate and commander of the Twelfth Infantry on D-Day.

223. Reeder, Col. "Red" (Russell P., Jr.). *Ulysses S. Grant, Horseman and Fighter* (A Discovery Book). Illustrated by Ken Wagner. Champaign, Ill.: Garrard, 1964. 80 pages. (Ages 7–10) *Biography*

In the easy-to-read text common to all the books in this series, this fictional biography presents brief highlights of the life of Ulysses S. Grant. Mention is made of some of his boyish pranks, but for the most part themes of courage and bravery underlie serious episodes depicting his military career. The story begins with eleven-year-old Ulysses displaying his horsemanship at a circus in Georgetown, Ohio, and moves quickly into his period of training at West Point. During his first assignment at Jefferson Barracks near St. Louis, he met Julia Dent, whom he later married. While little attention is given to her role in his life, she and their children are mentioned as living at various places where he was stationed. The final chapter deals briefly and superficially with his presidency and final years, omitting the tragic realities of those years. Chapter headings and maps of the major battlefields add interest and clarity for the reader. The value of the book, as with others in the series, lies in its usefulness as an introduction to biography and to research in new areas.

224. Rees, Ennis. *Windwagon Smith*. Illustrated by Peter P. Plasencia. Englewood Cliffs, N.J.: Prentice-Hall, 1966. Unpaged. (Ages 8–12) *Fiction*

In unrhymed verse, Rees tells the tale of Windwagon Smith as his prairie schooner rolls over the great plains toward the fabled land of American tall tales. Practically everyone in Westport, Missouri, laughed at Mr. Smith and his strange wagon until a man from St. Joseph offered him money to build others like it for "hauling trade to Santa Fe and all points west." Then the windwagon became Westport's pride and joy, at least for a while. Some of the leading citizens went for a ride in the "Prairie Clipper" which "was ten times as large as a regular wagon and built with a platform, or bridge, on top where Windwagon Smith